MY
REVISION
NOTES

Pearson Edex

A-level

POLITICS
UK GOVERNMENT AND POLITICS
POLITICAL IDEAS
GLOBAL POLITICS

Sarra Jenkins
John Jefferies

HODDER
Education

Orders: please contact Hachette UK Distribution, Hely Hutchinson Centre, Milton Road, Didcot, Oxfordshire, OX11 7HH. Telephone: +44 (0)1235 827827. Email education@hachette. co.uk. Lines are open from 9 a.m. to 5 p.m., Monday to Friday. You can also order through our website: www.hoddereducation.co.uk

ISBN: 978 1 3983 8501 6

© 2023 Sarra Jenkins and John Jefferies

First published in 2023 by
Hodder Education
An Hachette UK Company
Carmelite House
50 Victoria Embankment
London EC4Y 0DZ

www.hoddereducation.co.uk

Impression number   10 9 8 7 6 5 4 3 2 1

Year   2027 2026 2025 2024 2023

Cover photo © xyz+/stock.adobe.com

Typeset by Integra Software Services Pvt. Ltd., Pondicherry, India

Printed in Spain

A catalogue record for this title is available from the British Library.

Get the most from this book

Everyone has to decide their own revision strategy, but it is essential to review your work, learn it and test your understanding. These Revision Notes will help you to do that in a planned way, topic by topic. Use this book as the cornerstone of your revision and don't hesitate to write in it — personalise your notes and check your progress by ticking off each section as you revise.

Tick to track your progress

Use the revision planner on page 4 to plan your revision, topic by topic. Tick each box when you have:

+ revised and understood a topic
+ tested yourself
+ practised the exam questions and gone online to check your answers and complete the quick quizzes

You can also keep track of your revision by ticking off each topic heading in the book. You may find it helpful to add your own notes as you work through each topic.

Features to help you succeed

Exam tips

Expert tips are given throughout the book to help you polish your exam technique in order to maximise your chances in the exam.

Now test yourself

These short, knowledge-based questions provide the first step in testing your learning. Answers are at **www.hoddereducation.co.uk/ myrevisionnotesdownloads**

Key terms

Essential key terms are highlighted in bold in the text, with clear, concise definitions provided alongside.

Use the glossary at the end of the book for quick reference and revision of terms from the specification.

Summaries

The summaries provide a quick-check bullet list for each topic.

Revision tasks

These activities will help you the understand each topic in an interactive way.

Exam skills

These summaries highlight how the specific skills identified or applicable in that chapter can be applied to your exam answers.

Exam practice

Practice exam questions are provided for each topic. Use them to consolidate your revision and practise your exam skills.

Online

Go online to check your answers to the exam questions at **www.hoddereducation.co.uk/ myrevisionnotesdownloads**

3

My Revision Notes: Pearson Edexcel A-level Politics: UK Government and Politics, Political Ideas and Global Politics

My revision planner

Answers at **www.hoddereducation.co.uk/myrevisionnotesdownloads**

Countdown to my exams

6–8 weeks to go

- ✚ Start by looking at the specification — make sure you know exactly what material you need to revise and the style of the examination. Use the revision planner on page 4 to familiarise yourself with the topics.
- ✚ Organise your notes, making sure you have covered everything on the specification. The revision planner will help you to group your notes into topics.
- ✚ Work out a realistic revision plan that will allow you time for relaxation. Set aside days and times for all the subjects that you need to study, and stick to your timetable.
- ✚ Set yourself sensible targets. Break your revision down into focused sessions of around 40 minutes, divided by breaks. These Revision Notes organise the basic facts into short, memorable sections to make revising easier.

REVISED ◯

2–6 weeks to go

- ✚ Read through the relevant sections of this book and refer to the exam tips, summaries and key terms. Tick off the topics as you feel confident about them. Highlight those topics you find difficult and look at them again in detail.
- ✚ Test your understanding of each topic by working through the 'Now test yourself' questions in the book. Look up the answers at **www.hoddereducation. co.uk/myrevisionnotesdownloads**
- ✚ Make a note of any problem areas as you revise, and ask your teacher to go over these in class.
- ✚ Look at past papers. They are one of the best ways to revise and practise your exam skills. Write or prepare planned answers to the exam practice questions provided in this book. Check your answers at **www.hoddereducation.co.uk/ myrevisionnotesdownloads**
- ✚ Use the revision activities to try out different revision methods. For example, you can make notes using mind maps, spider diagrams or flash cards.
- ✚ Track your progress using the revision planner and give yourself a reward when you have achieved your target.

REVISED ◯

One week to go

- ✚ Try to fit in at least one more timed practice of an entire past paper and seek feedback from your teacher, comparing your work closely with the mark scheme.
- ✚ Check the revision planner to make sure you haven't missed out any topics. Brush up on any areas of difficulty by talking them over with a friend or getting help from your teacher.
- ✚ Attend any revision classes put on by your teacher. Remember, he or she is an expert at preparing people for examinations.

REVISED ◯

The day before the examination

- ✚ Flick through these Revision Notes for useful reminders, for example the examiners' tips, topic summaries and key terms.
- ✚ Check the time and place of your examination.
- ✚ Make sure you have everything you need — extra pens and pencils, tissues, a watch, bottled water, sweets.
- ✚ Allow some time to relax and have an early night to ensure you are fresh and alert for the examinations.

REVISED ◯

My exams

Paper 1: UK Politics and Core Political Ideas

Date:...

Time: ....

Location: ....

Paper 2: UK Government and Non-Core Political Ideas

Date:...

Time: ....

Location: ....

Paper 3: Comparative Politics — Global

Date:...

Time: ....

Location: ....

1 Democracy and participation

1.1 What types of democracy are present in the UK?

Democracy is from the Greek 'demos' and 'kratos', meaning rule of the people. There is more than one type of democracy, however. The UK uses a number of types of democracy, including direct and representative (Table 1.1).

Table 1.1 Types of democracy in the UK

	Direct democracy	Representative democracy
Features	People are engaged directly in political decision-making, making decisions for themselves.	People vote for someone to engage in political decision-making on their behalf.
	Such decisions are usually made on specific, and limited, issues at a time.	Usually, representatives are elected by smaller sections of a society in constituencies in free and fair elections.
Use in the UK	The most common form of direct democracy in the UK is the use of referendums, e.g. the referendums on devolution in 1997 and 1998, the Scottish independence referendum in 2014 and the Brexit referendum in 2016.	The UK has a range of representatives at different levels of government, e.g.: + Members of Parliament (MPs) elected to serve in UK Parliament + Scottish, Welsh and Northern Irish representatives elected to serve in devolved bodies + local councillors elected to local councils
Example	**The Brexit Referendum, 2016** + Citizens voted on whether the UK should remain part of the European Union (EU) or not. + 72% of eligible voters turned out. + 52% of voters voted to 'leave' the EU, while 48% voted to 'remain'. + This gave the Conservative government at the time the mandate to take the UK out of the European Union, which was achieved on 31 January 2020.	**The general election, 2019** + Citizens voted on which party they wished to govern the country for up to the next 5 years, based on manifestos that covered lots of issues. + 67% of eligible voters turned out. + 43.6% voted for the Conservative Party, 32.1% voted for the Labour Party and 11.6% voted for the Liberal Democrats. + This gave the Conservative Party under Boris Johnson the mandate to govern the UK.

While it appears that there are distinct differences between direct and representative democracy, they do have similarities:
+ Both systems engage the population in political decision-making and encourage them to be politically educated in order to take part in the political system.
+ Both systems recognise the people as the source of political power, requiring the consent of the voters. In representative democracy, this consent gives legitimacy to elected officials; in direct democracy it gives legitimacy to the decision in the referendum.
+ Both systems try to balance competing interests within a country. Often citizens and politicians do not agree on a single course of action; both of these types of democracies try to provide answers and political direction.

> **Direct democracy** A political system in which the people make decisions themselves, rather than through an elected official acting on their behalf.
>
> **Representative democracy** A political system in which citizens elect a representative to make decisions on their behalf.

Now test yourself   TESTED

1 Distinguish between representative and direct democracy.
2 Identify three advantages of representative democracy.
3 Describe two different examples of the use of direct and representative democracy in the UK recently.

What are the advantages and disadvantages of direct and representative democracy?

REVISED

Table 1.2 Summary of direct and representative democracy

Advantages of direct democracy	Advantages of representative democracy
+ Everyone with the franchise is able to have their voice directly heard, making it the purest form of democracy. + It encourages the engagement of citizens in the political system and increases political education. + The decisions that are reached can have greater legitimacy. + It can solve controversial issues — these may be issues that are dividing a party or controversial issues for society. The resulting decision therefore has a clearer mandate.	+ Electing representatives works on a large scale in a country with millions of citizens. + Elections for representatives allows them to be held to account for their actions and decisions, allowing good representatives to continue their role and poor ones to be removed. + It can help to avoid tyranny of the majority, allowing for minority representation to be better heard and acted upon. + Many decisions are complex and elected representatives have the time and responsibility to understand them before making decisions.
Disadvantages of direct democracy	**Disadvantages of representative democracy**
+ In countries with millions of citizens, it is difficult to use direct democracy frequently given the number of decisions that need to be taken. + It removes accountability for the decisions that politicians carry out, as they can say they are carrying out the will of the people. + It can lead to tyranny of the majority, as the minority are unlikely to have their voices heard. + Referendums can be on highly complex issues and citizens do not necessarily have the time or full context to be able to understand these issues.	+ Although everyone gets to vote for a representative, it is not possible for that representative to make the voice of each of their constituents heard. + It can encourage political apathy, with people believing that politics is not for them, but only for the elected representatives. + Decisions that are reached can lack legitimacy as they may be made by representatives who were elected a number of years ago in entirely different national circumstances.

Legitimacy The rightful exercise of political power, usually by a government that gains legitimacy for its decisions from winning a free and fair election.

Tyranny of the majority A situation where the will of the majority of people in a country is used to make decisions, ignoring the will or needs of the minority.

7

What other types of democracy are there in the UK?

The UK uses a number of other types of democracy. The features of these can be seen in Table 1.3.

Table 1.3 Features of other types of democracy

Liberal democracy	Pluralist democracy	Elitist democracy
+ Free, fair and frequent elections + Free media, without censorship + Tolerance of a wide range of views + Protection of the rights of citizens + Government is limited in the extent of its power	+ Tolerance of a wide range of views + Many centres/locations of political powers + Competing parties/groups between which power can, and does, change hands	+ Power is concentrated in the hands of the few + Usually, political decision-making is dominated by a small number of people, often those who are wealthy or well-educated

For each of these democracies, aspects of them can be seen in UK politics to varying degrees, and this often also changes over time.

> **Now test yourself**
>
> TESTED
>
> 4 Identify three advantages of direct democracy.
> 5 Identify three disadvantages of representative democracy and direct democracy.
> 6 Briefly outline the features of liberal democracy.

> **Exam tip**
>
> It is not necessary to discuss every possible type of democracy being used in the UK in your essays. Instead, you should pick the types that are most relevant to the question that you have been asked.

How could aspects of UK democracy be reformed?

There are several concerns with the effectiveness of UK democracy today. Some of these are detailed in Table 1.4.

Table 1.4 Reasons for reform of UK democracy

Concern	What types of democracy is it a problem for?	Possible reform/s?
Falling voter engagement. Turnout at UK elections rarely exceeds 70%.	Representative democracy — officials elected by a low turnout may lack legitimacy.	Make voting compulsory or introduce online voting. ✓ Could increase turnout and improve legitimacy. ✗ Would not necessarily increase political education, meaning votes could be cast without political knowledge. There is also a concern over the security of online voting.
The extent of the franchise. A number of citizens cannot vote, for example under-18-year-olds.	Liberal democracy — protection of rights of citizens. Pluralist democracy — allows power to be concentrated in fewer hands.	Lowering the voting age — perhaps to 16. ✓ Could encourage political engagement of young people and increase legitimacy. ✗ Questions over whether 16-year-olds are mature enough to exercise the vote.
Lack of opportunities for engagement between elections.	Direct democracy — elected officials may have years to make decisions without listening to the public.	Increase the use of referendums or **e-democracy** such as e-petitions. ✓ Could increase public engagement on specific issues and improve legitimacy of decisions taken. ✗ Could undermine representative democracy and make elected officials less accountable for their decisions.
Representatives can only be held to account at election time.	Representative democracy — elected officials are supposed to represent the views of their constituents.	Improve the ability of constituents to use acts such as the Recall of MPs Act of 2015. ✓ Could improve the relationship between an MP and their constituency and the effectiveness of representation. ✗ Could lead to elected officials being unable to use their expertise and judgement, instead relying on the opinions of their constituents.

E-democracy The use of ICT to improve citizens' education and access in the political system. This could include e-petitions, online voting and the use of social media.

1.2 The franchise

The franchise in the UK has been extended considerably over time (Table 1.5).

Franchise The right to vote. It is also called 'suffrage'. The extent of the franchise refers to those with the right to vote, for example over-18s in the UK.

Table 1.5 Extension of the franchise in the UK over time (UK Parliament)

1832 Reform Act	1867 Reform Act	1918 Representation of the People Act	1928 Representation of the People Act	1969 Representation of the People Act
This gave the vote to middle-class men.	This gave the vote to working-class men.	This gave the vote to all men over 21, and many women over 30.	This gave the vote to all men and women over 21.	This lowered the voting age from 21 to 18.

However, there are still limits to those who can vote. The following people cannot vote in elections to the UK Parliament:
+ people aged under 18 years old
+ prisoners
+ members of the House of Lords

Now test yourself   TESTED ◯

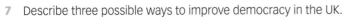

7   Describe three possible ways to improve democracy in the UK.

8   Explain how e-democracy could be used in the UK.

9   List three groups of people in the UK who do not have the vote.

How can people participate in democracy in the UK?

REVISED ◯

It is possible to participate in democracy in the UK by doing any of the following:
+ **Vote** — in a local, national or general election. The extent of participation can be judged by the turnout.
+ **Stand in an election** — those who are 18 or over, are a British citizen and pay a £500 deposit can run in a general election.
+ **Join a political party** — citizens can join a party and shape the policy direction of that party; many parties have youth memberships for those under 18.
+ **Join a pressure group or political movement** — with social media, groups such as Extinction Rebellion, Black Lives Matter and #MeToo allow people to be involved in issues that are significant to them.
+ **Sign an e-petition** — the House of Commons runs an e-petition website where petitions with 10,000+ signatures will get a response from the government and those with 100,000+ may be debated.

Is there a participation crisis in the UK?

One way to evaluate whether the UK has a **democratic deficit** is by reviewing whether the electorate participate in politics or not.

Yes	No
+ Turnout in elections is not high enough. The 2010, 2015, 2017 and 2019 general elections all had turnout between 65–69%, meaning around one-third of UK voters are not taking part in these elections.	+ Turnout in recent elections has been higher than previous elections in the 2000s, and the results have been much closer. The 2010 election resulted in a coalition, 2015 in a very small majority and 2017 in a supply and confidence agreement. Close results can increase turnout.
+ Only around 50% of 18–24-year-olds have voted in the last three general elections.	+ There were calls for second referendums regarding Scottish independence and Brexit, demonstrating the public's demand to take part in this form of democracy.
+ Turnout in local elections is often even lower. The turnout at the 2012 Police and Crime commissioner elections was just 15.1%.	+ Social media has allowed voters to mobilise quickly and be heard by the government in a different forum. Sacking of government ministers and U-turns can be seen as a result of public participation.
+ UK political parties have a total membership of less than one million people, compared to a population of nearly 70 million.	+ The use of e-petitions, both government run and independent sites such as change.org, have seen substantial participation. Between 2015 and 2019, the Parliament-run e-petitions site gathered nearly 23 million unique signatures (around 35% of the UK population).
+ While those taking part in political movements such as Extinction Rebellion have made headlines, the numbers at their protests are far fewer than their presence on social media suggests.	+ The Labour Party increased its membership substantially, at one point having over 500,000 members, up from 200,000 in 2014.
+ Some petitions have had millions of signatures, but the lack of impact has undermined the relevance of this method of participation. In 2019, a petition to cancel Brexit passed more than 6 million signatures.	

Participation crisis A situation in which few people take part in the political process and decision-making, undermining democratic legitimacy.

Democratic deficit A lack of democratic ideals seen in a political system, or where political decisions are taken by those without sufficient legitimacy.

Exam tip

When evaluating participation, it is often useful to look both at the number of people participating *and* the impact that they have had. Large social media movements that have had little impact may negatively affect participation in the future.

Now test yourself

TESTED

10 List the ways in which people in the UK can participate in democracy.

11 Explain what is meant by the term 'participation crisis'.

12 Explain the link between participation and legitimacy in a democratic system.

1.3 Pressure groups

Pressure groups seek to make change by influencing those in power, and they use a range of methods to try to achieve this. The nature of pressure groups and how they are classified changes over time. However, there are some useful basic definitions. Pressure groups are often classified as in Table 1.6.

The definitions given in Table 1.6 can be problematic in an era of social media. This has led to the emergence of 'movements' rather than groups. Instead of signing up to be a formal member of a group, people can simply participate by getting involved. Groups such as Extinction Rebellion, Black Lives Matter and #MeToo do not have formal membership structures yet have organised mass protests through social media.

Pressure group A group of like-minded individuals who seek to influence those in power on a specific issue.

Exam tip

Insider and outsider classifications come from a 1978 book by Wyn Grant. These classifications are not necessarily easily applied to groups that have emerged on social media, so ensure you have up-to-date and recent examples of pressure groups or movements, and ideally of their success and/or failure.

Table 1.6 Classification of pressure groups

Sectional		Causal
A sectional group represents a relatively narrow, or specific, section of society, often on a number of issues, e.g. trade unions represent specific industries but on all issues relevant to their profession.	Or	A causal group represents a wide cross-section of society but often on a single, or narrowly focused issue, e.g. Liberty is a group defending rights in the UK but which anyone is welcome to join.

Insider		Outsider
Insider groups often have some link with government, giving them the ability to influence the government directly. This might be due to being policy experts, or having an ideology that aligns with the current government, e.g. both Boris Johnson and Keir Starmer have given keynote speeches at the Confederation of British Industry's (CBI) annual conference.	Or	Outsider groups are those that do not have any links to the government, and therefore have to seek alternative methods to gain influence. Often these may therefore engage in high profile methods to try to gain public support, e.g. Extinction Rebellion and Just Stop Oil carried out protests such as gluing themselves to the M25 to cause disruption and raise the profile of their groups and their aims.

Think tanks and lobbyists

REVISED

Think tanks and lobbyists also act to try to influence the government. While they are different from pressure groups, there are aspects of similarity and cross-over (Table 1.7).

Table 1.7 Comparison of think tanks and lobbyists

	Think tanks	Lobbyists
Features	+ Groups of experts that carry out research into public policy areas that they hope will then influence government policy. + Often, they will have a specific political view that their research will aim to progress.	+ An individual or organisation that can be hired either for their political expertise or for their connections to policy makers. + Often lobbyists may have previously worked in government.
Example	**The Institute for Fiscal Studies** In May 2022, the group warned that the government would need to do more to help people with their energy bills, as bills were likely to be even higher in 2023 than they were in 2022.	**The Hanbury Strategy Group** In late 2022, this group set up a dedicated unit that would help their clients 'engage with the Opposition and prepare for the prospect of a Labour government'.
Concerns	+ Some think tanks have close ties to government, which gives them undue influence. + The development of policy by think tanks has removed some of the functions that parties have in doing this.	+ The close links between lobbyists and government raises concerns over elite or wealthy groups being able to 'buy' influence with the government. + There have been numerous scandals involving **lobbying** that have undermined government credibility.

Think tank A group of experts on a particular policy area that produces research to try to influence the government. These groups may have a specific political leaning.

Lobbyist A person or company that is paid to try to influence those in power, particularly when legislation is being considered.

Lobbying The act of 'seeking the ear of government', getting the government to listen to a particular point of view.

Exam tip

Do not confuse lobbying and lobbyists. Lobbying is the act of trying to influence the government and is a key principle of democracy. For example, a constituent raising a local issue with their MP is engaging in lobbying. Lobbyists are paid consultants who offer either political expertise, political access, or both. This is more controversial as it seems to suggest those with money should have greater influence than those without.

Now test yourself

TESTED

13 Define sectional and causal pressure groups.

14 Define insider and outsider pressure groups.

15 Explain the difference between pressure groups, think tanks and lobbyists.

What methods do pressure groups use?

Pressure groups and movements can use a range of methods when trying to raise their profile and influence the government (Table 1.8).

Table 1.8 Methods used by pressure groups

Direct action	Mobilising the public
This includes protests and advertising in order to raise public awareness of an issue. This may include civil disobedience or breaking the law. ✦ Greenpeace protestors interrupted Truss's conference speech in October 2022. ✦ Led by Donkeys used social media and paid-for advertising to highlight its concerns over Conservative government policy.	If a group can demonstrate to the government that a lot of voters care about an issue, they may have more chance of gaining influence. They may do this through social media, mass demonstrations or petitions. ✦ A vigil was held following the murder of Sarah Everard for people to pay their respects and to highlight concerns over the safety of women. ✦ A petition begun by Marcus Rashford gained over 1 million signatures to expand the free school meals programme.
Legal action	**Political action**
Groups can challenge government policy in the courts if they have the means and the legal standing to do so. ✦ Reclaim the Streets won a case against the Metropolitan Police for their actions at the vigil for Sarah Everard. ✦ The government was prevented from implementing its policy to process asylum seekers in Rwanda by the European Court of Human Rights (ECtHR).	If groups can work alongside politicians, they may be able to directly influence policy, or pay lobbyists to do so. They can also submit their views to the government or even donate to political parties. ✦ Action on Smoking and Health helped to shape government legislation on various smoking bans. ✦ The National Farmers Union (NFU) has submitted a number of responses to government plans regarding badger culling.

Factors that affect pressure group success

Pressure groups' success may be down to a wide variety of factors:

✦ **Their methods:** it is more difficult for the government to be seen to be working with groups that break the law.

✦ **Their status:** insider groups who have good relationships with the government may find getting influence easier than outsiders.

✦ **The government in power:** a government that has a similar ideology, or ideological sympathy, with a group may be more inclined to listen to it.

✦ **Their wealth:** groups that can afford expensive lobbyists or advertising campaigns do not need to resort to methods such as civil disobedience. This can make them more legitimate.

✦ **The extent of support:** if a group can demonstrate wide public support, the government may be more inclined to listen to it, as it represents a greater number of voters.

✦ **The timing of the next election:** the government may be more concerned about the feelings of voters the closer to an election that it is.

Now test yourself

16 Outline three different methods of pressure groups.

17 Explain the difference between lobbyists and lobbying.

18 List four factors that can affect pressure group success.

TESTED

1.4 Rights in the UK

Where are rights protected in the UK?

Citizens enjoy both rights and responsibilities (civil liberties) as members of their country. Common rights that citizens have include the right to vote, the right to life and the right to education. Citizens are also expected to carry out certain responsibilities, such as abiding by the law, paying taxes and voting. It is important to understand where the key rights of UK citizens are protected:

✦ **Magna Carta 1215:** first outlined that no one should be imprisoned unlawfully, later developed into the Habeas Corpus Act 1679.

✦ **Human Rights Act 1998:** enshrined the European Convention on Human Rights (ECHR) into UK law, and includes the right to education, freedom of expression and freedom from torture.

Civil liberties The rights that a citizen of a country is given by their government or constitution.

Answers at **www.hoddereducation.co.uk/myrevisionnotesdownloads**

+ **Freedom of Information Act 2000:** allowed the public to request information from public authorities about their work to ensure government transparency. However, there are a number of exceptions, for example regarding the security services.
+ **Equality Act 2010:** protects people against discrimination based on a number of protected characteristics including age, sex, race and disability.

How are rights protected in the UK?

While there are a number of pieces of legislation that protect rights in the UK, *how* rights are actually protected is another matter (Table 1.9).

Table 1.9 How rights are protected in the UK

The judiciary	UK Parliament	Devolved parliaments	Pressure groups	The ECtHR
The courts can protect rights in the UK through judicial review. If someone believes that the government has exceeded its authority, they can challenge this in court.	As Parliament is sovereign, Parliament can protect rights, or even challenge them, through the passage of new legislation.	The devolved bodies in Scotland, Wales and Northern Ireland can also pass legislation to protect rights, provided it does not clash with law made by Parliament.	Pressure groups can seek influence on matters of rights protection. This may be through the courts, through the media or through their relationship with the government.	The **European Court of Human Rights (ECtHR)** is the court of the Council of Europe. It can hear challenges under human rights law.
Example: In 2022, the UK Supreme Court ruled that abortion clinics in Northern Ireland could create 'buffer zones' which prevented protesters from going within an area around the clinic to protect users and staff.	**Example:** In 2022, the government passed the Police, Crime, Sentencing and Courts Act, which restricted protesting rights, but the government said this was to protect the public from disruption.	**Example:** In 2023, the Scottish government passed the Gender Recognition Reform (Scotland) Bill, although the implementation of this law was prevented by UK Parliament.	**Example:** In 2023, thousands of demonstrators protested at Downing Street regarding the government anti-strike legislation. Many of the strikers were trade union members.	**Example:** In 2022, the ECtHR temporarily blocked the UK government from introducing its policy to fly asylum seekers to Rwanda until the policy had been properly scrutinised and cases heard.

European Court of Human Rights (ECtHR) This court is part of the Council of Europe, a body set up after the Second World War to protect human rights. This has nothing to do with the European Union, and the UK remains a member state of the ECtHR.

Exam tip

In discussing rights protection, it is important to recognise what Parliament *can* do and what Parliament *will* do. While Parliament is sovereign, and therefore in theory can make or remove any rights that it wishes, whether this would be politically possible is an important consideration and will help you to evaluate rights protection in the UK.

Now test yourself

TESTED

19 Identify three pieces of parliamentary legislation that protect rights in the UK.

20 Describe, with examples, three ways in which rights are protected in the UK.

21 Outline why Brexit did not affect the rulings of the ECtHR.

13

How healthy is the UK democracy?

To answer this question, you may draw on a range of factors from across your course. But from this topic alone, there are a number of arguments that can be made about the health of UK democracy.

UK democracy is healthy:

+ Voter participation in recent elections has increased from some of the lows of the 2000s, improving representative democracy and legitimacy of government.
+ The development of social media has allowed people to become more involved with pressure group movements to raise awareness of current issues, improving pluralist democracy.
+ Citizens' rights have been increasingly enshrined in parliamentary legislation, improving liberal democracy.
+ The creation of the UK Supreme Court from 2005 (opened in 2009) added a body that can challenge the power of the government, improving both pluralist and liberal democracy.
+ Increasing devolution has spread power throughout the UK, improving pluralist democracy.
+ Referendums have become an increasing and accepted feature of the UK political system, improving direct democracy.
+ The UK's elections are free and fair, and there is universal suffrage, all of which are key principles of liberal democracy.

UK democracy is not healthy:

+ Voter participation may have increased, but turnout is only around 65–69% for general elections, and lower for many other elections. This undermines the legitimacy of elected representatives and the government that is formed.
+ Participation in the form of party membership has broadly declined too, meaning that the few citizens who are party members are playing a large role in shaping party policy, undermining pluralist democracy.
+ The Supreme Court can be ignored by the UK government as Parliament is sovereign which could limit the power of the court to challenge government, undermining liberal democracy.
+ Parliament has made laws that restrict the rights of citizens, including the right to strike, the right to protest and bringing in stricter voter identification laws, and there is little that can be done to challenge this legislation. This undermines liberal democracy.
+ Referendums are called only when the government wishes, as seen with the Scottish government's request for a second independence referendum. This undermines the use of direct democracy in the UK.
+ The UK's use of first-past-the-post could undermine voter choice as minor parties are unlikely to win, and under-18-year-olds and prisoners still do not have the right to vote.

It is possible to add factors from other topics to these lists and evaluate their impact on UK democracy such as the House of Lords, the monarchy, the impact of other electoral systems in the UK, the role of the media, and so on.

Exam tip

In a broad question like this, it is crucial that you do not try to include absolutely every factor you can think of. Instead, you are going to need to consider which factors are the most significant and how many you have time to write about. If you include too many factors, your work will become overly descriptive (AO1) and will lack analysis (AO2) and evaluation (AO3).

Now test yourself

22 Explain three factors that suggest that the UK's democracy has become healthier.

23 Give two examples that suggest the UK's democracy has become more under threat.

TESTED

Answers at **www.hoddereducation.co.uk/myrevisionnotesdownloads**

How effectively are rights protected in the UK?

Table 1.10 outlines the arguments concerning how effectively rights are protected in the UK.

Table 1.10 Are rights well protected in the UK?

Rights are well protected	Rights are not well protected
+ Parliamentary sovereignty means that Parliament can pass legislation to enshrine new rights for citizens as society advances, e.g. the Marriage (Same Sex Couples) Act of 2013 made marriage between two people of the same sex lawful in England and Wales.	+ Parliament is able to make law that challenges rights, or undoes previous legislation, e.g. the Strikes (Minimum Service Level) Bill restricted the ability of people to take strike action and the Police, Crime, Sentencing and Courts Act restricted the right of citizens to protest.
+ The Supreme Court can challenge national and devolved governments, and other bodies, if they infringe on the rights of citizens, e.g. in the *Ashers Bakery* case (2018) the Supreme Court ruled it would violate the baker's religious rights to write a pro-gay marriage slogan on a cake.	+ The Supreme Court can be challenged by the UK government, which is ultimately sovereign. This means that not only could the court be ignored, but any laws it is using in its cases could ultimately be changed by Parliament.
+ The establishment of the Supreme Court in 2005 (opened in 2009) means the court is more independent and neutral than its predecessor and may therefore be willing to challenge the government.	+ The Supreme Court can also rule in favour of the government, which may challenge rights, e.g. Shamima Begum lost her Supreme Court case to return to the UK so that she could argue her case to not lose her UK citizenship.
+ The UK is a member of the European Court of Human Rights, and has enshrined the European Convention on Human Rights into UK law as the Human Rights Act, e.g. when the UK government tried to deport asylum seekers for processing in Rwanda, the ECtHR granted an interim measure preventing the removal of some people until a full UK judicial review of their case had taken place.	+ The UK has previously ignored rulings from the ECtHR, e.g. in the case of *Hirst* v *UK* 2005, the ECtHR ruled that prisoners should be given the vote, which the UK government ignored, and there has been considerable debate in the Conservative government from 2019 about the UK's membership of the ECHR, e.g. Rishi Sunak said he was prepared to withdraw the UK from the ECHR if it continued to challenge the government's plans on illegal immigration.

Conflict between individual and collective rights

When considering the protection of rights, it is important to remember that by protecting the rights of one group, the rights of another may be infringed. In the *Ashers Bakery* case (above), although the rights of religious groups were protected, this came at the expense of LGBTQ+ rights. Similarly, the restrictions on the rights to protest and strike protected the rights of society to function. This conflict between the rights of different groups means it can be difficult to ensure complete protection of rights for all groups.

> **Exam tip**
>
> When analysing pros and cons, it can also be useful to evaluate recent trends and developments. So rather than just discussing whether rights are well protected or not, you could evaluate whether it is getting better or worse. This is a good use of analytical (AO2) and evaluative (AO3) skills.

> **Now test yourself**
>
> 24 Explain three ways in which rights are protected in the UK.
>
> 25 Explain three ways in which rights are at risk in the UK.
>
> 26 Explain the importance of parliamentary sovereignty when considering rights protection.
>
> TESTED

> **Case study**
>
> **A British Bill of Rights**
>
> In 2015, the Conservative Party manifesto introduced a commitment to a British Bill of Rights. This would repeal the Human Rights Act 1998, which itself was an incorporation into UK law of the European Convention on Human Rights. In 2020, the Conservative government set up a review of the Human Rights Act. By 2022, the British Bill of Rights had become the Bill of Rights and in the Queen's Speech Lobby Pack, the government said:
>
> ```
> My ministers will restore the balance of power between
> the legislature and the courts by introducing a Bill of
> Rights.
> ```

15

The Bill of Rights, drawn up by the then Justice Secretary, Dominic Raab, said that it would ensure that 'spurious cases do not undermine public confidence in human rights so that courts focus on genuine and credible human rights claims'. This bill, however, would not have seen the UK leave the ECHR. Just a month after the Queen's Speech was delivered in May the ECtHR intervened on the UK government's plan to deport asylum seekers to Rwanda for processing. This intervention increased the calls by some Conservatives for the UK not only to develop its own Bill of Rights but to withdraw entirely from the ECHR.

Summary

+ There are several different types of democracy in the UK — you must know direct, representative, liberal, pluralist and elitist.
+ Electoral systems turn votes into seats, allowing governments to be formed as part of a representative democracy.
+ Each system has different outcomes and creates different party systems.
+ Referendums have been increasingly used in the UK since 1997, but have both advantages and disadvantages to their use.

Revision tasks

1 For each of the key types of democracy — liberal, representative, direct, pluralist, elitist — copy and complete the table below.

Type of democracy	Key features	One way the UK is effective at this type of democracy	One way the UK is ineffective at this type of democracy

2 Identify the ways in which pressure groups could have influence on the government and evaluate which are most likely to be successful and why.

3 Create a timeline of recent developments in UK democracy, including rights and pressure groups. Use it to assess whether democracy has become more or less secure.

Exam skills

Determining factors

+ Many questions that you will face in an exam will have a range of factors that could be discussed in the answer. However, it is vital that you decide at the start what factors you are going to discuss and ensure that you have not chosen to cover too many.
+ Many factors can be discussed from differing viewpoints. In this chapter, we have seen how the ECtHR has both protected rights and been ignored by the UK government.
+ You need to ensure that factors are distinct and that you do not repeat yourself. In this chapter, we have seen that pressure groups may undertake protests, civil disobedience or even law breaking. These are not three factors; instead, they are all examples of direct action and writing about each of them separately would limit the breadth of your essay.

Exam practice

1 Evaluate the view that democracy in the UK is increasingly under threat. (30 marks)

2 Evaluate the view that pressure group success is determined entirely by the ideology of the government in power. (30 marks)

3 Evaluate the view that the most significant protector of civil rights in the UK is now the Supreme Court. (30 marks)

Answers at **www.hoddereducation.co.uk/myrevisionnotesdownloads**

2 Political parties

2.1 The UK political spectrum

What do 'left-wing' and 'right-wing' describe?

REVISED ⬤

Left-wing and right-wing are descriptions of different sides of the political spectrum. In the UK, these two wings are associated with different types of policy. The general principles of each wing are listed in Table 2.1 along with the key policies associated in the UK with these ideologies in a YouGov survey.

Table 2.1 Summary of left- and right-wing principles and policies associated with them in the UK

	Left-wing principles and policies	Right-wing principles and policies
General principles	+ Greater state intervention + Protection of collective rights + Greater industry regulation	+ Stronger policies on law and order + Support of free market ideals + Protection of individual rights
Key policies	+ Supporting a higher minimum wage + Support for trade unions + Supporting higher tax for wealthier people, including a bigger role for the government in wealth redistribution + Believe that welfare support is too low + Greater support for nationalisation of industries	+ Support capitalism and limited government intervention in business + Support tighter immigration controls + Believe in greater private sector involvement including in the NHS + Believe that welfare support is too high + Believe in less government involvement in wealth redistribution

> **Left-wing** Describes a set of political ideals that support increased social and economic equality, favouring increasing government intervention and challenging existing structures such as capitalism.
>
> **Right-wing** Describes a set of political ideals that support individual rights and capitalism, which may result in inequality, often challenging increased government intervention in society.

> **Exam tip**
>
> When discussing party policies, avoid using generalisations such as 'Labour supports high tax and the Conservatives support low tax'. Instead, you need to support your argument with specific party policies from recent manifestos or legislation from recent governments.

What are the functions of parties?

REVISED ⬤

Parties have a range of functions, many of which overlap:
+ **To fight elections:** elections in the UK are mostly fought on a party basis, with party manifestos informing people how to vote. This could also include encouraging people to turn out and vote.
+ **To form government:** parties fight in an election to try to gain a majority of seats so that they can form a government and carry out their manifesto.
+ **To recruit and select leaders:** from joining a party, to running in an election, to forming government, parties are often where people are trained for government roles.
+ **To represent the electorate:** MPs are elected to represent the views of their constituents.
+ **To educate:** through the formulation of manifestos and scrutiny of the government, parties can educate the public on important issues of the day.
+ **Policy formulation:** through party conferences, and in keeping with party ideals, parties produce a manifesto to show the policies they would carry out if they won in an election.

> **Now test yourself**
>
> 1 Define left- and right-wing politics.
> 2 List two left-wing beliefs and two right-wing beliefs.
> 3 Explain three functions of a political party.
>
> TESTED ⬤

Parties and democracy

Do parties in the UK help or hinder democracy?

Parties help democracy	Parties hinder democracy
✦ They help to ensure that those who take office have sufficient experience and training to do so. ✦ They encourage the electorate to participate, through mechanisms such as party membership, educating voters, or giving them a clear choice between who to vote for. ✦ Parties are the way in which government is organised and able to function coherently in the UK. ✦ Adversary politics mean that parties scrutinise the policies of other parties, ensuring good policy formulation. ✦ They ensure representation of the public, by carrying out the will of the electorate from an election.	✦ Where **adversary politics** exists, scrutiny can often be for poor reasons such as to humiliate a competitor party, rather than to produce good policy. ✦ There is concern that at the centre of UK politics, there is too much **consensus** between the two main parties, limiting voter choice. ✦ Falling party membership and low voter turnout levels suggest parties are not working as a mechanism for political engagement. ✦ Factions within political parties make it difficult to create a manifesto that the whole party agrees on. ✦ Parties may educate the public selectively in order to win support for their own view.

Adversary politics A political situation in which there is broad disagreement over political principles between the main parties.

Consensus A political situation in which there is broad agreement over key political principles between the main parties, even if there is disagreement on the detail or on how policies should be carried out.

Party finance in the UK

Parties are funded by a number of key sources in the UK:

✦ **Party membership fees.** The Conservative Party increased its fees by 56% in 2022 to £39 per year following a slump in people joining the party. In 2020, Labour reported an income of £34.5 million from membership fees.

✦ **Donations.** Parties must report donations over £7,500 to the Electoral Commission in the UK, but there are no limits on donations. The Conservative Party reported £3 million in donations from July to September 2022, down from £5.4 million in the previous quarter.

✦ **Public funding**
  ✦ The main source of public funding is 'short money', introduced in 1975. This is given to opposition parties to support them carrying out their parliamentary duties, but not electioneering.
  ✦ Cranborne money was introduced in 1996 to support the main and second-largest opposition parties in the House of Lords.
  ✦ Policy development grants from the Electoral Commission were introduced in 2000, given to parties to develop the policies in their manifestos.

Exam tip

When dealing with a small topic such a party funding, remember to look at how it applies to other areas that you have studied in order to broaden the scope of your essay. In discussing whether parties should be state funded, there are links to their representative role, to elitism and pluralism, and to party systems in the UK.

Should increased state funding be provided for political parties?

For	Against
✦ It would give smaller parties a greater chance to be competitive in elections, which could increase voter choice and reduce two-party dominance in the UK. ✦ It would reduce the excessive influence of an elite few wealthy donors, and create more transparency in party funding and greater pluralism. ✦ It would allow parties to focus on governing rather than fundraising. ✦ Perceived influence of donations undermines trust in MPs to do their job for the whole of society.	✦ If state funding was based on the current electoral success of parties, it could actually reinforce the two-party system rather than challenge it. ✦ Fundraising by parties ensures that they have to listen to their supporters, increasing the claim they have to be representing them. ✦ Spending public money on political parties is not popular. Even capping the level of donations that political parties should receive is controversial, with more than 40% of people saying they 'don't know' what level such a cap should be set at (and 15% saying there should be no cap).

Answers at **www.hoddereducation.co.uk/myrevisionnotesdownloads**

Now test yourself

TESTED ◯

4 Give two arguments that show parties help democracy and two that show they hinder it.

5 List the three main ways in which parties are funded in the UK.

6 Explain why state funding of UK political parties is controversial.

2.2 Political parties

The Conservative Party

REVISED ◯

One-nation conservatives A Conservative Party faction that has a greater appreciation of the need for a welfare state due to the responsibilities of the *noblesse oblige*.

New Right A Conservative Party faction that favours a smaller government, less state intervention and more responsibility for the individual.

Table 2.2 Summary: the Conservative Party

General beliefs	Main factions
+ Slow, evolutionary change (to conserve) rather than radical change + Individual rights, which results in a preference for lower taxes + The right to own private property + General support for free markets and capitalism with limited state intervention + Safeguard traditional institutions in the UK + A greater stress on security, including rule of law, law and order, and crime and punishment	**One-nation conservatives** + Focus on the idea of paternalism + Believe in the need for a welfare state to ensure a level of social equality, based on a belief in *noblesse oblige*, that the rich have an obligation to the poor + Believe the state has a key role in ensuring economic growth + May be called 'compassionate conservatism' today **New Right** + Greater focus on the individual, including reducing individual taxation + Believe in a free-market economy and private property with limited government intervention, resulting in privatisation and deregulation + Take a stronger stance on law and order, including immigration
2019 Manifesto	**Examples up to spring 2023**
+ Leave the EU — to carry out the Brexit referendum result and take the UK out of the EU + No income tax, VAT or national insurance rises + A pledge that pensions will rise by 2.5% per year + Commitment to net zero carbon emissions by 2050 + Commitment to spending £6.3bn upgrading the energy efficiency of over 2 million homes + The introduction of a points-based immigration system + The launch of a 'Democracy Commission' to review the balance of political power following the government's loss in the *Miller* v *PM* Supreme Court case in 2019 + Likely freeze of student finances at £9,250 while assessing the Augar Review + Create 250,000 childcare places for primary-age children in the school holidays + A commitment to 'levelling up', to reduce economic imbalances across the UK	+ Energy Bills Support Scheme saw every household in the UK be given £400 towards their energy bills in 2022–23 due to soaring energy costs. + The Police, Crime, Sentencing and Courts Act 2022 placed restrictions on the right to protest. + The Strikes (Minimum Service Levels) Bill aimed to restrict the right to strike. + The government's plan to curb illegal immigration across the Channel was to fly asylum seekers to Rwanda for processing. + Government was re-organised under Rishi Sunak, including the announcement of four new government departments including Energy Security and Net Zero. + In January 2023, over £2 billion was shared with projects around the UK in the second round of 'levelling up' funding.

7 List three of the main beliefs of the Conservative Party.

8 Outline three specific examples of Conservative Party policy from 2019 to 2023.

9 Using examples in Table 2.2 and any additional examples since spring 2023, explain which ideological faction of the Conservative Party is most applicable to the party today.

Exam tip

You are not expected to know every policy that a party has enacted, but you should know the details of some.

The Labour Party

REVISED

Old Labour A Labour Party faction that prioritises government intervention and control in order to achieve social equality.

New Labour A Labour Party faction that accepts a greater role for the private sector and prioritises equality of opportunity.

Table 2.3 Summary: the Labour Party

General beliefs	Main factions
+ A belief in socialism and social democracy, ensuring that there is equality within society + A greater role for government intervention to ensure this equality, often through intervention in and regulation of the economy + A belief in protecting collective rights, including rights of workers and rights of minority groups + Support for the welfare state and measures to tackle poverty through the provision of universal services + A belief in common ownership, sometimes seen in nationalisation of key industries	**Old Labour (social democracy)** + A clear focus on social equality, to be achieved through the redistribution of wealth by the government + Regulation of capitalism and the nationalisation of some key economic industries, resulting in a 'mixed' economy of public and private ownership + A strong welfare state with universal services provided for all including a strong NHS and comprehensive education system **New Labour (Third Way)** + A focus on equality of opportunity over social equality, reducing the importance of redistribution of wealth by the government + An acceptance of economic regulation by the market itself rather than by the government + Support of the welfare state but targeted to those most in need rather than universally available
2019 Manifesto	**Examples up to spring 2023**
+ Increase the NHS budget by 4.3%, while scrapping prescription charges, dentistry charges and car parking charges for hospitals + Hold a second Brexit referendum + Raise the real living wage (minimum wage) to £10 per hour (it was £8.21 in 2019) + Keep the pension age at 66 + Substantial cuts to carbon emissions by 2030 + Nationalise key industries such as the energy firms, Royal Mail and BT broadband + Scrap Universal Credit + Abolish private schools' charitable status + Free bus travel for under-25s + Build 100,000 new council homes	Keir Starmer took over leadership of the Labour Party in 2020 from Jeremy Corbyn. This took the party in a different direction. Starmer pledged: + to increase tax on the top 5% of earners + a Clean Air Act to tackle local pollution + to introduce a Prevention of Military Intervention Act to ensure military action is lawful + end privatisation of the NHS The Labour Party has also criticised policies of the Conservative government: + It criticised the restrictions in protesters' and strikers' rights. + Starmer called the Rwanda plan 'unethical'. + Labour called for an energy bill freeze in 2022 and a windfall tax on energy company profits. But Labour supported the Conservative Party in seeking an agreement with the EU on the Northern Ireland Protocol.

Now test yourself

10 List three of the main beliefs of the Labour Party.

11 Outline three specific examples of Labour Party policy from 2019 to 2023.

12 Using examples in Table 2.3 and any additional examples since spring 2023, explain which ideological faction of the Labour Party is most applicable to the party today.

The Liberal Democrats

REVISED ○

Table 2.4 Summary: the Liberal Democrats

General beliefs	Main factions	2019 election promises
+ **Liberty**: a focus on individual rights and freedoms + **Equality:** ensure that equality is necessary for liberty, which may require state intervention + **Democracy:** a belief in limited government created by checks and balances + **Community:** the decentralisation of power to the regions and nations within the UK + **Human rights:** a focus on ensuring human rights are upheld, and rejecting discrimination and prejudice + **Internationalism:** favouring working collaboratively with other countries, including re-joining the EU + **Environmentalism:** promoting sustainability	Classic (Orange Book) liberals + A focus on personal, individual freedoms + A belief in limited government, including limited intervention in the economy and government spending Modern liberals + Individual freedom can be achieved through government intervention to ensure equality of opportunity	+ Stop Brexit + 1p increase to income tax to fund the NHS + 35 hours of free childcare for children aged 2–4 + Legalise cannabis + Build 300,000 new homes annually

The Scottish National Party (SNP)

REVISED ○

Table 2.5 Summary: the SNP

General beliefs	2019 Manifesto
+ A belief in Scottish independence + A desire for a close relationship with the EU and to reverse Brexit (at least for Scotland) + A belief in greater state intervention, including protecting the rights of workers, increasing benefits and protecting the healthcare system + Opposition to nuclear weapons such as Trident (nuclear-armed submarines)	+ Stop Brexit + Hold a second independence referendum for Scotland + Increase healthcare spending and introduce an NHS Protection Act to ensure the NHS remains publicly owned + Scrap Trident nuclear-armed submarines + Tackle the climate emergency, with all new cars to be electric by 2032 + Increase paternity leave to 12 weeks

Other minor parties

REVISED ○

Nearly 100 parties and more than 200 independent candidates ran in the 2019 general election. These independent candidates gained collectively 0.64% of the national vote and 40 of these parties gained less than 500 votes. However, some minor parties are well known — national parties such as Plaid Cymru in Wales, and the Democratic Unionist Party (DUP) and Sinn Fein in Northern Ireland. Other parties such as the Green Party and Brexit Party also ran hundreds of candidates. While minor parties may stand little chance of forming a government, if they can develop policies that are popular, they can have an impact as these policies may be adopted by the major parties — this was evident in 2015 when the rise of UKIP led to the Conservative Party including a referendum on the EU in its election manifesto.

Now test yourself

13 List the main beliefs of the Liberal Democrats.

14 List the main beliefs of the SNP.

15 Explain why the Conservatives adopted the policy of a referendum on the EU in 2015.

21

2.3 Party policies

How have party policies changed over time?

When trying to identify whether parties are acting in line with their traditional principles, it is useful to understand how their beliefs and policies may have changed in recent years. Table 2.6 gives a small selection of policies from each party on a wide range of policy areas.

Table 2.6 Party policies changing over time

Conservatives			
	2010	**2015**	**2017**	**2019**
Party leader	David Cameron	David Cameron	Theresa May	Boris Johnson
Economy	Cut corporation tax to 25%	No rise in VAT, national insurance or income tax	Cut corporation tax to 17%	No income tax, VAT or national insurance rises
Education	Develop free schools	Open 500 more free schools	At least 100 new free schools per year	Freeze student tuition fees at £9,250
Health	Access to GPs at weekends	Extra £8bn for the NHS per year	Extra £8bn for the NHS per year	Increase number of nurses by 50,000
Rights	Replace the Human Rights Act with a British Bill of Rights	Replace the Human Rights Act with a British Bill of Rights	Repeal the Human Rights Act	Replace the Human Rights Act with a Bill of Rights
Society	Tax breaks to promote marriage	Double free childcare to 30 hours a week	People with more than £100,000 of assets must pay for social care	No one will have to sell their home to pay for social care

Labour			
	2010	**2015**	**2017**	**2019**
Party leader	Gordon Brown	Ed Miliband	Jeremy Corbyn	Jeremy Corbyn
Economy	No increase to income tax	50p income tax rate for those earning over £150,000	50p income tax rate for those earning over £150,000	Nationalise key industries
Education	1,000 secondary schools to be part of a chain	Ensure all young people study English and maths to 18	Scrap tuition fees for university	Abolish private schools' charitable status
Health	Maximum 18-week waiting list	Invest £2.5bn more than the Conservatives	Maximum 18-week waiting list	Increase health budget by 4.3%
Rights	Increase paternity leave to 1 month	Increase paternity leave to 1 month	Enforce all workers' rights to trade union representation	Raise minimum wage to £10 an hour
Foreign policy	No adoption of the Euro without a referendum	No further transfer of power to the EU without a referendum	Support the renewal of Trident	Hold a second referendum on Brexit

Liberal Democrats			
	2010	**2015**	**2017**	**2019**
Party leader	Nick Clegg	Nick Clegg	Tim Farron	Jo Swinson
Economy	No increase to income tax	Tax policy where the rich pay 'their fair share'	1p increase to income tax	1p increase to income tax
Education	Scrap tuition fees for university	Extra £2.5bn for education	Extra £7bn for education	Recruit 20,000 new teachers
Health	Cut the Department of Health in half	Increase NHS budget by £8bn per year	Increase NHS budget by £6bn per year	Increase NHS budget by £7bn per year
Rights	A freedom bill including scrapping ID cards	Create a Digital Bill of Rights	Protect the Human Rights Act	Protect the Human Rights Act
Society/ Environment	Shared parental leave of 18 months	Carbon net zero target by 2050	Carbon net zero target by 2050	Generate 80% of energy from renewable sources
Foreign policy	No like-for-like replacement of Trident	End continuous nuclear weapons patrols	Second referendum on Brexit	Stop Brexit

Answers at **www.hoddereducation.co.uk/myrevisionnotesdownloads**

Now test yourself

TESTED ◯

16 Give an example of a party policy that remained consistent throughout the four elections from 2010 to 2019.

17 Give an example of a party policy that changed over the course of the four elections from 2010 to 2019.

2.4 Party systems

What are party systems?

REVISED ◯

A party system is used to describe the number of parties in any election that have a realistic chance of forming government. This means it is not about how many parties run in an election, but how many might win enough seats to form a government.

It is important to understand that party systems are a result of the electoral system that is used. It would be very difficult to choose a particular party system, but it would be possible to pick an electoral system that might lead to a particular party system.

+ Majoritarian and plurality electoral systems such as first-past-the-post (FPTP) and supplementary vote (SV) usually result in a two-party system as it is unlikely that minor parties will get enough votes to win many seats.
+ Proportional systems such as the additional member system (AMS) and single transferable vote (STV) tend to result in multi-party systems as parties do not need a high number of the votes to win seats.

Party system Describes the number of parties in an election that have a realistic chance of forming government. This is usually the result of a chosen electoral system.

Electoral system A process by which votes cast can be turned into seats in an elected body. These are usually categorised as proportional, majoritarian, or plurality systems.

The party systems that could be argued to be in effect in the UK today are outlined in Table 2.7 (below), and arguments for and against each one are set out in Table 2.8 (over the page).

Table 2.7 Party systems in the UK

Type of system	Explanation	Example
One-party system	A system in which one party experiences long periods in office over multiple elections, and dominates the legislative system.	From 1997 to 2010 the Labour Party was in power and from 2010 to 2024 the Conservative Party was in power in the UK Parliament.
Two-party system	A system in which two parties have a realistic chance of forming government in an election and dominate the legislative system.	Throughout the twentieth century, the Conservatives or Labour Party controlled every government.
Two-and-a-half-party system	A system in which two main parties compete for power, but a third party is strong enough to be considered as a coalition partner.	From 2010 to 2015 the Conservative Party was in coalition with the Liberal Democrats. While the Liberal Democrats had relatively few seats, they had enough to create a majority alongside a major party.
Multi-party system	A system in which many parties have a realistic chance of forming government or having influence over the legislative process.	In the Scottish Parliament in 2007, the SNP gained 47 seats, Labour 46, Conservatives 17, Liberal Democrats 16 and Green Party 2; 69 was needed for a majority. Ultimately the Green Party worked with the SNP to form a government.

Exam tip

When dealing with party systems, remember there are far more elections in the UK than those for UK Parliament. You should consider devolved assemblies, mayoral elections and others when assessing what party system best describes the UK.

Table 2.8 Arguments for and against the different party systems the UK

	Arguments for	Arguments against
One-party	+ At national level, the impact of FPTP ensures that one party often has a substantial majority and can hold control of Parliament. + Parties with small majorities, or who have suffered backbench rebellions, have still controlled Parliament.	+ The existence of an official opposition that holds a substantial number of seats can reduce the dominance of one party. + Recent coalitions and confidence and supply agreements suggest that a one-party model may no longer be appropriate.
Two-party	+ The use of majoritarian and plurality systems results in a battle between major parties. + Popular policies from small parties, such as a Brexit referendum, can be co-opted by major parties.	+ Third parties and minor parties have seen increasing success where proportional systems have been used. + Factions within major parties suggest that they are not as cohesive as they once were.
Two-and-a-half-party	+ Third parties have been partners in recent national governments. + Policies from **third parties** have been adopted by major parties.	+ These parties are still dominated by the two major parties, even when they do get into government. + Without a partner, they would stand little chance of gaining political power.
Multi-party	+ In devolved assemblies, it has become common for coalitions to occur or for parties other than the Conservatives or Labour to hold power.	+ Even in the Scotland and Wales, the main UK parties have retained a presence. + This exists only where proportional systems are used.

> **Third party** A party that takes part in an election but is not one of the two main competitors and is likely to receive a limited vote share in comparison to those parties. Also known as a 'minor party'.

Now test yourself TESTED ◯

18 List the four types of party systems and briefly explain them.

19 Define the term 'party system'.

20 Outline the difference between an electoral system and a party system.

2.5 The success of parties

What impact have minor parties had? REVISED ◯

Minor parties often struggle to break through in elections due to factors beyond their control:

+ They are often less well financed than the major parties, and therefore getting recognition can be difficult.
+ The electoral systems in use, especially plurality and majoritarian systems, make it difficult for minor parties to be successful.
+ The major parties in the UK have a long tradition and also cover a wide range of policies and of the political spectrum, meaning voters can often find a reason to vote for the major parties.

The existence of smaller parties can create an impact even if they do not win in an election:

+ Their popular policies can be co-opted by larger parties (co-optation) who may fear losing votes to them. While this may limit the success of smaller parties, their policies can still be impactful. This happened to UKIP in 2015 over the Brexit referendum.
+ They can divert votes away from major parties. In Scotland, the SNP has taken votes from all of the major parties and even managed to form a majority government under a proportional system (in 2011).

> **Co-optation** When a larger party takes on the popular policy of a smaller party. In this instance, the policy has been co-opted.

- They can also 'split' the vote. When parties of a similar ideology run against each other, they might split the voters of that same ideology between them. Sometimes this can result in a party of an opposing ideology winning because their voters have rallied around one party. Commonly in the UK, the Liberal Democrats and Labour Party might 'split' the left-wing vote, and this can allow Conservative victory in constituencies that may have a majority of left-wing voters.
- Their vote share can raise questions about the legitimacy of election results and incoming governments. In 2015, UKIP won 13% of the vote but only 1 seat, which highlighted the electoral unfairness of first-past-the-post.

What factors affect party success?

 REVISED

A range of factors may affect the success of parties in the UK:

- **The leader:** while elections take place at constituency level, voters may be swayed to vote for a party due to its leader. Factors such as their credibility, personality, media image and experience may all improve a party's chances.
- **The record of the government:** the party in power will often be judged on what it has delivered over the past electoral period. For opposition parties, they may be judged by how they have worked with, or challenged, the government in power.
- **Funding and organisation:** the more money a party has, the more it can spend on campaigning to ensure that people know what it stands for, and even simply to get them out to vote.
- **Party policy:** before each election, a party will publish a manifesto, and the policies in it may sway voters for or against a party depending on the issues that affect them.
- **Role of the press:** often newspapers and other media outlets support or oppose a specific party, and encourage their readers to do so too. This has been exacerbated with the role of social media.

> **Exam tip**
>
> Examples do not always have to be the most current, but avoid using really old examples when there are newer, better ones around. For example, many students still use a 1992 headline from *The Sun* to demonstrate media influence, but media has moved on considerably since then. In 2019, on election day *The Sun* urged its readers to 'Save Brexit, Save Britain' by voting Conservative.

> **Now test yourself**
>
> TESTED
>
> 21 List ways in which minor parties can be successful without winning an election.
>
> 22 Explain what is meant by 'splitting the vote'.
>
> 23 Outline the factors that affect party success.

> **Case study**
>
> **The Democratic Unionist Party**
>
> The Democratic Unionist Party (DUP) was formed in 1971 but has come to prominence since the 1998 Good Friday Agreement and re-opening of the Stormont Assembly in Northern Ireland. Since 2003 the DUP has been one of the two major parties in Northern Irish politics, the other being Sinn Fein. Being a unionist party, the DUP favours the union of Northern Ireland within the UK, as opposed to Sinn Fein which favours Northern Ireland joining the Republic of Ireland.
>
> In the general election of 2017, Theresa May won only 316 seats, falling 10 short of a majority. However, the DUP had gained 10 seats in the election and agreed to enter into a confidence and supply agreement with the Conservatives. This meant that on votes of confidence in the government or about the budget, the DUP would support the Conservatives. In return, the DUP was promised £1 billion for Northern Ireland for areas including infrastructure, the health service and broadband development. Despite its small size, it was therefore able to gain considerable concessions from the government due to the weak position of the Conservative Party following that election.

Summary

+ The left-wing and right-wing sides of the political spectrum have key defining ideologies on to which we can place UK parties.
+ Parties have a range of functions that they fulfil.
+ Each of the main UK parties has a number of ideological traditions that have evolved over time and can be compared to recent examples.
+ There are different party systems across the UK.
+ Minor parties can be successful in some ways, but face considerable hurdles to success.

Revision tasks

1 Compare the party policies from the four elections from 2010 to 2019. Outline which party saw the biggest changes in its policy and explain why.

2 Outline the factors that affect the chances of success for a party, and then try to rank them by order of importance. Explain your ranking.

3 Look at the 2019 manifestos for the main parties. For each policy decide which ideological tradition of the relevant party it could be used as an example of.

Exam skills

In all three of the politics papers, you will have to choose between questions. It is important that you are able to select questions quickly so that you can use your time for essay writing. You should assess what each question is actually asking you to do. In some cases, you might be comparing two sides, in others you might be comparing factors. It is important you know exactly what is required in order to answer the question well. For example, to answer the questions in the Exam practice box you would need to do the following:

1 Compare the Conservative Party to the New Right and other Conservative ideologies (One nation).

2 Show how a leader can help party success, and compare other factors directly to this factor to assess importance.

3 Evaluate the ways in which third parties could be considered to be successful and compare this to the word 'never'.

Exam practice

1 Evaluate the view that the Conservative Party today is most closely aligned to the New Right. (30 marks)

2 Evaluate the view that the most important factor for party success is its leader. (30 marks)

3 Evaluate the view that third parties can never be considered to be successful in the UK. (30 marks)

3 Electoral systems

3.1 Electoral systems in the UK

What is the purpose of an election?

The reasons for holding an election are shown in Figure 3.1.

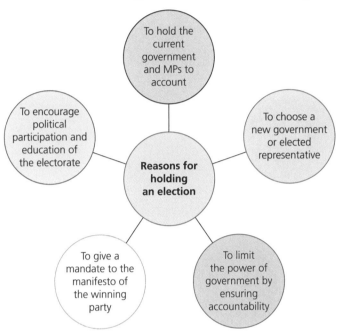

Figure 3.1 Summary of the reasons for holding an election

What is an electoral system?

An electoral system is a mechanism through which votes cast by the electorate are turned into seats for elected representatives. The different systems are summarised in Table 3.1.

Table 3.1 Electoral systems

Majoritarian systems	Plurality systems	Proportional systems
Require the winning candidates to gain a **simple majority** of 50%+1 or more of the valid votes cast, e.g. supplementary vote (SV)	Require the winning candidates to gain more votes than any other candidate, e.g. first-past-the-post (FPTP)	Allocate the number of seats gained roughly in proportion to the percentage of the vote gained, e.g.: ✦ additional member system (AMS) ✦ single transferable vote (STV)

Simple majority Mathematically, a simple majority is 50%+1 of the valid votes cast.

Elections in the UK

There is a vast array of elections that take place across the UK at different intervals using different electoral systems (Figure 3.2 on the next page).

My Revision Notes: Pearson Edexcel A-level Politics: UK Government and Politics, Political Ideas and Global Politics

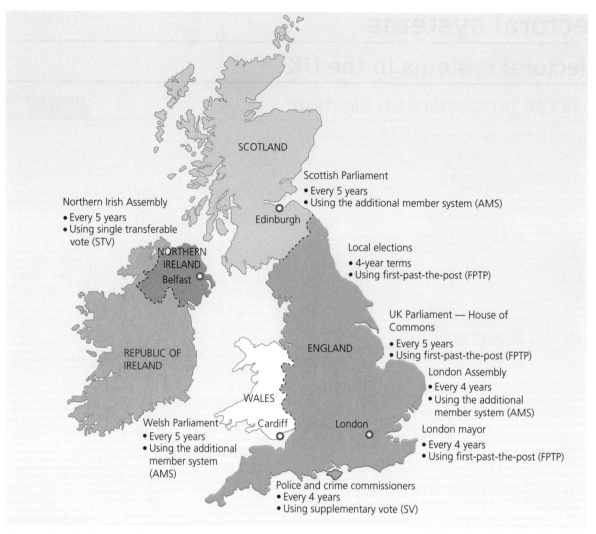

Figure 3.2 Elections in the UK

Table 3.2 lists and gives details of the elections that are held in the UK.

Table 3.2 Elections held in the UK

Area	Elections for	How often	System used	Name of elected representatives	Number of elected representatives
UK National	Parliament — Westminster	Up to every 5 years	First-past-the-post	Member of Parliament (MP)	650
Scotland	Scottish Parliament — Holyrood	Every 5 years	Additional member system	Member of Scottish Parliament (MSP)	129
Wales	Welsh Parliament — Senedd	Every 5 years	Additional member system	Member of the Senedd (MS)	60
Northern Ireland	Northern Irish Assembly — Stormont	Every 5 years	Single transferable vote	Member of the Legislative Assembly (MLA)	90
London	London mayor	Every 4 years	First-past-the-post	London Mayor	1

Exam tip

Ensure that you are aware of changes from 2022. The Dissolution and Calling of Parliament Act repealed the Fixed-term Parliaments Act (2011) and gave the power to call elections back to the prime minister. The Elections Act changed the election system for the London mayor from SV to FPTP.

Now test yourself

1 Outline three functions of an election.

2 Distinguish between a plurality and a majoritarian electoral system.

3 Define the purpose of an electoral system.

TESTED

Answers at **www.hoddereducation.co.uk/myrevisionnotesdownloads**

How does first-past-the-post (FPTP) work?

First-past-the-post is used for UK general elections.

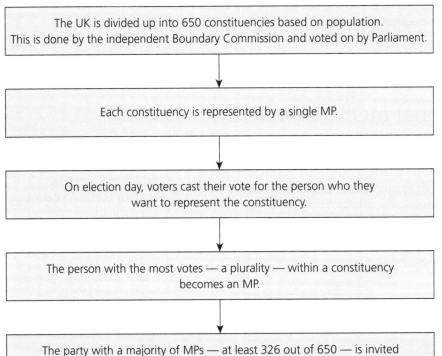

The UK is divided up into 650 constituencies based on population. This is done by the independent Boundary Commission and voted on by Parliament.
Each constituency is represented by a single MP.
On election day, voters cast their vote for the person who they want to represent the constituency.
The person with the most votes — a plurality — within a constituency becomes an MP.
The party with a majority of MPs — at least 326 out of 650 — is invited to form a government by the monarch.

Figure 3.3 How FPTP works

> **First-past-the-post** A plurality electoral system used for UK general elections to Parliament.
>
> **Safe seat** A constituency that is highly likely to be won by a specific party due to a concentration of its voters in this area.

FPTP has the following impacts:

+ It creates a two-party system, with only two parties having a realistic chance of forming government, and other parties have little impact.
+ It creates **safe seats** and marginal seats across the UK.
+ It usually leads to a strong, stable government of one party with a sizeable majority.
+ It creates a winner's bonus, where the winning party often has a higher percentage of seats than the proportion of the vote gained.

> **Exam tip**
>
> Assessing the 'impact' of something is a neutral interpretation, i.e. the impacts, or effects, are simply what happened, with no explanation of whether they are positive or negative. Being able to explain why these effects occur is analysis (AO2).

The advantages and disadvantages of FPTP

Advantages of FPTP	Disadvantages of FPTP
A simple system which should encourage higher turnout and increase the legitimacy of the resulting government	The simplicity of the system results in wasted votes because only the candidate with a plurality of the vote takes the seat
Usually creates a strong government with a majority of MPs, giving a mandate for its manifesto and the ability to carry it out in Parliament	The winner's bonus can give the government power in excess of the vote that they received
A single-member constituency means that local areas have a representative with a vested interest in that area and can be held accountable by local voters	Due to FPTP creating a two-party system, many people vote for the candidate standing for their preferred party rather than who will best represent their constituency
By creating a two-party system, more extremist parties are kept out of government and centrist policies, which are appealing to more people, are encouraged	Could encourage tactical voting, with voters casting their ballot for the 'least bad' of the two main parties, rather than their preferred party
A quick system, often giving a result on the day after an election, allowing the government to quickly carry on with the business of governing	Creates safe seats in which the value of an individual vote is reduced, going against the principle of universal suffrage and equal votes for all

29

4 Briefly outline how FPTP works, from voters casting their votes to the formation of a government.

5 Identify three advantages and three disadvantages of FPTP.

6 Identify what you believe to be the biggest advantage and disadvantage of FPTP and explain why you reached this judgement.

How does the additional member system (AMS) work?

REVISED ○

The additional member system (AMS) is used for elections to the Scottish Parliament at Holyrood and the Welsh Parliament or Senedd in Cardiff.

> **Additional member system (AMS)** An electoral system that uses two, separate, votes — one for a constituency representative and one for regional representatives on a top-up basis. It aims to create a more proportional result.

The voter casts **two** separate votes — a first vote for an MSP or MS to represent their constituency and a second vote for a party to represent their region.

↓

Scotland is divided into 73 constituencies that cover the whole of Scotland; Wales has 40 constituencies. Constituency MSPs are elected using FPTP from the first vote cast.

↓

The second votes are used to elect regional MSPs in eight large regions that cover the whole of Scotland; Wales has five regions. Using the d'Hondt formula takes the results of the constituency elections and the votes cast in the region to allocate remaining seats to parties more proportionally.

Figure 3.4 How the AMS works

The AMS has the following impacts:

✚ It creates a multi-party system, with a number of parties having a realistic chance of forming government as it is a more proportional system.

✚ Often, these governments may be minority or coalition due to the more proportional nature of AMS.

✚ Smaller parties often do better in the regional vote, which is more proportional, while major parties do well in the constituency vote, which is plurality.

✚ This has resulted in the growing success of nationalist parties in devolved assemblies — SNP in Scotland and Plaid Cymru in Wales.

How does the single transferable vote (STV) work?

REVISED ○

The single transferable vote (STV) is used for elections to the Northern Irish Assembly.

> **Single transferable vote (STV)** A voting system in which voting places the candidates in order of preference, and that uses the Droop quota to proportionately allocate seats to parties.

The STV has the following effects:

✚ It creates a multi-party system, with a number of parties having a realistic chance of forming government as it is a highly proportional system.

✚ In Northern Ireland, the Good Friday Agreement (not STV) means that the government resulting from an election must be power sharing. This means that both Sinn Fein and the DUP must hold roles within government. However, as STV is a proportional system, it would have a high likelihood of creating a coalition anyway.

✚ Smaller parties often do better in the regional vote, which is more proportional, while major parties do well in the constituency vote.

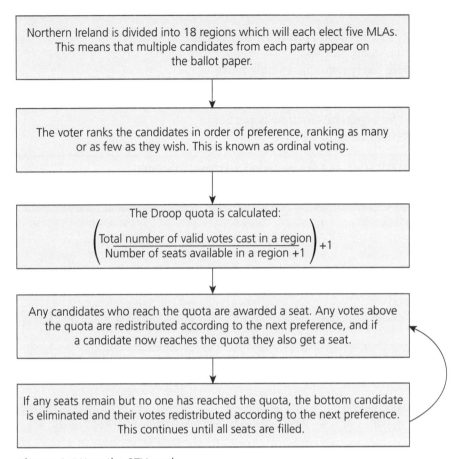

Northern Ireland is divided into 18 regions which will each elect five MLAs. This means that multiple candidates from each party appear on the ballot paper.

↓

The voter ranks the candidates in order of preference, ranking as many or as few as they wish. This is known as ordinal voting.

↓

The Droop quota is calculated:

$$\left(\frac{\text{Total number of valid votes cast in a region}}{\text{Number of seats available in a region} +1}\right) +1$$

↓

Any candidates who reach the quota are awarded a seat. Any votes above the quota are redistributed according to the next preference, and if a candidate now reaches the quota they also get a seat.

↓

If any seats remain but no one has reached the quota, the bottom candidate is eliminated and their votes redistributed according to the next preference. This continues until all seats are filled.

Figure 3.5 How the STV works

Exam tip

It is important to understand that the constituencies used in the AMS in Scotland and Wales, or in the STV in Northern Ireland, are entirely different ones to those used in general elections in the UK.

Now test yourself

7   Briefly outline how the AMS and STV work, from voters casting their votes to the formation of a government.

8   Explain why more proportional systems are more likely to create a multi-party system.

9   Outline the impact that proportional systems have had on national party representation.

TESTED ◯

How does the supplementary vote (SV) work?

REVISED ◯

The supplementary vote (SV) was used to elect the London Mayor from 2000 to 2021.

The voter has **one** vote but is able to identify a first and second choice on their ballot.

↓

Once all votes are cast, the first choices are counted.

↓

If anyone has 50%+1, or more, they are the winner and the election is over.

↓

If no one has 50%+1, all but the top two candidates are eliminated and their votes are redistributed according to second preference.

↓

Someone will now have at least 50%+1, and they are the winner.

Figure 3.6 How the SV works

> **Supplementary vote (SV)**
> A majoritarian electoral system in which voters can express two preferences, and a candidate needs to gain at least 50%+1 of the vote to win their seat.

The SV has the following impacts:

+ It creates a two-party system, especially as the second round eliminates all but the top two candidates, favouring two main parties.
+ If used on a large scale, this system would likely result in a single party government, with smaller parties likely to have little chance of gaining power.
+ SV would likely create safe seats if used for a general election as parties would need a high concentration of voters in order to win.

The advantages and disadvantages of majoritarian and proportional electoral systems

Advantages of majoritarian systems	Disadvantages of proportional systems
+ Relatively simple systems, which should encourage voter turnout + Give a clear result and a strong government, which increases legitimacy + Maintain a strong link between representative and constituency, which improves representation + Encourage major parties to have centrist policies with the broadest possible appeal	+ Usually more complicated systems which can increase voter apathy + Can create governments with smaller, or no, majority, which can undermine their **mandate** + Representatives are often elected in larger areas which can reduce direct representation of constituents + Smaller parties with more extremist policies can gain influence over government
Disadvantages of majoritarian systems	**Advantages of proportional systems**
+ Create more wasted ballots, which undermines representative democracy + The likely result of a two-party system can decrease voter choice, encourage tactical voting or lead to **spoilt ballots** + Disproportionate result, including a winner's bonus, can lead to an 'elective dictatorship' + Create a government that has the support of a single majority, which can create 'tyranny of the majority'	+ Create fewer wasted votes and safe seats, which can encourage turnout especially if voters can express their preference + Voters have a wider choice between parties, all of whom could play a role in government + A more proportionate result, which improves the legitimacy of the government + Create a weaker government that must cooperate with other parties to form a broadly popular government

Exam tip

The advantages of proportional systems are broadly the opposite of the disadvantages of a majoritarian system, and vice versa. Understanding this relationship by pairing them together to create comparative arguments can help to develop strong evaluation (AO3).

Mandate The authority to carry out the policies that are in a party's manifesto, and to govern the country.

Spoilt ballot A ballot that is made invalid either through leaving it blank, voting for more candidates than is allowed, or defacing the ballot paper.

Now test yourself TESTED

10 Briefly outline how SV works, from the voter casting their vote to the formation of a government.

11 Explain why more majoritarian systems are more likely to create a two-party system.

12 Outline three advantages of majoritarian and proportional systems, and explain the counter-argument to each point.

What happened in elections from 2010 to 2022?

Table 3.3 shows what happened in the various elections in the UK from 2010 to 2022.

Table 3.3 The outcome of elections in the UK, 2010–22

UK general elections

2010 (turnout 65%)

Conservative	36.1% vote	306 seats (47%)
DUP	0.6% vote	8 seats (1%)
Labour	29.0% vote	258 seats (40%)
Liberal Democrats	23.0% vote	62 seats (10%)
SNP	1.7% vote	6 seats (1%)
UKIP	3.1% vote	0 seats (0%)

Government: **coalition** of Conservatives and Liberal Democrats

2015 (turnout 66%)

Conservative	36.8% vote	330 seats (51%)
DUP	0.6% vote	8 seats (12%)
Labour	30.4% vote	232 seats (36%)
Liberal Democrats	7.9% vote	8 seats (1%)
SNP	4.7% vote	56 seats (9%)
UKIP	12.6% vote	1 seat (0%)

Government: Conservative majority

2017 (turnout 69%)

Conservative	42.3% vote	317 seats (49%)
DUP	0.9% vote	10 seats (2%)
Labour	40.0% vote	262 seats (40%)
Liberal Democrats	7.4% vote	12 seats (2%)
SNP	3.0% vote	35 seats (5%)
UKIP	1.8% vote	0 seats (0%)

Government: Conservative, with **supply and confidence** agreement with the DUP

2019 (turnout 67%)

Conservative	43.6% vote	365 seats (56%)
DUP	0.8% vote	8 seats (12%)
Labour	32.1% vote	202 seats (31%)
Liberal Democrats	11.6% vote	11 seats (2%)
SNP	3.9% vote	48 seats (7%)
UKIP	0.07% vote	0 seats (0%)

Government: Conservative majority

Other elections

Scotland 2021 (turnout 64%)

	Constituency vote	Constituency seats	Regional vote	Regional seats
Conservative	22%	5 (7%)	23%	26 (46%)
Green Party	1%	0 (0%)	8%	8 (14%)
Labour	22%	2 (3%)	18%	20 (36%)
Liberal Democrats	7%	4 (5%)	5%	0 (0%)
SNP	48%	62 (85%)	40%	2 (4%)

Government: SNP and Green Party power-sharing agreement

Wales 2021 (turnout 47%)

	Constituency vote	Constituency seats	Regional vote	Regional seats
Conservative	26%	8 (20%)	25%	8 (40%)
Labour	40%	27 (68%)	36%	3 (15%)
Liberal Democrats	5%	0 (0%)	4%	1 (5%)
Plaid Cymru	20%	5 (13%)	21%	8 (40%)

Government: Labour in cooperation with Plaid Cymru

Northern Ireland 2022 (turnout 64%)

Alliance	5% vote	9 seats (10%)
DUP	21% vote	25 seats (28%)
Sinn Fein	29% vote	27 seats (30%)
Ulster Unionist	11% vote	9 seats (10%)

Government: not formed at the time of going to press due to the DUP being unwilling to name a deputy first minister until issues with the Northern Ireland Protocol are resolved

London, 2021 (turnout 42%)

	First round vote	Second round vote
Conservative	35%	45%
Green	8%	55%
Labour	40%	–
Liberal Democrat	4%	–

Sadiq Khan (Labour) retained the post of Mayor of London

> **Supply and confidence** An agreement where one party agrees to support another in issues of 'supply' (money) and in votes of no confidence in Parliament.
>
> **Coalition government** A government formed after an election consisting of two or more parties that have formally compromised on common policy goals.

Exam tip

Knowing election statistics is less helpful than understanding what they suggest about each electoral system. A key part of analysis is comparisons. For example, it is notable that the Conservative vote increased by less than 1% between 2017 and 2019, and yet the number of seats went up by nearly 7%.

Now test yourself

TESTED ⦿

13 Explain what the trends in the recent FPTP elections suggest are the advantages and disadvantages of this system.

14 Explain which system could be best to replace FPTP using this data.

What has the impact of electoral systems been in the UK?

REVISED ⦿

The introduction of different electoral systems in the UK has had a range of impacts (Table 3.4).

Table 3.4 Impact of different electoral systems in the UK

Impact on type of government formed	Overall comment
+ Proportional systems often lead to coalitions or **minority governments**. In both Wales and Scotland, cooperation between parties has been needed to form government under the AMS. In Northern Ireland, although the Good Friday Agreement requires power sharing, the use of STV would likely result in it anyway. + However, the SNP did manage to gain an outright majority in the 2011 election, showing that proportional systems can lead to majority governments. + Majoritarian and plurality systems like the SV and FPTP are likely to lead to a strong, single party government. The only parties to win the seat of London Mayor under the SV were Labour or Conservative. + However, FPTP showed in 2010, 2015 and 2017 that it can give different results of coalition, a small majority and a supply and confidence agreement.	Although an electoral system has a likely impact on type of government formed, it is not guaranteed.
Impact on parties and party systems	**Overall comment**
+ Proportional systems encourage multi-party systems, where many parties have a chance of forming government. This is because it is unlikely that one party will gain an outright majority, meaning cooperation is required. This can mean that smaller parties can have immense power, as who they decide to cooperate with can often determine the party that forms a government — this makes small parties 'king-makers'. + The use of the AMS in Scotland has allowed Conservatives far greater success in the Scottish Parliament. + The use of proportional systems has encouraged the success of nationalist parties like the SNP and Plaid Cymru, compared to under FPTP. + The growth in success of smaller parties in the devolved regions has also led to their greater success under FPTP for Parliamentary elections. + Majoritarian and plurality systems are likely to result in a two-party system in which only the largest two parties have a realistic chance of forming government, excluding the impact of third parties.	The impact of smaller parties has certainly increased, although not uniformly across the UK and at national level two parties do remain dominant.
The impact on voter choice	**Overall comment**
+ The AMS has allowed 'split-ticket' voting. This is where voters can vote differently with their constituency vote and their regional vote, even voting tactically if they choose to. + The STV allows voters greater choice *within* as well as between parties through **ordinal voting**. This is because voters can rank as many candidates as they wish in order of preference. + In proportional systems, where there are fewer wasted votes, there is also a greater choice for voters as they know their vote is more likely to count, regardless of who they vote for. + The SV allows greater choice through preference ranking, although it only has a first and second choice. Given that only two candidates remain in the second round however, this could narrow voter choice to effectively one of the two main parties with the second vote. + The increase in voter choice has not seen an increase in turnout above that of national general elections.	There has been a substantial increase in voter choice but it has not resulted in increased turnout.

Minority government A government in which one party has a minority, but usually a plurality, of seats in Parliament, and chooses to form government alone.

Ordinal voting A system in which the voter ranks candidates in order of preference, ranking as many or as few as they wish.

> **Exam tip**
>
> In order to justify the most significant factor in an essay, you must be able to show how you reached your judgement. This often means showing which factor had the biggest *impact*, rather than just stating which is most important.

Now test yourself TESTED ◯

15 Describe two effects of electoral systems on voter choice and party systems.

16 Explain the impact of two different electoral systems.

Do elections improve UK democracy?

REVISED ◯

There are many types of democracy in the UK, and whether elections improve or hinder democracy may depend on which type of democracy is being discussed (Table 3.5).

Table 3.5 Ways that elections improve democracy in the UK

Democracy	Elections improve democracy by:	Elections hinder democracy by:
Liberal	+ holding a government accountable for its actions which means it limits its power + using a secret ballot, which means voters are free to exercise their choice without pressure + leading to parties publishing manifestos which increases voter choice and increases voter education + leading to a peaceful transition of power + allowing everyone over the age of 18 to vote (universal suffrage) which legitimises the resulting government	+ causing voter apathy through the increased number and frequency of elections following devolution, and a lack of **participation** can undermine the legitimacy of government + ensuring a two-party system through plurality and majoritarian electoral systems which undermines voter choice + encouraging political apathy as the public can effectively opt out of political engagement, leaving it to their elected representatives + allowing an 'elective dictatorship' and only giving accountability at election time
Representative	+ allowing voters to elect representatives in small constituency areas which allows for representation of local issues + enabling voters to elect representatives to government who have the full-time job of governing. The electorate can therefore expect them to be informed. This is a 'Burkean democracy' in which representatives can use their conscience to make decisions + holding representatives accountable through regular elections	+ causing confusion under the AMS and STV where voters are represented by multiple representatives + creating confusion and tension between governing bodies when voters in devolved regions are represented in a range of differing institutions + allowing MPs to vote with their conscience, which may mean they are more concerned with representing the majority — to ensure re-election — rather than representing everyone, including minorities

> **Exam tip**
>
> Whenever you are discussing whether something is 'democratic' or not, you should always identify the type of democracy that you are referring to — most commonly this will be representative, liberal or direct democracy.

35

Should FPTP be replaced?

FPTP should be replaced	FPTP should be retained
✦ Recent elections have resulted in coalitions and supply and confidence agreements. ✦ The winner's bonus means the results of FPTP lack proportionality. ✦ FPTP can deliver a government which is *too* strong — an 'elective dictatorship'. ✦ FPTP results in few **marginal seats** and unequal voter value. ✦ FPTP leads to wasted votes. ✦ Voter choice under FPTP is limited with only two parties having a realistic chance of gaining power.	✦ FPTP is simple and easily understood. Use of other electoral systems has not increased turnout. ✦ Regardless of the size of the majority, almost all UK governments have been 'strong and stable'. ✦ Smaller parties have had increasing success under FPTP, either through gaining seats or by being a threat and therefore having their policies co-opted. ✦ There is a clear voter choice, which makes education simpler for voters too. ✦ There is a strong link between MP and constituency.

Participation The act of taking part in the political process, most commonly through elections.

Marginal seat A constituency in which the winner in an election is not easily predictable and could be won by a number of parties. Also known as a 'swing seat'.

Now test yourself

TESTED ◯

17 Identify three reasons why FPTP should be retained.

18 Identify three reasons why FPTP should be replaced.

19 Outline three ways that elections enhance democracy.

3.2 What are referendums and why are they called?

Referendums in the UK have become a more common feature of political life, especially since 1997. It is now more common for issues of major constitutional change to be settled through referendums.

Referendum A 'yes' or 'no' vote offered to the public on a single issue.

Table 3.6 Differences between a referendum and an election

Referendum	Election
A vote on a single issue	A vote on a wide range of policy issues
A binary choice vote	A choice of options is available for the voter
Called when the government wishes	Called at intervals defined by law
The result is not legally binding	The result is legally binding
An example of direct democracy	An example of representative democracy

A referendum could be called:
+ to settle a controversial issue — this may be divisive for the public, or the party that is offering the referendum
+ to give legitimacy to an issue of constitutional significance by gaining clear public support
+ in response to public pressure

Exam tip

When discussing whether something 'works' or not, like an electoral system or referendums, it is important to consider what it is *supposed* to achieve. Then you can compare the outcome to what it is supposed to do.

How have referendums been used in the UK?

A number of referendums have been used in recent years. Key ones are identified in Table 3.7.

Table 3.7 Recent referendums in the UK

Year	Location	Issue	Yes vote (%)	No vote (%)	Turnout (%)
1975	UK	Should the UK stay in the European Community (the Common Market)?	67	33	63
1997	Scotland	Should there be a Scottish Parliament?	74	26	60
1997	Scotland	Should a newly formed Scottish Parliament have tax-varying powers?	64	36	60
1998	Northern Ireland	Approval of the Good Friday Agreement	71	29	81
2011	UK	At present, the UK uses the 'first-past-the-post' system to elect MPs to the House of Commons. Should the 'alternative vote' system be used instead?	32	68	42
2014	Scotland	Should Scotland be an independent country?	45	55	85
2016	UK	Should the UK remain a member of the European Union or leave the European Union?	52	48	72

Turnout The number of people who voted as a percentage of those eligible to vote.

What are the consequences of using referendums?

✚ Referendums are not legally binding on the government as Parliament is sovereign. Indeed, the government decides whether or not to offer a referendum. Even so, in each case in Table 3.7, the government followed the majority outcome. This can lead to questions over how sovereign the government actually is.

✚ The increased use of referendums has led to calls for more referendums. Following the Brexit referendum in 2016, in which a majority of Scotland voted to remain, there were calls for a second independence referendum. In 2022, the UK Supreme Court heard a case between the UK government and Scottish government on whether such a referendum could be called by the Scottish government alone — the Supreme Court decided it could not.

> **Now test yourself**
>
> 20 Outline three differences between a referendum and an election.
>
> 21 Outline three circumstances in which referendums have taken place in the UK.
>
> TESTED ◑

A second Scottish independence referendum?

After the result of the Brexit referendum, the issue of Scottish independence became important again. Although the result of the 2014 Scottish independence referendum was to remain with the UK, in the Brexit referendum Scotland overwhelmingly voted to remain in the EU. Therefore, when the UK voted to leave, Scottish nationalists debated whether independence from the UK and remaining in the EU would be better for Scotland.

In June 2022, First Minister of Scotland Nicola Sturgeon called for a second Scottish independence referendum. The UK government refused this request saying the issue had been settled in the 2014 referendum. The Scottish government responded that it would carry it out anyway. The dispute was sent to the UK Supreme Court to settle. In November 2022, the Supreme Court ruled that Scotland could not hold this referendum.

This controversy highlights the difficulties in deciding whether the UK should use referendums more frequently or not.

Should there be more referendums in the UK?

Yes	No
✦ Referendums can help to improve **political education**. The calling of the referendum on Brexit led to two key groups — Vote Leave and Britain Stronger in Europe — campaigning to explain the pros and cons of UK membership to the EU.	✦ Referendums **oversimplify** very complex issues. The 2016 Brexit referendum was fought on few issues, but took years to settle. Even after the UK left the EU, issues such as the Northern Ireland Protocol continued to be problematic.
✦ Referendums can improve the **legitimacy** of a specific decision and encourage **pluralist democracy**. The Scottish referendum in 2014 allowed the whole population of Scotland to decide on the issue of Scottish independence, rather than just a few elected officials.	✦ Referendums **undermine representative democracy**. By allowing the population to make key decisions, this makes politicians less accountable for carrying out these actions despite having the responsibility for doing so.
✦ Referendums can provide **clear answers** to controversial political issues. The Brexit referendum in 2016 gave an answer to the issue of UK membership of the EU while the governing Conservative Party was divided on the issue.	✦ Referendums are **called by the government** with no rules on when they should be called or on what issues. The Scottish government asked for a second independence referendum in 2022, but were denied by the UK Parliament and UK Supreme Court.
✦ Referendums can provide a **clear answer** to controversial social issues. The 1998 referendum on the Good Friday Agreement allowed the citizens to vote on a new settlement for Northern Ireland, and begin to heal societal divisions.	✦ Referendums encourage the **tyranny of the majority**. With only a slim majority, decisions can be carried out that may disadvantage the rest of the population. The Brexit referendum in 2016 saw 52% of citizens vote to leave the EU while 48% voted to remain. This was very close and therefore arguments have continued over the issue in the following years.
✦ Referendums hold the government **accountable** between elections. This helps to ensure limits on the government and ensure they do not become too powerful.	✦ Referendums can encourage **misinformation**, and education may depend on the **resources** of competing groups. The Vote Leave group campaigning to leave the EU claimed that this would result in an additional £350m a week for the NHS; the accuracy of this claim remains contentious.
✦ Referendums can increase **participation** in democracy. Both the 2014 Scottish independence referendum and the 2016 Brexit referendum saw turnout above that of recent elections.	✦ Increased use of referendums could actually increase **political apathy**, with voters becoming bored by overuse or only taking part in those they care about. The turnout for the AV referendum in 2011 was just 42%.

Now test yourself

TESTED ○

22 Outline three arguments in favour of using more referendums in the UK.

23 Outline three arguments against using more referendums in the UK.

Case study

2015 general election

Although the 2015 general election is not the most recent example, it had a number of unique outcomes that are excellent for understanding elections in the UK (Figure 3.7).

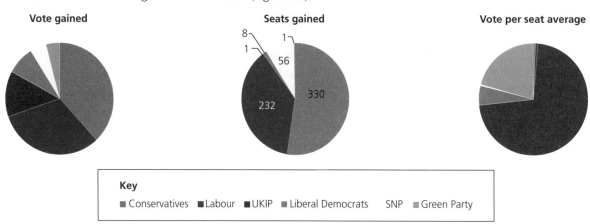

Figure 3.7 Summary of the outcome of the 2015 general election

Answers at **www.hoddereducation.co.uk/myrevisionnotesdownloads**

Notable problems highlighted by the 2015 election:

+ The difference in the average number of votes received per seat varied widely between parties, with UKIP gaining just one seat for nearly 4 million votes. This highlighted the lack of proportionality in the FPTP system.
+ The Labour Party increased the percentage of vote they received compared to the 2010 election, and yet lost seats.
+ The SNP gained a huge number of seats compared to their vote share, due to their concentrated support in a relatively small area. When compared to both the Liberal Democrat and UKIP seats gained, this seems highly unrepresentative.
+ The Liberal Democrats lost a lot of voters following decisions that had been taken during their coalition with the Conservative Party (2010–15), for example the decision to increase student tuition fees.
+ Despite gaining just over one-third of the vote nationally, the Conservative Party gained over 50% of the seats available and was therefore able to form a majority government.

Summary

+ The electoral systems used in the UK are first-past-the-post (FPTP), the additional member system (AMS) and the single transferable vote (STV), each of which has advantages and disadvantages.
+ Electoral systems turn votes into seats, allowing governments to be formed as part of a representative democracy.
+ Each system has different outcomes and creates different party systems.
+ Referendums have been increasingly used in the UK since 1997, but have both advantages and disadvantages to their use.

Revision tasks

1 Compare the results of elections in Parliament, Holyrood, the Senedd and Stormont between 2010 and 2022.

2 Copy and complete the table below for first-past-the-post (FPTP), the additional member system (AMS) and single transferable vote (STV).

System	How it works	Pros	Cons

3 Explain the arguments for and against replacing FPTP with a proportional system using examples from recent elections to support your arguments.

Exam skills

Introductions are crucial as they are the first time your examiner will 'meet' you, and it is your chance to lay out your argument. A simple structure to follow to succeed in introductions is the three Ds — **define, discuss, direction**.

+ **Define:** are there any key terms in the question that need defining to help you answer the question?
+ **Discuss:** what factors do you plan to discuss in your essays? These will likely become the topic of each paragraph that you write.
+ **Direction:** what are you going to argue? AO3 skills make up about a third of the marks in your A-level so you must have a clear line of argument throughout your essay.

Exam practice

1 Evaluate the view that the strengths of first-past-the-post no longer outweigh the weaknesses. (30 marks)

2 Evaluate the view that increasing the use of referendums is the most effective way to improve UK democracy. (30 marks)

3 Evaluate the view that the successful use of proportional electoral systems in the UK means that they should now be used for elections to Westminster. (30 marks)

4 Voting behaviour and the media

4.1 Factors affecting how people vote in elections

How does social class affect voting?

To divide people into classes in the UK, it is common to use their job type, and from this identify who they would have traditionally voted for (Table 4.1).

Table 4.1 Occupational class types in the UK

Grade	Occupation	Class	Would traditionally vote for:
A, B, C1	Higher/intermediate/junior managerial roles, administrative or professional	Middle	Conservative
C2, D, E	Skilled/semi-skilled/unskilled manual workers, unemployed, casual workers	Working	Labour

Between 1974 and 1992, over 50% of A, B, C1 class people voted for the Conservatives. However, this has changed over time (see Figure 4.1).

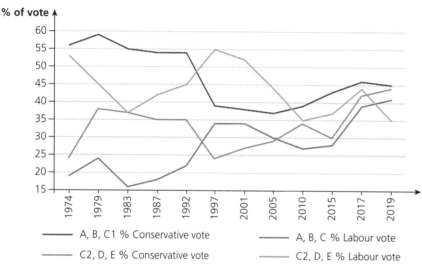

Figure 4.1 Voting by class over time

Is class still an important factor in voting behaviour?

Yes	No
✦ Despite a drop, a plurality of middle-class voters still vote Conservative. ✦ Working-class voters were increasing for the Labour Party until the 2019 election. ✦ Class may also link to other factors, such as education. ✦ There is a trend of middle-class voters voting Labour and working-class voters voting for the Conservatives in the twenty-first century. Even if classes are not voting for their 'traditional' party, it still seems there is a correlation between class and voting behaviour.	✦ The Conservative Party won a number of 'red wall' seats in the 2019 election, which had traditionally been held by Labour. ✦ A majority of voters no longer vote in line with the traditional expectations of their class. ✦ Other factors, such as age, region or ethnicity, seem to be more important in determining voting patterns across the UK.

Why has class voting changed?

✦ **Class dealignment:** as occupations in society have changed, people are less likely to associate themselves with a specific class.

✦ **Partisan dealignment:** as party policies have changed and political education has increased, people are less likely to have loyalty to one specific party, but vote on issues that are relevant and important to them at each election.

> **Class dealignment** The process of voters not associating themselves as belonging to a particular class.
>
> **Partisan dealignment** The process of voters not having a long-term loyalty to a particular party.

Exam tip

When dealing with issues that affect voting behaviour, it is useful to put each election in context and know what some of the key issues were at the time. For example, when evaluating the shifts between the 2015 and 2017 election, it is useful to contextualise that the Brexit referendum took place in 2016 and may help explain this shift.

Now test yourself

1 List the occupations that traditionally voted for Labour and Conservatives.

2 Outline the general trend in class voting behaviour between 1974 and 2019.

3 Define class dealignment and partisan dealignment.

Other factors affecting voter behaviour

Gender and voting behaviour

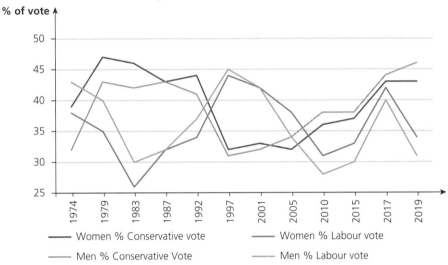

Figure 4.2 Voting by gender

✦ Over the last 50 years, there has been little evidence that gender affects voting behaviour in the UK.

✦ The graph (Figure 4.2) shows that the changes in party support in an election seem to be broadly mirrored in both sexes.

✦ In the twenty-first century, there has been a marginal trend that more men support the Conservative Party and more women support the Labour Party, but this is only by a small margin.

✦ Women and men may also prioritise different issues — women tend to favour increased spending and oppose cuts to public services.

Age and voting behaviour

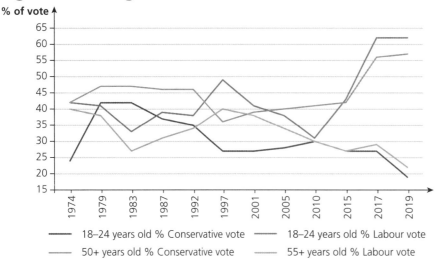

Figure 4.3 Voting by age

+ Traditionally, younger voters have been more likely to vote for Labour and older voters more likely to vote for the Conservative Party.
+ This trend has continued in the twenty-first century, with over 55s voting for the Conservatives in a majority, and 18–24-year-olds voting for Labour in a majority. Similarly, over 55 votes for Labour declined further and 18–24-year-old votes for the Conservatives declined further.
+ There was a sharp spike in this trend in the last three elections.

Ethnicity and voting behaviour

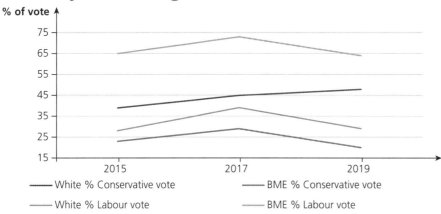

Figure 4.4 Voting by ethnicity

+ In recent elections, there is a notable trend for black and minority ethnic (BME) voters to vote for the Labour Party, with a clear majority doing so. The term 'BME' is used in the original data source but many minority groups prefer to be referred to as 'people of colour'.
+ The trend for white voters is less pronounced, but there is still a gap with more white voters voting for Conservatives than Labour.

> **Exam tip**
>
> When considering voting factors, always remember that how a person chooses to vote will be due to a series of factors, rather than just one — all of the factors together will play an influence, so be wary of over-generalising.

> **Now test yourself**
>
> 4 Outline recent voting trends by age, ethnicity and gender.
>
> 5 Explain which one of these factors appears to be the most important and why.
>
> TESTED ◯

Education and voting behaviour

Table 4.2 Education and voting behaviour

Qualifications	2017 % voted Conservative	2017 % voted Labour	2019 % voted Conservative	2019 % voted Labour
No qualifications	52	35	59	23
Other qualifications	46	39	44	33
Degree	33	48	34	39

Answers at **www.hoddereducation.co.uk/myrevisionnotesdownloads**

+ The general trend from the last two elections has seen those with no qualifications voting in a majority for the Conservative Party, and those with a degree voting in a plurality for the Labour Party.
+ Education may be closely linked to other factors, however.

Region and voting behaviour

Table 4.3 Region and voting behaviour

Region	% Conservative vote (change from 2017)	% Labour vote (change from 2017)
Northwest	37.5 (+1.3%)	46.5 (–8.4%)
East Midlands	54.8 (+4.0%)	31.7 (–8.8%)
London	32.0 (–1.1%)	48.1 (–6.4%)
Southwest	52.8 (+1.4%)	23.4 (–5.8%)
Scotland	25.1 (–3.5%)	18.6 (–8.5%)

+ Prior to 2019, there was a north–south divide, with Labour doing well in the north and the Conservatives in the south. There has also traditionally been an urban–rural divide, with Labour doing well in cities, and Conservatives in the countryside.
+ In the 2019 election, the Conservative Party gained a number of 'red wall' seats in traditional Labour heartlands in the north.
+ Labour continues to do well in cities.

Other factors affecting behaviour

+ Rational choice voting and governing competency expectations: the idea that voters are rational and will evaluate current circumstances and the policies that parties are offering to vote for a party that will best serve their needs. This is linked to issue voting.
+ Valence: how much a voter trusts that a party will be able to deliver on its promises. Often this is linked to 'governing competence', which is how much a voter believes the party in power have shown an ability to govern well.
+ Party leadership: while voting takes place in constituencies, voters may evaluate party leaders when determining how to vote. They may look at the leader's personality, reliability and trust, and experience.
+ Party manifestos: what policies a party is offering, especially in the context of current circumstances.
+ Tactical voting: if a constituency is a safe seat, a voter may choose to vote tactically in order to get the 'least bad' outcome for them.
+ Opinion polls: where it might appear that a specific party is highly likely to win from opinion polls, this may decrease turnout. If opinion polls suggest a close election, it may also affect the way a party chooses to campaign for the election.
+ Turnout: the number of people that turn out can affect an electoral outcome. Older people are more likely to turn out than younger people, which can help the Conservative Party.
+ The media: particularly traditional print media, as a newspaper may choose to back a particular party and encourage its readers to vote that way too.

> **Exam tip**
>
> Be very clear on the difference between a 'plurality' and a 'majority'. These terms have specific meanings and using them accurately in your work is vital to writing a good essay and advancing your argument.

> **Rational choice** This refers to the theory that a voter will vote for a party that best serves the interests of that voter.
>
> **Governing competency** The perceived ability of a party to carry out the roles of government effectively.
>
> **Issue voting** When voters consider current issues as the biggest factor in determining their voting behaviour.

> **Now test yourself** TESTED ◯
>
> 6 Explain recent trends in voting behaviour linked to education and region.
> 7 List four factors that might affect voting behaviour beyond social factors.
> 8 Define rational choice theory.

4.2 How important are factors affecting voting behaviour?

Table 4.4 Arguments for and against the different factors in voting behaviour

Factor	Arguments for importance	Arguments against importance
Class	Even if class allegiance to a particular party is changing, trends are still evident.	Class dealignment suggests this factor is increasingly difficult to determine.
Age	This has clearly been an important factor in recent elections.	This is a recent trend and may not continue.
Region	There are notable regional variations across the UK.	Regional variations have undergone significant changes recently, such as the red wall.
Gender	When gender and age are taken together, there does seem to be an impact.	There is little difference between gender and voting patterns for the main parties.
Rational choice	Issue-based voting, on issues such as Brexit, have played a significant role in recent elections.	Similarities between party **manifestos** can make it difficult to make a clear choice for voters.
Valence	Scandals that have dominated newspaper headlines, such as 'Partygate', seem to have had an impact on voter choice, seen in polling.	The public belief in politicians generally is low, with two-thirds of people seeing them as 'out for themselves'.
Party leadership	Headlines can cause problems for a party leader, such as Ed Miliband's 'bacon sandwich' or the 'Ed Stone'.	Popular party leaders have still not performed well, for example 'Super Nick' (Nick Clegg) in 2010. Leaders like Jeremy Corbyn divided those who supported the Labour Party in 2019.
Party manifestos	A poor party policy can create negative headlines, such as May's 'dementia tax' in 2017.	If a party is unlikely to win, what is put in its manifesto is of little value as it is unlikely to be held to those commitments.
Tactical voting	The existence of websites, such as **tactical.vote**, which outline the best way to vote tactically in any constituency suggest this is important.	Electoral Calculus suggests only ten seats changed hands due to tactical voting in 2019.
Opinion polls	Polling can change party policies/manifestos to try to improve their electoral chances.	Opinion polls have been inaccurate in recent elections and referendums, undermining their value.
Turnout	2017 saw young voters turning out in higher proportions for the Labour Party, which ultimately meant the Conservatives did not gain a majority.	While turnout has fluctuated over time, the proportion of each age group turning out has varied considerably less.
The media	Headlines and press support can expose issues and create image problems for parties, such as 'Partygate'.	Increasingly people get their news from social media, but this is not always accurate or balanced.
Overall	Changes in the last three elections seem to have produced some markedly different outcomes to those that went before. However, these three elections took place in a period of only 5 years, and whether these trends are a short-term blip, or are here to stay remains to be seen.	

Now test yourself

TESTED ⬤

9 Explain the difference between a mandate and a manifesto.

10 Which factors that affect voting behaviour can you use 'Partygate' as an example for?

11 Why it is unclear whether recent changes in these factors will continue?

Manifesto A document containing the principles and policies that are a party's pledges to carry out if it wins an election.

Exam tip

While Table 4.4 shows arguments for and against, in an exam it is important that you advance a specific argument. You might need to *show* both sides, but you need to evaluate which side is stronger and show why you reached this judgement — this is AO3. Simply balancing out arguments all the time is not creating a persuasive argument.

Answers at **www.hoddereducation.co.uk/myrevisionnotesdownloads**

4.3 General elections in the UK

Issues in recent elections

Table 4.5 Issues in recent elections

Year	Result	Turnout (%)	Notable national circumstances	Political circumstances
2010	Government: coalition of Conservatives and Liberal Democrats Conservatives: 36% vote, 306 seats Labour: 29% vote, 258 seats Liberal Democrats: 23% vote, 57 seats	65	+ The global economic crisis created division over whether the solution was austerity or spending our way out of the crisis. + The *Daily Telegraph* broke the story which became the MPs 'expenses scandal'.	+ This was the first time televised leadership debates had been used, in which Liberal Democrat leader Nick Clegg had been very successful, being dubbed 'Super Nick'. + Gordon Brown was caught on a microphone calling an older voter a 'bigoted woman'. + The *Sun* publicly switched its support from Labour to Conservatives. + New Conservative leader David Cameron reflected more centrist Conservative Party policy.
2015	Government: Conservatives Conservatives: 37% vote, 330 seats Labour: 30% vote, 232 seats Liberal Democrats: 8% vote, 8 seats	66	+ Greater public optimism in the economic outlook of the UK, but all parties supported continued austerity to some extent. + The rise of UKIP put the idea of a referendum on the EU in the public consciousness. + The possibility of another hung parliament.	+ Televised debates were expanded to include seven party leaders. + Despite a growth in social media, it ranked lowly among factors that influenced voting. + Inaccurate polls predicted a very close race between Conservatives and Labour, but the result was quite different. + The SNP became the third largest party in Parliament. + On the day after the election, three party leaders resigned within the same hour! (Labour, Liberal Democrat and UKIP).
2017	Government: Conservatives and DUP Conservatives: 42% vote, 306 seats Labour: 40% vote, 262 seats Liberal Democrats: 7% vote, 12 seats	69	+ Following the 2016 Brexit referendum result, the major economic issue was what the UK's relationship with both the EU and the rest of the world would look like after Brexit. + This was a snap election (under the Fixed-term Parliaments Act) to strengthen the government's ability to negotiate Brexit with the EU. + Less than 1 month before the election, a bomb was set off in the Manchester Arena.	+ Following Brexit, the UKIP vote collapsed, from 12.6% in 2015 to 1.8% in 2017. + The two major parties both saw a substantial increase in their vote share, with 82% of the vote between Labour and Conservatives + The Labour Party, notably Corbyn and Abbott, got considerable negative press for gaffes and inabilities to answer questions about the costs of their policies. + Theresa May commented that there was 'no magic money tree', before finding £1bn for Northern Ireland in the confidence and supply agreement with the DUP.

➡

4 Voting behaviour and the media

Year	Result	Turnout (%)	Notable national circumstances	Political circumstances
2019	Government: Conservatives Conservatives: 44% vote, 365 seats Labour: 32% vote, 202 seats Liberal Democrats: 12% vote, 11 seats	67	✦ All parties pledged an increase in spending for the NHS. ✦ The fear of a no-deal Brexit remained, meaning the economic future of the UK continued to be uncertain. ✦ This was another snap election, called after Boris Johnson replaced Theresa May in July 2019, and then failed to get Parliament to support a revised withdrawal agreement from the EU. ✦ The SNP called for a second independence referendum, with Scotland having voted remain in 2016.	✦ Not only did Jeremy Corbyn resign from the leadership of the Labour Party, the Liberal Democrat leader Jo Swinson lost her constituency seat and therefore also resigned. ✦ Numerous MPs resigned from their parties between 2017 and 2019, including some who went on to form the new Independent Group for Change in Parliament. ✦ Conservative Jacob Rees-Mogg had to apologise for comments made about the Grenfell Tower fire in the run-up to the election.

Exam tip

You should always try to use recent examples. This does not mean they have to be from a specific time period, but it could be considered odd if you are discussing issues affecting voting by talking about examples that are 20 years old when, for example, Brexit is so relevant today.

Now test yourself

TESTED

12 Explain why a general election was called in 2019.

13 Outline what happened to the votes for UKIP after the Brexit referendum was held.

Case studies of elections

1979 general election

Turnout and results
Turnout: 76%
Government: Conservatives led by Margaret Thatcher, 44% vote, 339 seats
Labour led by James Callaghan: 37% vote, 269 seats
Liberals led by David Steel: 14% vote, 11 seats

Impact of issues	Impact of the campaign
✦ 1978–79, Winter of Discontent — a series of strikes. ✦ A 40-year high of unemployment of 1.5 million people in 1978. ✦ 1979 — Scottish devolution was defeated, which led to a vote of no confidence in the government, which resulted in the 1979 election. ✦ All three main parties were led by new leaders, including the Conservatives, led by a woman for the first time.	✦ Given the social issues that existed, the Conservative party campaigned on the slogan, 'Labour isn't working', and its manifesto focused on economic balance and reducing the power of unions. ✦ Labour implied that the voters should not elect the Conservatives as they were led by a woman. ✦ Labour's manifesto was entitled 'The Labour way is the better way' and focused on inflation and improving industrial relations.
Impact of party leaders	**Impact of the media**
✦ Thatcher explicitly called on Labour voters to vote for her, saying the Labour Party was extreme. ✦ Callaghan was seen as oblivious to the industrial unrest the country faced. ✦ The advertising agency Saatchi & Saatchi worked on honing Thatcher's image, softening the 'Iron Lady'.	✦ The *Sun* supported the Conservative Party, and published a famous headline, 'Crisis? What crisis?' mocking Labour leader Callaghan. ✦ Televised debates were suggested, but ultimately Thatcher did not wish to take part in them.

1997 general election

Turnout and results
Turnout: 71%
Government: Labour led by Tony Blair, 43% vote, 418 seats
Conservatives led by John Major: 31% vote, 165 seats
Liberal Democrats led by Paddy Ashdown: 17%, 46 seats

Impact of issues	Impact of the campaign
✦ The Conservatives had been in power for 18 years, and the years leading up to the election had seen scandals emerge. ✦ The UK being forced out of the European Exchange Rate Mechanism (ERM) in 1992 led to Black Wednesday, questioning the Conservative's economic credibility. ✦ The Referendum Party pushed for a referendum on EU membership and threatened to draw Conservative voters to them.	✦ Labour had rebranded as 'New Labour', abandoning Clause IV and endorsing market economics. This 'third way' appealed to a broader range of voters. ✦ The Conservative manifesto, 'You can only be sure with the Conservatives', tried to emphasise stability. ✦ The 'New Labour, New Danger' poster demonstrated an aggressively adversarial campaigning method. ✦ For Labour, 'spin' became important, seeing the rise of spin doctors like Alastair Campbell.

Impact of party leaders	Impact of the media
✦ Blair was 43, a relatively young party leader and had proven himself charismatic on the campaign trail. ✦ By comparison, John Major was seen as dull; the satirical TV show *Spitting Image* portrayed him with a grey puppet emphasising the belief he was boring.	✦ *The Sun* supported Tony Blair and the Labour Party with the headline, 'The Sun backs Blair'. ✦ The internet was in its relative infancy but the BBC created the BBC Politics 97 service to document the election campaign.

2019 general election

Turnout and results
Turnout: 68%
Government: Conservative led by Boris Johnson, 44% vote, 365 seats
Labour led by Jeremy Corbyn: 32% vote, 202 seats
Liberal Democrats led by Jo Swinson: 12%, 11 seats

Impact of issues	Impact of the campaign
✦ Parliament's inability to find agreement on the Brexit withdrawal agreement was the backdrop to this election. ✦ This led to the formation of the Brexit Party in 2018 under Nigel Farage's leadership, which advocated a no-deal Brexit. ✦ Scottish independence was key in the SNP's manifesto, with Scotland having voted 'remain' in 2016, but being taken out of the EU with the rest of the UK. ✦ A few months before the election, Johnson had removed the whip from 21 MPs for voting against his Brexit plans, including party grandees such as Ken Clarke and Nicholas Soames. ✦ The Labour Party was under investigation for antisemitism going into the election. ✦ The climate was a key issue, with all parties having carbon pledges in their manifestos.	✦ The Conservative Party's slogan, 'Get Brexit done', was at the heart of its campaign. ✦ A number of parties campaigned on the platform of holding a second referendum on withdrawal from the EU. ✦ The Labour Party developed a 'My Campaign Map' app that allowed grassroots activists to see where their efforts would be most effective. ✦ A controversy arose over an edited clip of Keir Starmer put out by the Conservative Party which suggested he could not answer a question about Labour's policy on Brexit. →

Impact of party leaders	Impact of the media
+ Televised debates were held between Johnson and Corbyn alone, as well as those including other party leaders. + According to YouGov, voters saw Johnson as decisive and strong, but also untrustworthy and dishonest. They saw Corbyn as authentic, but also as incompetent, weak and indecisive.	+ **Social media** advertising was a well-used tool — it allowed parties to target specific demographics of voters. + Online news outlets also widely reported on the election — but 33% of them were committed to **impartiality** and did not endorse a party. + Only the *Guardian* and the *Mirror* endorsed Labour, while the *Express*, *Mail*, *Telegraph*, *Times*, *Sun* and *Standard* endorsed the Conservative Party. + When Johnson refused to attend a Channel 4 debate, they allowed the debate to go ahead with an ice sculpture in his place. 13 televised debates took place.

Now test yourself

TESTED ◯

14 Identify the key issues of the 1979 and 1997 elections.

15 Explain how important the leaders were in the 1979 and 1997 elections.

16 Outline the change in voting behaviour between the 1979 and 1997 elections.

Exam tip

One way in which you can create a convincing argument in an essay is to compare events and look for trends and change over time. This can help you to explain why one factor may **now** be more important than another.

Now test yourself

TESTED ◯

17 Explain how social media helped political parties to campaign in the 2019 election.

18 Outline the public perception of Johnson and Corbyn in 2019.

Social media Online websites or applications that allow users to share ideas with one another. This is not the same as, for example, a news website.

Impartiality A commitment from some news organisations to remain unbiased and balanced in their political reporting, not endorsing any candidate or party.

4.4 The media

The changing nature of the media

REVISED ◯

The media is an important way for voters to be informed about what is going on in the world. It is a way to reduce voter apathy. The advent of digital media has created notable changes in the way that people get their news. The statistics below outline some of the key changes in recent years:

+ Newspapers, both in print and online, have seen a decline in their impact, with only 38% of people using them in 2022, down from 47% in 2020.
+ The most common places people go for news are the television (74%) and the internet (66%).
+ The *Daily Mail* is the most-read printed newspaper, and the *Guardian* and *Daily Mail* are the most-read digital newspapers.
+ Social media has become an increasingly prominent news outlet. TikTok's reach for news was only 1% in 2020, but 7% by 2022. However, TikTok users get more of their news from 'people they follow' rather than from news organisations.
+ Younger voters tend to use social media and the internet to get news, while older voters use more traditional media. 39% of 16–24 year olds see social media as their most important source of news.

Voter apathy A process by which voters become disengaged with the political process. Also known as 'disillusion'.

Traditional media methods of mass communications that existed before digital methods, such as newspaper and radio.

Answers at **www.hoddereducation.co.uk/myrevisionnotesdownloads**

Decline of traditional media

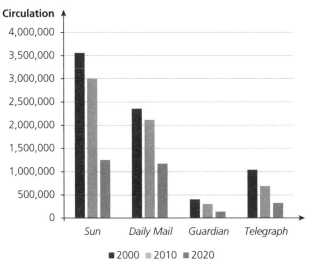

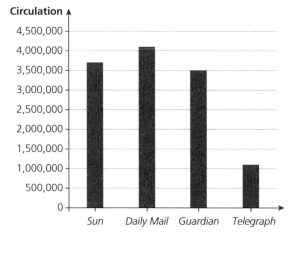

Figure 4.5 Print newspaper circulation

Figure 4.6 Daily online readership (2021)

Figures 4.5 and 4.6 show how traditional newspapers may have fallen in their print circulation but have remained a presence online. Newspapers such as the *Daily Mail*, the *Sun*, and the *Telegraph* are considered to be more right-wing leaning, while newspapers such as the *Guardian*, the *Mirror* and the *Independent* are more left leaning.

> **Exam tip**
>
> It is important to consider whether newspapers influence their readership, or whether readers seek out the news that aligns with their own political views. It is likely that this is a symbiotic relationship.

> **Now test yourself** TESTED ◯
>
> **19** Outline the changes to print media readership.
>
> **20** Explain the difference between where younger and older voters go for their news.

Do opinion polls matter?

Opinion polls are used to help predict the outcome of elections and to demonstrate the issues that are most important for voters. One form of opinion poll is an 'exit poll' — this is conducted by asking people how they voted as they leave a polling station to try to predict an election outcome before the votes are counted.

> **Opinion poll** An assessment of public opinion gathered by questioning a sample of people, usually the electorate.

How important are opinion polls?	
Important	**Not important**
✛ Opinion polls can help to shape government policy to better reflect public opinion. This is good for representative democracy and keeps the government accountable.	✛ Opinion polls have been inaccurate in recent elections, and therefore could mislead voters and/or politicians.
✛ Exit polls have shown accuracy in predicting electoral outcomes.	✛ Rather than informing party policy, opinion polls can be affected by party policies, simply reflecting changes in party manifestos.
✛ If opinion polls suggest an election might be close, it can help to encourage voters to turn out.	✛ They could influence the way that people vote and yet pollsters are broadly unregulated. This could therefore allow undue influence in elections.
✛ Opinion polls allow the public to have an impact on government policy between elections.	✛ Politicians are elected in a representative democracy to act as trustees not delegates. They should be acting in the country's best interests as they see it, and not reacting to every opinion poll.
✛ They reflect a measure of political engagement, reducing political apathy.	✛ There is no way to determine voter honesty in their responses, especially when compared to a voter's action at the ballot box.
✛ They protect political freedoms by allowing the public to raise issues that politicians may otherwise ignore.	✛ It can be difficult to ensure that a sample is representative of the electorate at large, which could skew outcomes.

How influential are the media?

Given that voters have a choice in the media they consume, it is important to consider factors around whether the media could be considered to be persuasive or not in politics:

+ While the use of social media is increasing, it rates poorly in 'trust' from those who use it.
+ Only 51% of people say that they trust the news most of the time.
+ 70% of people are concerned about whether the news they get is real or fake.
+ Those of a higher social grade are more active in sharing news via social media.
+ Voters for the Liberal Democrats and Labour are more likely to follow the news than Conservative voters.
+ 52% of over-45s use the television as their main source of news, but only 27% of under-45s. 63% of under-45s get most of their news online, compared to 6% of over-45s.
+ There are pronounced differences between social grades. Higher social grades are more likely to use multiple sources of offline and online news while lower social grades use fewer sources. Higher social grades are more likely to use the BBC, *Times* or *Guardian*, and lower social grades are more likely to use ITV, the *Sun* and the *Mirror*.

Now test yourself

21 List three arguments in favour of opinion polls.

22 List three arguments against the use of opinion polls.

23 Outline two ways in which the media has an influence on voters.

TESTED

Exam tip

The media could be considered as a factor that might influence voting behaviour. However, it has clear overlaps with other factors such as age and social class. Where overlaps like this occur, try to consider the cause of this relationship. For example, are some social media outlets more left leaning because of who they are used by, or are users attracted by its political outlook?

Case study

Opinion polling and the Brexit referendum

In 2016, there was a UK-wide referendum on the UK's membership of the European Union. In the lead-up to the referendum, opinion polls routinely predicted that the outcome would be 'remain'. Of 168 polls carried out after the exact wording of the question was decided, only 55 predicted that the UK would vote to leave the EU, and only 16 polls predicted the outcome of 52% voting to leave with 48% voting to remain.

This was particularly concerning as polling had also failed to accurately call the 2015 general election as a Conservative majority. Lots of questions then followed about why the polls were so wrong with several possible reasons:

+ Younger voters were more in favour of remaining in the EU in polling, but their turnout was low on the polling day.
+ The murder of MP Jo Cox happened days before the referendum, and made it more difficult for people to admit in polling that they were going to vote to leave the EU.
+ Polls undercount some voters and overcount others — for example, less-highly educated people tend to be under-represented while graduates tend to be over-represented.
+ There was a substantial difference in outcome depending on whether the polls were conducted online or by telephone, with telephone being less accurate. Online polls suggested outcomes more like 50% for each side, whereas telephone polls suggested 55% remain and 45% leave.
+ There were differences in how pollsters dealt with those voters who said they 'didn't know' how they were going to vote, and how they weighted the answers they were given.

Summary

+ There is a range of social factors that affect voting behaviour, including class, gender, age, ethnicity, education and region.
+ There is a range of non-social factors that affect voting behaviour such as party leadership, valence, tactical voting, opinion polls and the media.
+ Traditional media sources are declining while social media sources are increasing, however both still have a level of influence.
+ Opinion polls have proved problematic in recent elections. However, there are arguments supporting and opposing their use.

Revision tasks

1 List five factors that could affect voting behaviour and give a specific example of each at a recent election.

2 Outline the changing trends in voting behaviour over the last 20 years and give reasons to explain the changes you identify.

3 Outline the arguments for and against the use of opinion polls.

Exam skills

Defining key words

Many words have multiple meanings or can be interpreted in different ways. Sometimes it is necessary in an introduction to define the key terms in a question to set the parameters of your essay. These might be words that have a political meaning, or sometimes words that could simply be interpreted in different ways.

For example, in the questions in the Exam practice box, you may choose to define:
+ 'social class' — do you mean working/middle/upper class? Or do you mean A, B, C1, C2, D, E?
+ 'UK democracy' — which type of democracy are you going to discuss?
+ 'failure' – this is a very binary word that you may choose to define. Have opinion polls 'failed', or is the truth more nuanced than that?

Exam practice

1 Evaluate the view that social class is no longer an important factor when determining voter behaviour in the UK. (30 marks)

2 Evaluate the view that the role of the media is damaging to UK democracy. (30 marks)

3 Evaluate the view that the failure of opinion polls means that they should now be banned. (30 marks)

5 The UK constitution

5.1 Nature and history of the UK constitution

Features of the UK constitution

A constitution should outline several things:
+ the limits of government power
+ the relationship between the various branches of government
+ what makes someone a citizen
+ how rights are protected
+ how to amend the constitution

The UK's constitution has features that are quite rare (Table 5.1).

Table 5.1 Features of the UK constitution

Uncodified	The UK constitution is not written down in one single document, but is drawn from different sources. In a country with a codified constitution, the constitution would be written in a single document (perhaps with amendments made to it).
Unentrenched	There is no protection offered for the UK constitution such as a formal amendment process. Instead, it can be changed easily, for example by a single Act of Parliament. In a country with an entrenched constitution, the amendment process would be formalised. For example, in the US amendments to the Constitution require Congressional and state approval.
Unitary	Political power in the UK all resides in one place — in Parliament. This means that Parliament is sovereign. While Parliament might give power out, for example to devolved bodies, it remains the ultimate decision-maker. In countries with a codified constitution, usually the constitution itself is sovereign.
'Twin pillars'	Because of the **uncodified** and unentrenched nature of the UK constitution, it is based on the '**twin pillars**' which underpin the UK constitution: 1 **Rule of law** — everybody is equal under the law and the law applies equally to all. 2 Parliament is sovereign.

Constitution A set of principles that outline the political system and division of political power within a country.

Uncodified A constitution that is not written in one single document, but drawn from a range of sources.

Twin pillars Refers to the two key principles upon which the UK constitution rests — the rule of law and parliamentary sovereignty.

Rule of law The law passed by Parliament applies equally to everyone.

Exam tip

Ensure you absolutely understand that the UK constitution is uncodified, **not** unwritten. Many sources of the UK constitution are written down, they are just not collected into one document.

What is Parliamentary sovereignty?

A. V. Dicey described parliamentary sovereignty as Parliament's right to 'make or unmake any law whatever' in his book *An Introduction to the Study of the Law of the Constitution*. Parliamentary sovereignty encompasses a number of principles:
+ Parliament can make law on any topic.
+ No Parliament can be bound by its predecessors.
+ No Parliament can be bound by its successors.
+ Parliamentary law is supreme.

How did the UK constitution develop?

Table 5.2 outlines the key documents that shaped the UK constitution.

Table 5.2 The development of the UK constitution

Magna Carta 1215	A guarantee of certain basic rights including that citizens should not be imprisoned without trial (enshrined in the Habeas Corpus Act, 1679).
Bill of Rights 1689	The establishment of a constitutional monarchy in the UK in which the monarch's power is not limitless, outlining the rights of Parliament.
Act of Settlement 1701	Outlines the succession to the throne in the UK, including Scotland, Wales, Northern Ireland and England.
Act of Union 1707	Created Great Britain by formally joining Scotland to England and Wales (although retaining a separate Scottish legal system).
Parliament Act 1911	Removed the power of the House of Lords to reject money bills or reject a bill three times. The life of Parliament cannot be extended without consent of the Lords.
Parliament Act 1949	Reduced the power of the House of Lords to delay bills to 1 year.
European Communities Act 1972	Britain joined the European Community, later called the European Union.
European Union (Withdrawal Agreement) Act 2020	Britain left the European Union on 31 January 2020.

> **Now test yourself**
>
> 1 Explain what 'uncodified' and 'unentrenched' mean.
> 2 Outline the four principles of parliamentary sovereignty.
> 3 List the documents that have shaped the UK constitution.
>
> TESTED ◯

What are the sources of the UK constitution?

As the UK constitution is uncodified, it is important to recognise the sources from which the constitution is actually drawn (Table 5.3).

Table 5.3 Sources of the UK constitution

Source	Explanation	Examples
Statute law	A law made by Parliament, also known as an 'Act of Parliament'.	✚ The Succession to the Crown Act 2013 changed the line of succession for the monarchy. ✚ The Marriage (Same Sex Couples) Act 2011 protected the rights of same sex couples.
Common law	Rules made by judges who have had to interpret statute law when it has been unclear. This is often done through judicial review.	In *Miller* v *PM* 2019, the Supreme Court of the UK ruled that the prime minister did not have the right to prorogue Parliament in the circumstances that he had.
Conventions	Unwritten traditions that have influence over how a political system works.	✚ The Salisbury Convention is that the House of Lords cannot reject bills that have been promised in a party's manifesto as a party won a mandate to carry out these policies at an election. ✚ Royal assent is expected from the monarch on bills passed by Parliament.
Authoritative works	Books written by political scholars outlining how the UK political system works. They have no legal standing but are recognised as useful guides.	✚ A. V. Dicey outlined the principles of parliamentary sovereignty. ✚ Walter Bagehot described the 'fused' powers of the UK government in his book *The English Constitution*. ✚ *Erskine May* is considered the 'bible' of Parliament, and outlines procedures such as the humble address, which was used in 2017 to force the government's impact assessments on the effect of Brexit.
Treaties and agreements	Agreements that have been made between the UK and other countries or supranational organisations.	The UK is a founding member of the Council of Europe. The Council's court is the **European Court of Human Rights**, which has influence over the UK. The European Convention on Human Rights was adopted by the UK as the Human Rights Act 1998.

Statute law An act that is passed by UK Parliament, for example the Human Rights Act 1998.

Common law Rules made by judges interpreting the legislative landscape.

Conventions Unwritten traditions of the UK political system that influence how politics works.

Authoritative works Works written by political experts that have become recognised as useful guides to the UK political system.

European Court of Human Rights The court of the Council of Europe, where cases regarding the European Convention on Human Rights can be tried.

Treaty Formal agreement between the UK and other governments or supranational organisations.

Despite the range of sources, it is important to remember that Parliament is sovereign. Therefore, it can ignore or pass a new statute law to overturn any source that Parliament dislikes. For example:

✚ The UK government ignored the ruling of *Hirst v UK 2005* from the European Convention on Human Rights, which said that prisoners should have the right to vote.

✚ The UK government used statute law to both enter the European Community and then later leave what had become the European Union.

✚ The Salisbury Convention was suspended for the duration of the coalition as no party had won a majority for its manifesto.

How has the constitution changed over time?

REVISED

✚ Parliament has become more important and the role of the monarch has decreased. This is enshrined in the 1689 Bill of Rights, but today the monarch has very limited powers indeed.

✚ The constitution has become increasingly written down, although still in a vast range of sources.

✚ Parliamentary sovereignty and the unitary nature of the UK has been challenged — for example by judicial review and devolution. Nonetheless, Parliament remains sovereign as shown in the 2022 ruling on Scotland's second independence referendum.

✚ The 'fused' powers of UK government have become more separated. The addition of a Supreme Court removed the judicial role of the House of Lords, and the prime minister and cabinet have been chastised by the Speaker of Parliament for failing to brief Parliament on policy before they brief the press.

Exam tip

Be aware of the different types of sovereignty, especially legal and political sovereignty. Legal sovereignty is where power lies in theory, but political sovereignty is where power lies in reality. These may not always be the same.

Now test yourself

TESTED

4 List the sources of the UK constitution and give an example for each one.

5 Outline how the UK constitution has evolved over time.

6 Distinguish between legal and political sovereignty.

5.2 Reforms since 1997

Reforms passed under the Labour government, 1997–2010

When the Labour Party swept to power in 1997, it promised a range of reforms that would modernise and democratise the UK (Table 5.4).

Table 5.4 Key reforms passed by Labour 1997–2010

Reform	Impact	Limitations
Referendums on **devolution** in Scotland, Wales and Northern Ireland 1997/1998	+ This was the first time since 1975 that referendums had been used. + Turnout was high for the Scottish and Northern Irish referendums. + An example of direct democracy.	+ The Welsh referendum had only limited turnout. + The government decided on the wording, timing and other logistical issues.
Government of Wales Act 1998	+ Established the Senedd in Wales. + The Senedd would be elected using the additional member system (AMS), trialling proportional representation in the UK.	+ Only gave Wales secondary legislative power. + There have been a series of coalitions in Wales that have limited the power of government.
Scotland Act 1998	+ Established Scottish Parliament at Holyrood with primary legislative powers and limited tax-varying powers. + Created a more pluralist democracy, with power shared to the regions.	+ Did not quell nationalism in Scotland. + Created asymmetrical devolution between Scotland and Wales. + Challenged parliamentary sovereignty.
Human Rights Act 1998	+ Enshrined the European Convention on Human Rights into UK law, protecting rights in the UK. + Allows neutral and independent judges to defend human rights, rather than being dependent on the ideology of the government in power.	+ This is only an Act of Parliament and therefore can be overturned by another Act of Parliament, therefore not adequately protecting rights. + Gives too much power to unelected judges.
House of Lords Act 1999	+ Removed all but 92 hereditary peers from the House of Lords. + Extended the number of life peers (first introduced in 1958), which increased the number of experts in the House of Lords. + The House of Lords has become more willing to challenge the government.	+ Hereditary peers still remain, which is arguably the most undemocratic aspect of the House. However, all members are unelected. + The reforms extended the power of the prime minister over who sits in the House of Lords.
Freedom of Information Act 2001	Allowed the public to access documents detailing how government decisions have been reached.	+ Broad freedom of information requests can be denied for being too time-consuming for government. + There are several exemptions.
Constitutional Reform Act 2005	Creates a separate Supreme Court for the UK, removing this role from the Law Lords in the House of Lords.	Gives power to an unelected and unaccountable branch of government that has directly challenged the government.

Exam tip

When dealing with the Human Rights Act, it is imperative that you understand that it has nothing to do with the EU. It is UK law, enshrining the European Convention on Human Rights (ECHR) into statute law. The UK may have left the EU but it remains a member of the Council of Europe, which created the ECHR.

Devolution The sharing of political power, but not sovereignty.

Now test yourself

TESTED

7 List three reforms carried out by the Labour government between 1997 and 2010.

8 Outline the effectiveness and limitations of the House of Lords Act 1999.

9 Outline the effectiveness and limitations of the Constitutional Reform Act 2005.

Reforms passed under the coalition government, 2010–2015

When no party gained a parliamentary majority in 2010, the Conservative Party and the Liberal Democrats formed a coalition. This meant that both parties had to compromise on their manifestos. Ultimately, they created the Coalition Agreement, a 36-page document that outlined all of the policies they planned to carry out in the coming Parliament.

Table 5.5 Key reforms passed by coalition government 2010–2015

Reform	Effectiveness	Limitations
Fixed-term Parliaments Act 2011	+ Removed control of the calling of a general election from the government and created set dates instead. + Ensured stability for a coalition government, which was an uncommon political situation for the UK.	+ Snap elections could still be called with the support of two-thirds of MPs. + The Act could be repealed at any time, or by any future Parliament.
AV referendum 2011	+ A nationwide referendum was held on replacing FPTP with the alternative vote system. + It settled the debate on replacing FPTP for at least the duration of the coalition.	+ Turnout was very low, undermining the use of referendums. + AV was not the system the Liberal Democrats wanted as it is a majoritarian system. + Furthered the expectation that matters of constitutional importance be settled by a referendum.
Welsh devolution referendum 2011	+ A referendum was held in Wales and ultimately extended primary legislative powers to Wales. + Reduced asymmetrical devolution across the UK.	+ Turnout was just 35%, which raised questions over the legitimacy of the result.
Succession to the Crown Act 2013	+ Changed the line of succession for the crown from the first-born male heir to the first-born heir (removing primogeniture), and further enshrined a **constitutional monarchy** in the UK. + Recognised the equality of women's rights in the UK.	+ Had little impact beyond the monarchy, and as it transpired the first-born heir to Prince William was a son anyway.
Wales Act 2014	+ Gave Wales the power to determine certain taxes, extended Senedd terms to 5 years and precluded members of the Senedd from also being MPs.	+ Limits were still placed on Wales by UK government including limiting their debt. + Further threatened **parliamentary sovereignty** in the UK.
Referendum on Scottish Independence 2014	+ A 'once in a generation' vote to settle the place of Scotland in the UK. + The turnout was high. + 16- and 17-year-olds were able to vote.	+ Following the result of Brexit, the issue of Scottish independence continued to be controversial.

Recall of MPs Act 2015	+ Sets out provisions for constituents to be able to recall their MP to face an election in certain circumstances:
	  + if they are convicted of a crime
	  + if they produce false expenses claims
	  + if they are suspended from the House of Commons for at least 10 days
	+ Was successfully invoked twice in 2019.
		+ The low limits of petitioners required, just 10% of a constituency, raise questions of legitimacy.
		+ It has only been used three times, and one of those the required number of signatories failed to be reached.

Constitutional monarchy A monarchy that is limited in the extent of its power and shares power with another governmental body.

Parliamentary sovereignty The principle that Parliament is the source of all political power in the UK.

Answers at **www.hoddereducation.co.uk/myrevisionnotesdownloads**

Now test yourself TESTED ◯

10 List three reforms carried out by the Coalition government between 2010 and 2015.

11 Outline the effectiveness and limitations of the Fixed-term Parliaments Act 2011.

12 Outline the effectiveness and limitations of the Recall of MPs Act 2015.

Reforms passed under the Conservatives since 2015

REVISED ◯

Following the 2015 election, the Conservative Party gained power, and remained in power in some form in the following elections of 2017 and 2019. Some of the constitutional reforms during this time reversed some of the reforms of the previous governments, and some continued to develop them (Table 5.6).

Table 5.6 Key reforms passed by the Conservative Party since 2015

Reform	Effectiveness	Limitations
English Votes for English Laws 2015	✚ Allowed for English MPs alone to vote on legislation or parts of legislation that only affected England. ✚ Allowed England a form of devolution that Wales, Scotland and Northern Ireland already had.	✚ Scotland argued that due to the way that Scotland was funded, even legislation that may only affect England could end up affecting Scotland's funding. ✚ The Act was repealed in 2021 and therefore is no longer used.
Wales Act 2017	✚ Moved Wales to a 'reserved matters model', the same as Scotland, meaning it could rule on any matter that was not reserved for UK Parliament to rule on (as opposed to a 'conferred matters model' where it could only rule on what UK Parliament allowed it to). ✚ Further eroded asymmetrical devolution in the UK. ✚ Changed the name of the National Assembly for Wales to the 'Welsh Parliament' from May 2020.	✚ Further challenged the sovereignty of UK Parliament. ✚ Raised further questions over the need for devolution to England, to match that of Scotland, Wales and Northern Ireland.
Referendum on the UK's membership of the EU 2016	✚ A nationwide referendum was held on whether the UK should remain in the European Union or leave it. ✚ Turnout was high (72%). ✚ It gave legitimacy for the government to carry out negotiations on Brexit.	✚ The result was very close — 52% leave and 48% remain, which led to questions over the legitimacy of the result. ✚ Different nations in the UK voted different ways, which increased nationalism, especially in Scotland.
EU (Withdrawal Agreement) Act 2020	✚ Enacted the result of the 2016 referendum.	✚ There was little agreement in Parliament on this, leading to two snap elections and numerous backbench rebellions and House of Lords defeats.
Elections Act 2022	An Act which introduced a requirement for photo identification for elections in the UK and changed mayoral elections from supplementary vote to FPTP.	Raised concerns over the protections around suffrage with the introduction of voter ID. ➔

57

Reform	Effectiveness	Limitations
Police, Crime, Sentencing and Courts Act 2022	A bill which introduced restrictions on 'unacceptable' forms of protests, to reduce disruption to the public from protests.	Raised concerns over the rights to protest and the power of the government.
Dissolution and Calling of Parliament Act 2022	Repealed the Fixed-term Parliaments Act 2011 and gave the power to call elections back to the prime minister.	Gave more power back to the prime minister over Parliament, challenging the sovereignty of Parliament.

Exam tip

Lots of the reforms to the UK constitution are known by abbreviations — HRA 1998 for the Human Rights Act, CRA 2005 for the Constitutional Reform Act, and so on. This can be a real time saver in the exams.

Now test yourself

TESTED

13 List three reforms carried out by the Conservative government since 2015.

14 Outline the effectiveness and limitations of the English Votes for English Laws Act 2015.

15 Outline the effectiveness and limitations of the Dissolution and Calling of Parliament Act 2022.

5.3 Devolution in the United Kingdom

What does devolution look like in Scotland?

REVISED

Table 5.7 Key events of Scottish devolution

1997	Referendum held in Scotland on two issues: ✦ whether a Scottish Parliament should be created — 74% yes, 26% no ✦ whether that parliament should have tax-varying powers — 63% yes, 37% no Turnout was 60%.
1998	Scotland Act provides for a Scottish government to be set up with primary legislative powers and a range of devolved powers including education, health, justice, tax, elections to Scottish government and agriculture.
2014	Referendum held in Scotland on whether Scotland should become an independent country - 45% no, 55% yes. Turnout was 85%, and 16/17-year-olds were allowed to vote.
2016	Referendum held UK-wide on the UK's membership of the European Union. In Scotland, the turnout was 67%, with 62% voting to remain in the EU. The national result was to 'leave' the EU, which therefore led to increased Scottish nationalism.
2022	First Minister Nicola Sturgeon said that Scotland would have a second referendum without the UK's approval. This was denied by the UK Supreme Court.

As a devolved nation, Scotland made a number of policy decisions that differed from the UK:

✦ In 2006, Scotland banned smoking in public places, a year before the UK did.

✦ In its Covid response, Scotland had levels 1–4, where England had 5 levels.

✦ Scotland has a separate education and exam system, with free tuition fees for Scottish citizens at Scottish universities.

Answers at **www.hoddereducation.co.uk/myrevisionnotesdownloads**

What does devolution look like in Wales?

Table 5.8 Key events of Welsh devolution

1997	Referendum held in Wales on whether Wales should have a National Assembly with secondary legislative powers — yes 50.3%, no 49.7%. Turnout was 50%.
1998	Government of Wales Act sets up a National Assembly with conferred powers and secondary legislative powers.
2006	Government of Wales Act allowed for powers to be granted to Wales more easily.
2011	A referendum was held on whether Wales should gain primary legislative powers — yes 63%, no 37%. Turnout was 37%.
2014	The Wales Act devolved further powers to Wales including some tax setting powers.
2017	The Wales Act changed the National Assembly of Wales to a **reserved matters model** and changed its name to the Welsh Parliament (Senedd Cymru).
2020	The Senedd was recognised as a Parliament with law- and tax-making powers following the passage of the Senedd and Elections (Wales) Act 2020.

> **Reserved matters model** A model of devolution by which a devolved assembly can make law on anything that has not been explicitly reserved to UK Parliament. An example of a reserved matter might be foreign policy.

As a devolved nation, Wales made a number of policy decisions that differed from the UK:

+ In 2013, Wales changed its laws around organ donation to a 'opt out' model, rather than 'opt in'.
+ In 2022, Wales made the smacking of children illegal.
+ Wales held Covid lockdowns at different times to England, including a 'firebreak' lockdown in October 2020.

What issues have Welsh and Scottish devolution caused?

+ Asymmetrical devolution — where different national assemblies in the UK have been given different powers.
+ The West Lothian Question — the perceived imbalance of voting rights of MPs in the UK Parliament, where Scottish and Welsh MPs could vote in English matters, but English MPs had no voting rights in regional assemblies.
+ One result of this is questions over whether there should now be an English Parliament for English-only matters.
+ The Barnett formula — this is the formula that calculates the funding level of Wales and Scotland, which means changes to funding in England can affect Wales and Scotland. For example, the building of HS2 was deemed to be an English and Welsh project, despite not going to Wales. This meant that Wales was not eligible for the 'Barnett consequentials' funding that Scotland did benefit from.
+ There have been challenges to the unitary nature of the UK, especially with Scotland pushing for a second independence referendum.

> **Barnett formula** The formula that determines the funding levels of the devolved regions.
>
> **Unitary** The idea that legal sovereignty resides in one place. In the UK, this is parliament.

> **Exam tip**
>
> It can be easy to miss the changes that have happened incrementally to Welsh devolution that have made it increasingly like the Scottish settlement. Ensure you recognise that today, Scottish and Welsh devolution is almost identical.

> **Now test yourself** TESTED
>
> 16 Describe three policy differences enacted by the Scottish government.
> 17 Describe three policy differences enacted by the Welsh government.
> 18 Explain why Scottish and Welsh Devolution have raised issues over the need for an English parliament.

What does devolution look like in Northern Ireland?

REVISED

Northern Ireland has a much longer history of devolution than Wales or Scotland. However, it is unique due to the political circumstances it encounters with regards to Irish nationalism. Therefore, Northern Ireland is sometimes described as 'a place apart' as its devolved settlement is different to that of Scotland and Wales.

Table 5.9 Key events of devolution in Northern Ireland

1920	Government of Ireland Act created the Parliament of Northern Ireland, which ran from 1921 to 1972.
1960–98	The Troubles — this was a period of conflict in Northern Ireland over the status of Northern Ireland in the Union. From 1972, the Parliament of Northern Ireland was suspended, and Northern Ireland was ruled from Westminster.
1998	The Good Friday Agreement proposed a new power-sharing government in Northern Ireland and creation of a Northern Ireland Assembly and Northern Ireland Executive. A referendum was held on the agreement — 71% yes, 29% no. Turnout was 81%.
Suspensions	On five occasions since 1998, the Northern Ireland Assembly has been suspended: ✦ 11 February–30 May 2000 — failure to strike a deal on IRA decommissioning ✦ 10 August 2001 — continued failure to strike a deal on IRA decommissioning ✦ 22 September 2001 — continued failure to strike a deal on IRA decommissioning ✦ 14 October 2002–May 2007 — following a police raid of Sinn Fein's offices, the party withdrew from the power-sharing agreement ✦ 9 January 2017–11 January 2020 — a scandal over spending on a renewable heat initiative saw Sinn Fein withdraw from power-sharing while DUP leader Arlene Foster remained in power
2022	The DUP first minister resigned, causing the deputy first minister to also lose her position and leading to new elections. While Sinn Fein gained the most seats in the May election, the DUP would not nominate a deputy FM and therefore no government was formed.

As a devolved nation, Northern Ireland has made several policy decisions that differed from the UK:
✦ Until 2019, when a UK law forced change, Northern Ireland did not allow abortions in many circumstances.
✦ Northern Ireland held lockdowns at different times to England, including a 4-week 'circuit breaker' lockdown in October 2020.

What might devolution look like in England?

REVISED

England does not have its own national assembly like Scotland, Wales and Northern Ireland, which has created some of the concerns listed above. There have been suggestions that there should be an English Parliament.

Should there be an English Parliament?

Yes	No
+ Devolution is currently asymmetrical with England as the only one of the four nations of the UK without its own parliament. + It would resolve the West Lothian Question. + It could resolve concerns over the Barnett formula and funding of the other regions. + It would continue the increasing trend for devolution already evident in UK politics. + A version of this has been trialled through English votes for English laws (EVEL). + It may allow a new constitutional settlement that would make it easier to maintain the union in a time of rising nationalism.	+ The population and therefore number of MPs that England has already dominates UK Parliament, so why would an English Parliament be needed? + If it did exist, it would raise the question of the legitimacy and powers of the UK Parliament. + There is little public desire for this change. + The government is able to enact legislation that has the effect of an English Parliament without creating one, for example EVEL or the government's **levelling up** agenda. + The government has also overcome this problem by devolving power to the regions of the UK, for example the plan to create a 'Northern Powerhouse'.

> **Exam tip**
>
> The evolutionary nature of the UK constitution means that it is constantly changing. You do not need to know every reform being debated or enacted currently, but it would be useful to keep an eye on current affairs for any major changes.

> **Levelling up** A policy of the Conservative Party to reduce the economic imbalance across the regions of the UK.

> **Now test yourself**   TESTED ◯
>
> 19 Describe two policy differences enacted by the Northern Irish government.
> 20 Outline three arguments for and against having an English Parliament.

5.4 Possible reforms to the UK constitution

How could the UK constitution be further reformed?

REVISED ◯

While many reforms have been enacted since 1997, there are a number of ways in which the UK could be further reformed (Table 5.10).

> **Gridlock** A situation where two or more branches of government have the power to stop each other from acting and therefore no governance takes place.

Table 5.10 Possible areas of reform to the UK constitution

Issue	Advantages of reform	Disadvantages of reform
House of Lords remains an unelected chamber	+ A fully or partly elected House of Lords would have greater legitimacy to challenge the House of Commons. + It would democratise the UK.	+ Another elected chamber could create **gridlock** in government. + Rules over how often elections would be held, term lengths, etc. are unclear.
The use of proportional representation for general elections	+ FPTP produces disproportionate results. Reform would allow more minor parties to have a chance of succeeding. + If there were fewer wasted votes people may be more likely to turn out.	+ Proportional systems make it more likely that governments resulting from elections will be coalitions, which could lack legitimacy and are more fragile.
The role of the monarchy in the UK	+ The UK could retain its traditional monarchy while removing their influence from the legislative process, which would enhance representative democracy.	+ This could increase the power of the prime minister further who may take up the role of head of state if the monarchy were weakened or abolished.

61

Issue	Advantages of reform	Disadvantages of reform
A parliament for England	*Refer to 'What might devolution look like in England?' above.*	*Refer to 'What might devolution look like in England?'*
Further devolution to the regions	+ Existing policies such as 'devo-max' and 'levelling up' show that further devolution can be successful. It could quell nationalism in the nations of the UK and strengthen the union.	Further devolution can always be revoked by Parliament while it remains sovereign, making all reforms precarious.
The UK's place in the EU	+ There is already agreement across a number of UK parties which all had a second referendum on EU membership in their 2019 manifesto. + An increasing amount of polling suggests that the majority of the population either now favour 'remain' or see Brexit as a mistake.	+ If referendums can simply be reversed by holding another one, this could set a precedent in which referendums are held so frequently they mean very little.
Scottish independence	+ Allowing Scotland a second referendum on independence would increase direct democracy in the UK and further devolution.	+ If referendums can simply be reversed by holding another one, this could set a precedent in which referendums are held so frequently they mean very little.
The UK Supreme Court	+ The role of the UK Supreme Court could be enhanced, especially if the UK constitution was codified, to allow it to overturn decisions by the government, limiting government power.	+ The unelected nature of the Supreme Court raises questions over whether it should challenge the mandate of the elected government.
A codified constitution	*Refer to 'Should the UK constitution be codified and entrenched?' below.*	*Refer to 'Should the UK constitution be codified and entrenched?' below.*
Protection of Rights	+ Rights protection in the UK relies on statute law which can be overturned. Finding a way to permanently protect rights would secure freedoms for citizens.	+ There is no mechanism to protect rights from parliamentary sovereignty while the UK constitution remains uncodified.
The UK's place in the Council of Europe/ECHR	+ Removing the UK from the ECHR would free the government from restrictions to carry out policies such as the Conservative government's Rwanda policy for asylum seekers.	+ Removing the UK from the ECHR sends a negative signal about the view of rights and rights protection in the UK.

Exam tip

Make sure you are clear about the difference between the European Court of Human Rights and the European Convention on Human Rights. They are often both abbreviated to ECHR, which can be infuriating. It may be easier for you to abbreviate the Court to ECtHR for the clarity of your essays. This book uses ECHR for the Convention and ECtHR for the Court.

Now test yourself

TESTED

21 List three possible areas of reform for the UK constitution.

22 Outline the arguments for and against reform to the UK's place on the Council of Europe.

23 Outline the arguments for and against reform to the House of Lords.

Debates surrounding the UK constitution

REVISED

Should the UK constitution be codified and entrenched?

As much of the UK constitution is already written down, and the UK's political system seems to function relatively well, there are many arguments for and against whether the UK constitution should be codified into one document.

Should the UK constitution be codified?

Yes	No
+ A codified constitution would better lay out the relationship between the three main branches of government, and could reduce the power of the prime minister over Parliament. + A codified constitution would enhance the ability of the Supreme Court to strike down actions of the government that are 'unconstitutional', making the government more accountable. + Codified constitutions have amendment mechanisms contained within them and therefore would still be able to react to changing national circumstances. + It would allow for better protection of rights. + A codified constitution would provide greater clarity to the electorate, who could then gain more information about the political system and their rights, and hopefully increase voter engagement. + Conventions that are currently unwritten would be included, increasing transparency of government. + Codifying the constitution would also entrench the constitution and therefore make it more difficult to change by a government with a large majority.	+ There is no clear process by which this would be done. As the extent of the UK's unwritten constitution is so vast, how this could be done impartially and without creating a huge document is unclear. + It would undermine the 'twin pillars' of the UK constitution as Parliament would no longer be sovereign. + There is little public demand for it, as the current system works reasonably well. + Other countries that do have a codified constitution have found that it leads to government gridlock. + Other countries with an entrenched constitution have found amendments difficult to make, which can make the constitution archaic. + By limiting parliamentary sovereignty, a codified constitution could limit the responsiveness of government to national emergencies.

Should there be a British Bill of Rights?

Conservative governments since 2010 have included in their manifestos a pledge to replace the Human Rights Act with a British Bill of Rights. Some of this has been due to anti-European sentiment following the Brexit referendum and the perception that parliamentary sovereignty is being challenged by bodies outside of the UK.

Debates around creating a British Bill of Rights

Arguments for a British Bill of Rights	Arguments against a British Bill of Rights
+ It would secure parliamentary sovereignty, rather than allowing the ECtHR to have influence over the UK's political system. + It would also ensure that within the UK political system Parliament is clearly sovereign over, for example, the UK Supreme Court. + It would allow rights to be defined within the UK political context. For example, the UK limits freedom of speech more than some other countries. + Current human rights legislation has prevented the government from carrying out some of its policies. + It could offer greater protection to rights by gaining greater support and therefore less chance of a Bill of Rights being challenged by government.	+ It could suggest that the rights of citizens can be made and unmade on a whim of the government. + It could further enhance the power of the prime minister and Parliament. + It would limit the ability of citizens to use courts such as the ECtHR, giving them few ways to challenge the power of government. + It could politicise the judiciary, reducing their independence and neutrality. + There is no clear benefit, especially as many of the rights proposed seem to be the same as existing rights.

Exam tip

It can be quite easy in the argument over codification to repeat the same argument using different words. For example, a paragraph about the flexibility of the constitution would basically be the same as one about how the constitution is easy to change. Be wary of accidentally repeating paragraphs.

Now test yourself

24 Outline two arguments for a codified constitution and two against.

25 Outline two arguments for a British Bill of Rights and two against.

TESTED

63

The Northern Ireland Protocol

A key issue affecting both devolution and the UK constitution following the Brexit decision was the place of Northern Ireland in the union.

When the UK voted to 'leave' the European Union in 2016, it created a key problem. Given that the Republic of Ireland was a member of the EU but Northern Ireland would not be, how would the border between these two countries now work?

✚ Northern Ireland did not want to see the return of a 'hard border', meaning checkpoints being set up between these two nations.

✚ Northern Ireland also did not want trade checks to have to take place on goods leaving England, Wales or Scotland and arriving in Northern Ireland, as this could threaten its place in the union.

The solution was the Northern Ireland Protocol. This allowed Northern Ireland to remain part of the EU's single market for goods, with customs checks taking place if these goods then crossed the Irish Sea. However, this solution did not satisfy many parties and the issue continued to be debated.

In 2023, the UK government introduced the Windsor Framework to replace the Northern Ireland Protocol. It created 'red lanes' and 'green lanes' — 'green lanes' for goods leaving the UK and only going to Northern Ireland that would avoid customs checks. However, concerns remain over the place of Northern Ireland in the union following Brexit, highlighting the complexities of devolution and the UK constitution.

Summary

✚ The UK constitution has some relatively rare features such as being uncodified, unentrenched, unitary and relying on the 'twin pillars'.
✚ There are five key sources of the UK constitution.
✚ Numerous reforms have taken place to the UK constitution to modernise and democratise its political system.
✚ Key debates remain over what reform still needs to be carried out, how well rights are protected, the extent and impact of devolution and whether the UK needs a codified constitution.

Revision tasks

1 List the five sources of the UK constitution and give examples of them in action.

2 Outline three changes that have been made to the UK constitution by each of the following: (a) the Labour government 1997–2010, (b) Coalition government 2010–15 and (c) the Conservative governments since 2015. For each reform copy and complete the table below.

Reform	Problem it solved	Any problems it created or did not solve	How it could go further

3 Outline the arguments for and against a codified constitution, and give examples for each argument.

Exam practice

1 Evaluate the view that a codified constitution is now a necessity for the UK. (30 marks)

2 Evaluate the view that devolution has gone too far in the UK. (30 marks)

3 Evaluate the view that the most significant problem within the UK constitution is the power of the prime minister. (30 marks)

Structuring your essay

You should ideally aim for three paragraphs in your essay. Each paragraph should deal with a separate factor relevant to the question, analysing it, evaluating both sides of the argument around that factor and reaching a judgement about its importance. It is important that if a factor is named in the question, you deal with that first, and compare to it any new factors that you introduce.

For example, in question 3 in the Exam practice box, you may want to discuss devolution and rights protection in the UK. But your first paragraph should be on the power of the prime minister, and when you write about other factors you should show whether they are more or less significant than the power of the prime minister.

6 Parliament

6.1 Structure of Parliament

What is the structure of the UK Parliament?

REVISED

Most political systems are made up of three branches of government — the executive, the legislature and the judiciary. Often, these three branches will be separate from one another, to ensure that the government that is formed has limitations upon its power.

> **Parliament** The legislative branch of the UK political system, consisting of the House of Commons, House of Lords and the monarchy.

JUDICIARY

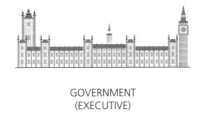

GOVERNMENT
(EXECUTIVE)

PARLIAMENT
(LEGISLATURE)

Figure 6.1 The three branches of government

A key feature of parliamentary government is the fusion of the executive and legislative branches of government — in the case of the UK, the fusion of the prime minister and cabinet with Parliament. This is because the prime minister and the ministers who form the cabinet are also sitting MPs within Parliament. It also means the executive can often dominate Parliament as the prime minister will usually command a majority of MPs, so provided the prime minister can keep their MPs in line, they should be able to pass most votes.

What is the structure of the House of Commons?

REVISED

The House of Commons is made up of 650 MPs, individually elected in constituencies from the whole of the UK. These 650 can be divided into different categories:

+ **Frontbenchers:** those MPs who hold a ministerial role within government, and those that shadow them from the opposition (known as the 'shadow cabinet').
+ **Backbenchers:** MPs without a role in the government.
+ **The speaker, and deputy speakers:** preside over the debates that take place in the House of Commons. They are politically neutral, although they are sitting MPs elected in a constituency.

> **House of Commons**
> One of two chambers of UK Parliament, forming the legislative branch. Considered the primary legislative chamber due to its elected status.

As part of its control over the House of Commons, the government can usually rely on the 'payroll vote'. This refers to those MPs expected to vote for the government as they hold a salaried role. Usually this is ministers, junior ministers and whips, although it may also include private parliamentary secretaries (but this is not a paid role).

What is the structure of the House of Lords?

The House of Lords is made up of around 800 peers, drawn from three categories:

+ **Hereditary peers:** 92 peers who hold their position due to inheriting it from their father (or less frequently their mother). When vacancies occur, the Lords vote to replace them with those other hereditary peers who wish to stand for election.
+ **Life peers:** appointed by the Appointments Commission, these are people who usually have expertise in a particular field. They make up most of the House of Lords members, and were originally created in the 1958 Life Peerages Act.
+ **Lords spiritual:** 26 bishops and archbishops of the Church of England.

> **House of Lords** One of two chambers of the UK Parliament. Considered the secondary legislative chamber due to being unelected.

> **Exam tip**
>
> Remember that 'life peers' were not created in the House of Lords reform of 1999. While their numbers increased dramatically during this reform, the position of life peer was created in the 1958 Life Peerages Act.

What is the relationship between Parliament and government?

It is crucial to understand that government and Parliament are not synonyms. Parliament is made up of the two chambers, and technically the monarchy. It includes MPs and Lords from all parties. By comparison, government refers to the party in power, or more specifically those who hold a role within the government.

> **Now test yourself**
>
> **TESTED**
>
> 1 List the types of MP in the House of Commons.
> 2 List the types of Lords in the House of Lords.
> 3 Explain the difference between Parliament and the government.

6.2 The functions of Parliament

Parliament has three key roles:
+ representation
+ legislation
+ scrutiny (of government)

How does Parliament represent people?

In carrying out the function of representation, MPs can represent a range of interests (Table 6.1).

Table 6.1 Summary of the representative function of MPs

Representing	Explanation	Example	Concern
Party	When MPs stand for office, they usually run as part of a party. They will usually vote the way their party expects in Parliament. A party can indicate how important a vote is by placing a one-, two-, or three-line whip on the vote.	In 2019 Prime Minister Johnson faced a rebellion over his Brexit deal from his own MPs. He removed the **whip** from the 21 MPs who voted against him. This meant these MPs were no longer considered part of the Conservative Party.	The expectation of voting with the party may clash with constituency or self-representation. The dominance of the governing party means that party-line votes may lack scrutiny.
Self	The UK's representative democracy is based on the Burkean model of 'trustees'. This means that MPs can use their conscience when making decisions.	In 2014 Nicky Morgan voted against the Marriage (Same-Sex Couples) Act, saying that her Christian faith was part of the reason. She also said she had received more letters from constituents asking her to vote against the bill than for it.	MPs can use **parliamentary privilege** to speak on issues, but this can challenge the rule of law. For example, using parliamentary privilege to break judicial injunctions.
Constituency	As MPs are elected to represent a specific geographical area, they may need to represent issues that are specific to their local area in parliament, such as funding or infrastructure issues.	In 2022 Mark Menzies gave a speech in Parliament criticising the government's plans about fracking due to the impact it would have on his constituency.	Those who hold a role in the government are not allowed to speak on the floor of the Chamber other than to answer questions, limiting their ability to represent their constituency.
Functional representation	This is the representation by MPs of groups sharing socioeconomic descriptors. For example, women, ethnic minorities, LGBTQ.	In 2019 the number of women elected to Parliament was a record, with 220 elected (34%). However, this remains far below the percentage of women in the national population (51%).	The diversity within Parliament is increasing. However, it is still below the levels within the UK population.
Pressure groups	Due to any of the factors above, an MP may have a link with a pressure group to try to enact change.	In 2010 Nicky Morgan took part in oral questions to ask about the building of a waste incinerator in her constituency, something she and the pressure group CHAIN stood against.	The links between MPs and pressure groups has led to lobbying scandals, and raises questions over who MPs should listen to.

Whips MPs appointed by their party to organise the parliamentary business of that party, ensuring their MPs know how a party expects them to vote on any issue.

Parliamentary privilege The right of MPs to speak freely on the floor of the House of Commons.

Exam tip

As there are several different ways in which Parliament can fulfil its representative function, it is important to identify which type/s of representation you are discussing in an essay, and not simply write about 'representation'.

Now test yourself   TESTED ◯

4   List the three key functions of Parliament.

5   Explain why party-line voting could raise concerns.

6   Outline the different groups that MPs might represent.

The scrutiny function of Parliament

Parliament has a range of ways in which it can scrutinise policies and laws put forward by the government. Scrutiny is a very important function of Parliament as by carrying it out it provides legitimation to the government.

> **Legitimation** As Parliament is sovereign in the UK, ruling through Parliament gives legitimacy to the actions of the government, and this includes scrutiny of the work of government.
> **Backbencher** An MP who does not hold a position within the government.

Table 6.2 How Parliament scrutinises policies and laws

Method	Explanation	Example	Issues
Prime Minister's Questions	A weekly 30-minute session in which the prime minister faces questions from the Opposition and from **backbenchers**.	In 2022 Liz Truss faced difficult questions from Keir Starmer following the dropping of her economic plan and a 40-year high inflation rate.	PMQs can often be more theatrical than in-depth questioning, with MPs looking for a media headline rather than scrutiny.
Ministerial Question Time	Held for 1 hour on Monday–Thursday, each day a different government department faces oral questions from the House of Commons.	In 2022 Priti Patel faced questions, including a request to disclose the cost of the plan to deport asylum seekers to Rwanda for processing.	Any minister from a department can be sent to answer questions, not necessarily the cabinet minister.
Select committees	Made up of backbench MPs, select committees shadow the work of a government department, including calling witnesses and producing reports on the work of the government.	In 2017 David Davis said to the Brexit Select Committee that Parliament would get a vote on Brexit but it might be after the UK had left. This led to his department issuing a clarification that Parliament would get a vote.	The government has 2 months to reply to select committee reports but does not have to take on board their suggestions.
The legislative process	All MPs can take part in debates, committees and voting on the legislative process.	In 2022 all Conservative MPs voted for the Police, Crime, Sentencing and Courts Bill (third reading), and all Labour MPs voted against it.	Party whips can limit the amount of scrutiny that takes place.
Opposition days	These are 20 days in the parliamentary calendar in which the opposition can choose the subjects for discussion.	In 2022 Labour used an opposition day to bring a vote on fracking, which was one of the factors leading to Truss's resignation.	Votes taken on opposition days are usually not binding, and the Opposition does not choose when the days take place.
Humble address	This is a request from the House of Commons for the release of documents named in the address. If passed, this is binding.	In 2017 Labour used a humble address to get the government to release its Brexit impact assessments.	This requires a vote in favour, and as the government has a majority in the House of Commons, that can be difficult to achieve.
Backbench Business Committee	This committee is given 35 half days per parliamentary session to choose what subjects will be discussed.	In 2011 a Backbench Business Committee debate passed a motion to give all government documents to the inquiry into the Hillsborough disaster.	The impact has been relatively limited, with few identifiable successes.
Petitions Committee	The Petitions Committee considers e-petitions on the House of Commons website. Those with 10,000 signatures get a government response, and those with 100,000 are eligible for debate.	During the 2017–19 parliamentary session, the petition to 'Revoke Article 50 and remain in the EU' gained over 6 million signatures.	While the government will respond to petitions with over 10,000 signatures, it is not bound to accept the requests they make.

Now test yourself

TESTED

7 List three ways backbenchers can scrutinise the government.

8 Explain the limitations of Prime Minister's Questions.

9 Define the 'humble address'.

The legislative function of Parliament

REVISED

How does Parliament create legislation?

A bill in Parliament (legislative bill) can begin in either the House of Commons or the House of Lords. In each it goes through roughly the process shown in Figure 6.2.

Legislative bills These are bills created by Parliament. If they pass through the entire legislative process and gain royal assent, they become 'Acts of Parliament'.

Public bill committee A committee created to consider a piece of legislation. These committees are created for a specific bill.

First reading
MPs are given the title of the bill and scheduled time for the second reading.

↓

Second reading
A debate is held in the House of Commons on the principles of the bill, after which a vote takes place to refer the bill to a committee.

↓

Committee stage
The bill is given to a **public bill committee** created specifically for that bill. Backbench MPs in this committee scrutinise the details of the bill and suggest amendments.

↓

Report stage
The bill is passed back to the House of Commons and a debate takes place with amendments being voted upon.

↓

Third reading
A final debate takes place on the whole bill as it has been finalised, with a vote ending the reading.

Figure 6.2 Process of legislation creation

After the third reading, the bill is sent to the other House for consideration. If the House of Lords makes changes to a bill put forward by the Commons, the Commons must consider and approve any changes as they are the elected house.

Once a bill has been fully approved by Parliament, it is sent to the monarch for royal assent.

Exam tip

When dealing with a process such as 'how a bill becomes a law', try not to simply describe the order in which it happens. Instead, look at the question you have been asked and select aspects of the process that either support or challenge the argument that you are making.

69

What are the different types of legislation?

+ **Public bills:** bills put forward by the government, often drawn from its manifesto.
+ **Primary legislation:** major pieces of law, passed by Parliament.
+ **Secondary legislation:** law created by the government or ministers using the powers given to them in primary legislation.
+ **Private Members' bills:** bills introduced into Parliament by members who are not part of the government.

What role do the Lords have in legislation?

The House of Lords is a revising chamber. This means it can scrutinise legislation passed to it by the House of Commons and make suggested amendments. There are limits to its powers, however:

+ Under the 1911 and 1949 Parliament Acts, the Lords can only delay a bill for 1 year, can only reject a bill three times, and cannot veto money bills.
+ The Salisbury Convention says that the Lords should not oppose bills that are in the winning party's manifesto, as they won a mandate for their policies.

Now test yourself TESTED ◯

10 List the stages of a legislative bill.

11 Explain what 'primary legislation' means.

12 Define 'public bill committee'.

Comparing the House of Commons and the House of Lords

REVISED ◯

Table 6.3 The powers and limitations of the House of Commons and the House of Lords

	House of Commons	House of Lords
Powers	+ The right to 'veto' any legislation as the elected House with a mandate from the electorate. + Call a vote of no confidence in the government to remove them from power. + Accept, amend, delay and reject legislation put forward by the government. + Scrutinise the government through a range of methods including select committees and questions. + Power of monetary legislation, due to the 1911 Parliament Act.	+ The power to scrutinise legislation and suggest amendments. + Delay the passage of legislation for up to 1 year, due to the 1949 Parliament Act. + Hold the government to account through question time and debates. + An absolute veto on Parliament extending its life beyond 5 years. + Lords may have expertise in a policy area that MPs do not have.
Limitations	+ The government usually holds a majority and using the whips can limit the effectiveness of scrutiny.	+ 1911 Parliament Act — removed the Lords' power to reject money bills, and allowed the Lords to delay a bill by only 2 years. + 1949 Parliament Act — removed the Lords' power to delay bills to just 1 year. + **Salisbury Convention** — a convention that the Lords will not reject a bill put forward in a government's election manifesto. + The Lords cannot question the prime minister or other government ministers, only government spokespeople. + Select committees do not scrutinise the work of departments.

Salisbury Convention A convention that the Lords will not reject a bill put forward in a government's election manifesto.

How many times has the government been defeated by the House of Lords?

The House of Lords can defeat government legislation and make amendments to it. As the House of Lords is not elected, the House of Commons can vote to ignore suggestions from the Lords. However, as the Lords make their recommendations from their expertise, a defeat in the House of Lords can be damaging for the government's chances of passing a bill. Such defeats have become more common (Figure 6.3).

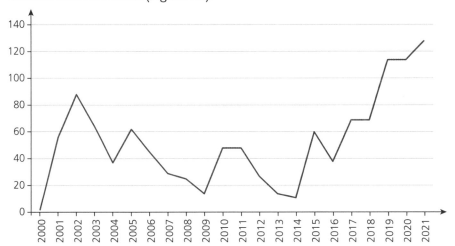

Figure 6.3 Government defeats by the House of Lords

Source: www.parliament.uk

Now test yourself TESTED ⭕

13 Outline three powers of the House of Commons.

14 Outline three powers of the House of Lords.

15 Identify the only issue over which the House of Lords retains a veto.

6.3 Parliament and the executive

What powers do backbenchers have? REVISED ⭕

+ Take part in a select committee.
+ Take part in the Backbench Business Committee.
+ Use parliamentary privilege.
+ Introduce a Private Members' bill — either as a ballot bill, or as a Ten Minute Rule bill.
+ Take part in the legislative process — debating, voting or on a public bill committee.
+ Ask questions — at Prime Minister's Questions or Ministerial Question Time (oral questions) or in writing.
+ If they chair a select committee, they can also take part in the Liaison Committee.
+ Bring urgent questions to the speaker.

Private Members' bill A bill introduced by an MP or Lord that is not from the government.

Ten Minute Rule bill A ten-minute slot on a Tuesday and a Wednesday for a member of Parliament to introduce a piece of legislation with a ten-minute speech.

71

What are urgent questions?

MPs can apply to the speaker for an urgent question to be asked of a government minister at short notice. This is meant to deal with important and time-sensitive issues, but as other methods of parliamentary scrutiny have been limited by a government majority, the number of urgent questions has increased.

No. of urgent questions asked by session

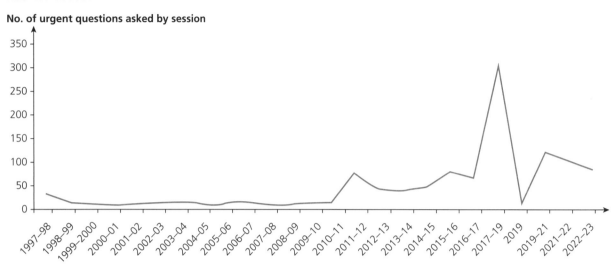

Figure 6.4 Number of urgent questions asked by session

Source: House of Commons Library

How effective are backbenchers in Parliament?

Are backbenchers effective?

Yes	No
+ Oral questions can raise the profile of an issue, causing the media to pick it up. + There have been successful Private Members' bills passed, such as the Live Music Act 2012. + Reforms to select committees have made them more independent and therefore more able to scrutinise the government effectively. Select committee reports routinely make headlines. + The Backbench Business Committee and Petitions Committee have power over the agenda of Parliament on some days.	+ When a government has a clear majority, there is little that a backbencher can do to have an impact on the government. + Party whips can enforce party discipline and prevent backbench rebellions. + Select committees cannot enforce their reports. + MPs can take part in oral questions, but PMQs especially can be mostly theatre. + The government does not have to send the cabinet minister to answer urgent questions, it can send junior ministers.

Exam tip

It is important to remember that almost every process of scrutiny in Parliament is carried out by backbenchers, so backbench power and the effectiveness of scrutiny are closely linked.

Now test yourself   TESTED ⭕

16 List three ways in which backbenchers can scrutinise government.

17 Outline two limitations to the power of backbenchers.

18 Explain why the number of urgent questions has increased.

Answers at **www.hoddereducation.co.uk/myrevisionnotesdownloads**

Committees and the opposition in Parliament

REVISED

Types of committees

Table 6.4 outlines the various committees in Parliament.

Table 6.4 Committees in Parliament

Committee	Explanation	Example
Select committee	Most select committees scrutinise the work of a government department and are named after that department. These are also known as departmental select committees. The number of select committees changes with the number of government departments. Some select committees can scrutinise the work of any department but in a specific area. For example, the Public Accounts Committee looks for efficiency and effectiveness of government spending. These are known as non-departmental select committees.	A candidate for the Bank of England Deputy Governor resigned in 2017 following criticism from the Treasury Select Committee of her 'incomplete answers' to them. The Environmental Audit Committee interviewed Environment Secretary George Eustice in the summer of 2022, following headlines about raw sewage being released into rivers and the sea around the UK.
Liaison Committee	A committee made up of the chairs of all of the select committees, which comes together twice a year to scrutinise the prime minister.	In July 2022, Prime Minister Johnson was scrutinised by the Liaison Committee about 'Partygate' while dozens of ministers were announcing their resignation from his government.
Public Bill committees	These are committees set up to scrutinise proposed legislation.	Most amendments made to bills are made by the party of the government; these were 84% of amendments in 2018.
Backbench Business Committee	Control the subjects Parliament will debate for 35 half days each Parliamentary session. MPs can apply to this committee for a debate to be held.	In 2011, the committee scheduled a debate on holding a referendum on the UK's membership to the EU which, while defeated, saw 81 Tories defy the whip.
Petitions Committee	Reviews the e-petitions on the House of Commons website for government response and debate.	In 2017, a petition to prevent President Trump from having a state visit to the UK gained nearly 2 million signatures and a 4-hour debate was held on this topic.

What is the role of the opposition?

The UK's system of adversarial politics means that the government is challenged in Parliament by His Majesty's Most Loyal Opposition, or more commonly the Official Opposition. This title is given to the party with the second largest number of seats in the House of Commons, however MPs from any party that is not in government are opposition MPs. The Leader of the Opposition is able to ask more questions at PMQs than other MPs.

The role of the opposition is to scrutinise policies put forward by the government. They can do this through the methods available to backbenchers. They can also put forward their own policy proposals and use opposition days to try and shape the parliamentary agenda.

Select committee A committee of backbench MPs that scrutinises the work of a specific government department.

Opposition MPs and Lords who are not from the governing party.

Exam tip

It is important to understand the distinction between Departmental Select Committees and non-departmental select committees as these can have different effects on scrutiny of the government.

Now test yourself

TESTED

19 Outline the role of the Liaison Committee.

20 Distinguish between a departmental select committee and a non-departmental select committee.

21 List the main roles of the opposition in Parliament.

6.4 Parliament and reform

What reforms have taken place to Parliament?

1911	**Parliament Act** — limiting the power of the House of Lords and removing its **veto** except for extending the life of Parliament
1949	**Parliament Act** — further limiting the power of the House of Lords
1958	**Life Peerages Act** — introducing life peerages into the House of Lords
1999	**House of Lords Act** — removing all but 92 hereditary peers and expanding the number of life peers
2005	**Constitutional Reform Act** — removing the law lords from the House of Lords, along with its role of the highest judiciary in the UK, and creating the UK Supreme Court
2010	**Wright Committee Reforms** • reducing the number and size of Select Committees • electing the Chairs of Select Committees by secret ballot • creating the Backbench Business Committee to schedule backbench business • introducing an e-petitions system
2011	**Fixed-term Parliaments Act** – fixing the date of the next election to Parliament
2015	**Recall of MPs Act** – allowing constituents to recall MPs under a limited number of circumstances
2022	**Dissolution and Calling of Parliament Act** – repealing the Fixed-term Parliaments Act

Figure 6.5 Key dates in the reform of the UK Parliament

Veto The right to reject a decision.

Exam tip

When considering possible reforms, it can be easy to get distracted by considering 'what ifs' — trying to guess what might happen. Instead, focus on what problem a suggested reform might improve.

What are the possible future reforms of Parliament?

Despite these changes, there are still concerns that could be addressed by further reform. Some of these are identified in Table 6.5.

Table 6.5 Potential reforms to UK Parliament

Concern	Possible reform
Does not represent the range of society in the UK	Party shortlists that are made up of, for example, all women. This is more of a party reform than a parliamentary one.
Unelected House of Lords	Reform the House of Lords to a fully or partially elected chamber. The Liberal Democrats wanted to do this as part of their 2010 Coalition, but plans were abandoned in 2011.
Time-consuming voting methods	Introduction of electronic voting for MPs to better use their time.
Ineffective parental leave practices that do not allow for MPs to have someone to cover their work while absent	Reform of the parental leave practices.
Late night sittings of Parliament, making it an unattractive career for some	There have been various calls to end late-night sittings.
The government may brief the media on policy issues before Parliament	From 2019 Speaker Hoyle has raised this with the Conservative government and allowed the use of urgent questions to ensure that the government did come to Parliament.
Parliament's role in the approval of military action is only a convention	A formalisation of Parliament's role in approving military action beyond the convention set in August 2013 when Parliament voted against military action in Syria.

Now test yourself

TESTED

22 List three reforms to Parliament in the twenty-first century.

23 List three remaining concerns about Parliament.

Answers at **www.hoddereducation.co.uk/myrevisionnotesdownloads**

6.5 The effectiveness of Parliament

Is Parliament effective?

Role	Yes	No
Representation	<ul><li>Record numbers of women and minority groups have been elected to Parliament in recent elections.</li><li>There are a number of parties represented in Parliament beyond the main two parties.</li><li>In the House of Lords, experts from many areas have been appointed, and many sit on the crossbenches.</li><li>There are examples of MPs acting on behalf of their constituency.</li></ul>	<ul><li>Parliament still does not effectively reflect the make-up of society.</li><li>Parties are not represented proportionately to the vote that they received.</li><li>The unelected nature of the House of Lords undermines a key principle of representative democracy.</li><li>The whips prevent the independence of MPs to act as they see fit.</li></ul>
Scrutiny	<ul><li>There are many methods of scrutiny including new ones such as urgent questions and the humble address, to challenge the government.</li><li>Around 40% of Select Committee recommendations are accepted by government.</li><li>High-profile methods of scrutiny, such as PMQs, are effective at raising issues in the media which can lead to change.</li><li>Recent elections have seen government formed with a small, or no, majority, which has enhanced the power of backbenchers.</li><li>Reforms, such as the Wright Committee reforms, have strengthened the power of Parliament.</li></ul>	<ul><li>Governments are still able to dominate Parliament with a large majority and the use of whips.</li><li>While some Select Committee recommendations are acted upon, a majority are not.</li><li>PMQs has increasingly become about grabbing media attention, rather than effective scrutiny with political pundits assessing who 'won' PMQs each week.</li><li>Scrutiny conducted by an unelected House of Parliament has questionable legitimacy.</li><li>The governing party has a majority on committees, and whips can be active in the work of committees.</li></ul>
Legislation	<ul><li>Both the Lords and the Commons have inflicted defeats on the government to their proposed legislation.</li><li>Backbench MPs and Lords can introduce Private Members' bills, and have done so successfully.</li><li>The Lords have become increasingly willing to challenge the House of Commons.</li></ul>	<ul><li>Legislation can be rushed through Parliament with little time for scrutiny.</li><li>MPs can vote on legislation without taking part in the debates, at which attendance can be poor.</li><li>Whips can enforce party discipline in voting on legislation.</li><li>The House of Commons can ignore amendments suggested by the House of Lords.</li><li>The House of Lords is limited in power by the Parliament Acts and the Salisbury Convention.</li></ul>

Exam tip

Understanding an example of a few pieces of legislation well can be very helpful in supporting your argument, and certainly better than being able to name lots of legislation but without being able to show why it is important to your answer.

Now test yourself

 TESTED

24 Outline two arguments for Parliamentary scrutiny being considered effective and two against.

25 Outline two arguments for the legislative process being considered effective and two against.

26 Outline two arguments for the representative function of Parliament being considered effective and two against.

75

Case study

Liz Truss and fracking

On 19 October 2022, an extraordinary event took place in Parliament. Labour used its opposition day to bring forward a vote to ban fracking. However, the motion put forward was to allow the Labour Party to take control of the parliamentary agenda, which would have made the vote effectively binding — something which most opposition votes are not.

This caused confusion and chaos throughout the day. Not wanting Labour to control the agenda, the Conservative whips' office said the vote was to be considered as a 'vote of no confidence' in the Prime Minister Truss and therefore ordered MPs to vote against it. However, a number of Conservative MPs, especially those who had constituencies in which fracking could take place, looked to the Conservative manifesto, which pledged a continued ban on fracking.

Throughout the day, it was unclear whether the vote was being seen as a 'vote of no confidence' or not. A Labour spokesman:

Every single Conservative MP stood on a manifesto in 2019 to ban fracking, and they are now faced with a clear choice. Do they follow Liz Truss and her collapsing leadership into yet another disastrous decision, or do they stand against her in the best interests of the British people?

Guardian, 19 October 2022

During the vote itself, there were accusations of bullying of Conservative MPs by other MPs, and the Conservative whip seemed to have resigned following a statement from No.10 saying it was not a vote of no confidence. Labour's motion was defeated 230–326 votes but 36 Conservative MPs did abstain. Ultimately, the chaos of the evening spelled the beginning of the end of Liz Truss's premiership, and she resigned the next day, suggesting considerable power of the use of an opposition day.

Summary

+ Parliament is made up of the House of Commons, House of Lords and the monarchy.
+ The House of Commons and House of Lords have different powers and limitations, but the House of Commons is the primary chamber.
+ Parliament has three main functions — representation, legislation, and scrutiny.
+ Parliament has undergone a number of reforms in the twentieth and twenty-first centuries, but a number of concerns remain.

Revision tasks

1 Outline the legislative process, and evaluate the strengths and weaknesses of each stage of the process.

2 Copy and complete the table below for the ways in which backbench MPs can scrutinise the government.

Method of scrutiny	Example	How it can be considered to be effective	How it can be considered to be ineffective

3 Compare the powers of the House of Commons and House of Lords and explain why the Commons is considered the primary chamber.

Exam practice

1 Evaluate the view that Parliament fulfils none of its functions adequately. (30 marks)

2 Evaluate the view that reform of the House of Lords is the most significant issue for UK democracy. (30 marks)

3 Evaluate the view that backbenchers are increasingly influential in Parliament. (30 marks)

Exam skills

Using evidence

Examples should be used throughout your essays to support the arguments that you are making. For example, in question 2 in the Exam practice box, it would be possible to argue that the House of Lords lacks legitimacy and therefore should not challenge the government. However, using the example of defeats that the Lords inflicted on the government over Brexit shows the extent of its influence as this was an issue decided by a national referendum, and was a key policy in the Conservative manifesto for two elections, therefore having a strong mandate from voters. The use of an example like this strengthens the argument and makes it easier both to contrast it to other examples and to evaluate the significance of the argument.

Answers at **www.hoddereducation.co.uk/myrevisionnotesdownloads**

7 The prime minister and the executive

7.1 Structure and power of the executive

What is the structure of the executive?

The prime minister is sometimes described as *'primus inter pares'*, or 'first amongst equals'. This is important as it means that the executive branch of UK government is not the prime minister alone. Instead, it is a collective of the ministers around them.

The prime minister heads the UK government. It is important to remember the distinction between government and parliament. Figure 7.1 shows the structure of the executive in the UK; this is what is referred to as the 'government'.

The prime minister usually has a majority in the House of Commons, and is also a sitting MP. This is part of the UK's 'fused powers' and means that the prime minister and government are sometimes able to dominate Parliament.

Table 7.1 explains the role played by the various parts of the executive with examples of those who have held these roles.

Table 7.1 Roles in the executive

Role	Explanation	Example
The prime minister	The head of government. Usually, this is the leader of the winning party in an election.	Rishi Sunak took over as prime minister on 31 October 2022.
Cabinet	A group of senior ministers, most of whom head a government department. They will meet together at least once a week. As ministers, they formulate policy and oversee the work of their departments. Many of these ministers hold the title 'secretary of state for…' but this may often be shortened in the media. For example, the secretary of state for foreign and Commonwealth affairs is usually referred to as the 'foreign secretary'.	Jeremy Hunt has held many cabinet roles: ✦ Secretary of state for culture, Olympics, media and sport (2010–12) ✦ Secretary of state for health and social care (2012–18) ✦ Secretary of state for foreign and Commonwealth affairs (2018–19) ✦ Chancellor of the exchequer (2022–)
Junior ministers	Reporting to each minister, several junior ministers oversee specific areas within a department. There are two tiers of junior ministers: ✦ minister of state ✦ parliamentary under-secretary of state	In the Education Department in 2023: ✦ Nick Gibb was the minister of state for schools. ✦ Robert Halfon was the minister for skills, apprenticeships and higher education.
Private parliamentary secretaries (PPS)	These are MPs appointed by ministers to assist them. This role does not come with an additional salary.	Nicky Morgan was the PPS to David Willetts when he was the universities minister. She later went on to be the education secretary.

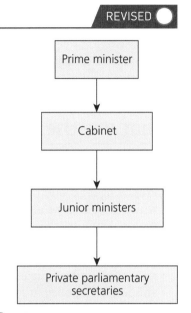

Figure 7.1 Structure of the executive

Executive The branch of government responsible for implementing and enforcing law from the legislative branch.

Cabinet A group appointed by the prime minister that includes senior government ministers.

77

Now test yourself

TESTED ⚪

1 Distinguish between Parliament and government.
2 Outline the different roles within the executive in the UK.
3 Define the term 'cabinet'.

What are the main roles of the executive?

REVISED ⚪

As the executive branch, the prime minister and cabinet have a number of roles:

+ **Proposing legislation.** Some of this will be taken from the manifesto on which they won an election, while other legislation will be a response to national circumstances. This is often known as 'primary legislation', for example the Coronavirus Act 2020.
+ **Making policy decisions.** This is the government determining how legislation will be implemented. For example, in 2022 the government announced a policy to send those seeking asylum in the UK to Rwanda for processing. This is often done through secondary legislation.
+ **Proposing a budget.** This can be the annual budget announcement by the chancellor of the exchequer, but there may also be budget statements throughout the year responding to emerging circumstances.
+ **Running domestic policy.** The government must determine the services that are provided for the population.
+ **Conducting foreign policy.** This can be through attendance at meetings such as the G7 and NATO, through the development of treaties and agreements, or through military action.

> **Secondary legislation**
> Powers of the government to make changes to the law within specific limits.

What roles and powers does the prime minister have?

REVISED ⚪

Table 7.2 The roles and powers of the UK prime minister as head of government

Roles	Powers
+ Form a government + Organise the structure of government in the UK + Provide a vision and overall direction for government policy + Represent the UK on the national and international stage + Provide leadership for the country and for the government. This is especially important during a time of national crisis + Exercise the **royal prerogative** powers	+ The ability to choose members of the cabinet. This is called 'exercising patronage', which is the ability to hire and fire ministers. For example, Prime Minister Sunak fired Conservative Party Chairman Nadhim Zahawi in January 2023 following investigations into the tax that he had paid. + The ability to abolish or create new government departments. For example, in 2023, Prime Minister Sunak announced the creation of four new government departments including the Department for Energy Security and Net Zero following the energy crisis. + As leader of their party, the vision for the country is usually drawn from the party manifesto. However, around 50% of prime ministers in the twentieth and twenty-first centuries took office at a time other than an election, so their direction for government has also been on their personal ideology. + Chairing cabinet meetings and setting up Cabinet Committees. The PM can determine the length of the meetings, the agenda and the attendees. Prime Minister Sunak uses the Domestic and Economic Affairs (cabinet) Committee to set government strategy on the economy and home affairs. + Exercising prerogative powers. These are powers that the prime minister exercises on behalf of the monarch and include calling an election, proroguing Parliament, and deploying armed forces.

Royal prerogative A set of powers exercised by the prime minister on behalf of the monarch.

Now test yourself   TESTED ◯

4 List three roles of the executive branch.

5 Distinguish between a role and a power.

6 Outline three powers the prime minister has with an example for each.

The power of the executive   REVISED ◯

What factors affect the power of the prime minister?

Table 7.3 Factors that affect the power of the prime minister

Factor	Explanation	Example
Electoral mandate and majority	If a prime minister commands a big majority in the House of Commons, they are more likely to be able to get legislation passed and enforce party discipline as they have a strong electoral mandate.	In 2019, the Conservative Party under Boris Johnson gained a majority of 74 in the election.
Cabinet unity	How prime ministers use their cabinets may be linked to their personal style. However, a cabinet can remove a prime minister, or make their ability to rule very difficult. There is also the possibility that a prime minister will have to appoint 'big beasts' to their cabinet. These are members of the prime minister's party who have a lot of individual support. This can make it difficult to ignore them, compromise with them, or maintain cabinet unity.	Members of Prime Minister Johnson's cabinet were the first to resign in the summer of 2022, ultimately leading to Johnson's resignation. Prime Minister May included Boris Johnson in her cabinet. As he was a leading figure in the Brexit referendum, this made her Brexit negotiations more complex.
National circumstances	National events and crises are unpredictable and require the government to respond to them. This can affect the power of the prime minister as the events can be a distraction from their agenda. Depending on the success of their response, it may affect the popularity of a prime minister.	The handling of the energy crisis of 2022 by Prime Minister Truss was a factor in her short-lived time in office.
Party unity	If the party is fully united behind a prime minister, the PM may have more chance of getting their laws and policies passed, and be able to ensure **party-line voting** in Parliament.	The European Research Group (ERG) faction of the Conservative Party made Prime Minister Sunak's negotiations of the Northern Ireland Protocol in 2023 incredibly challenging.
Prime ministerial style	How a prime minister sees their role can affect their success. The growth of 'spatial leadership' has seen some prime ministers governing more like presidents, some relying on a core inner group of the cabinet, and some relying heavily on SpAds (special advisers).	**Presidential prime ministers:** Tony Blair **Core inner cabinet:** Cameron, Clegg and the Quad **Relying on SpAds:** Theresa May with Nick Timothy and Fiona Hill
Popularity	Polling is not always accurate; however, it is still important as a demonstration of public support for a Prime Minister and their ability to use their powers.	Two days before Prime Minister Truss resigned, she was polling at –70 points, the lowest ever popularity score for a British PM.
The media	Traditional media can have an allegiance to a specific party or ideology. However, beyond this the role of the media is to report on, and often to scrutinise, the performance of the government. Favourable coverage can help a prime minister's popularity, and negative coverage can damage it.	The *Mirror* broke, and continually pursued, the 'Partygate' story in 2021 and 2022, which ultimately led to the resignation of Prime Minister Johnson.

79

Big beasts Members of a party who have individual popularity and therefore are difficult for a prime minister to ignore.

Party-line voting The expectation that when a representative votes, they will vote for those policies supported by their party.

Spatial leadership The idea that a prime minister presents themselves as singularly powerful, for example in the media, rather than acting collectively with their cabinet.

Exam tip

Always look for links between factors as this can help you to identify which of them are the most significant. Often, if one factor led to another then the first factor would usually be considered more important, as it was a catalyst. This will also help you to avoid repeating factors by accident in your essays.

Now test yourself

TESTED

7 Explain why big beasts may have an impact on prime ministerial power.

8 Give three examples of different styles of prime ministerial leadership.

9 List four factors that may affect prime ministerial power.

Powers of the prime minister

REVISED

Is the prime minister now a president?

To be able to answer this question, it is necessary to understand what presidential government is:

✚ There is separation of powers between the branches of government.

✚ The president is directly elected and holds a personal mandate.

✚ The president holds all executive power, and the cabinet is therefore advisory.

Is the prime minister presidential?

Yes	No
✚ There has been a growth in 'spatial leadership'. ✚ Election campaigns have become more centred around the party leaders, as seen in the televised leadership debates. ✚ There has been a growth of the number of advisers around the prime minister personally, often known as the No.10 Machine or **SpAds**. ✚ The direction that the prime minister wishes to take the country in may differ from the party manifesto.	✚ Parliament remains sovereign in the UK and can remove a prime minister and limit their powers. ✚ The cabinet holds power beyond being advisory, and can remove a prime minister. ✚ Many prime ministers take office between elections, undermining their claim to a personal mandate. ✚ Many of the factors in the 'yes' column vary widely with each new prime minister.

Presidential government A government in which the executive is dominated by one person with an individual mandate, and where power is separated between the branches of government.

SpAds An abbreviation of 'special advisers', which are politically motivated appointments to give ministers party political advice.

Confidence and supply The right of Parliament to remove government or withhold funding (supply) from it. Also the name of an agreement between two parties in which support is promised in votes of confidence and supply in return for policies.

How powerful is the prime minister?

The prime minister remains powerful	The prime minister has limited power
✚ Prime ministers still exercise considerable patronage powers in appointing their cabinet. ✚ Prime ministers have regained the ability to call an election at a time of their choosing. ✚ Election campaigns focusing on party leaders have given them a personal mandate to lead. ✚ Even in times of coalition, **confidence and supply** and minority governments, prime ministers have managed to pass most of their policy. ✚ New prime ministers have been able to exercise considerable policy influence from their own ideology.	✚ The media can give power to 'big beasts' by focusing on them, undermining the prime minister's power. ✚ The cabinet remains a force that can and does remove a prime minister. ✚ Party factions have been able to exercise influence, and limit the success of the policy goals of a prime minister. ✚ SpAds have become a target for media scrutiny, and can be seen as unaccountable, undermining a prime minister's power. ✚ Prime Minister Johnson lost at the UK Supreme Court in 2019 over prorogation of Parliament, suggesting a new limit on the power of prime ministers.

Now test yourself

TESTED ⬤

10 List the features of a presidential government.

11 Explain what is meant by 'spatial leadership'.

12 Outline three ways in which the prime minister could be seen as limited in their power.

7.2 Ministerial responsibility

What is individual ministerial responsibility?

REVISED ⬤

Individual ministerial responsibility means that ministers are accountable to Parliament for the decisions taken by their department and should take responsibility for their own actions and the actions of their department. This has been set out in the Ministerial Code since 1997.

There are two types of responsibility:
+ **Legal responsibility:** the responsibility of ministers for what goes on in their departments.
+ **Political responsibility:** the responsibility of ministers over their personal conduct.

> **Individual ministerial responsibility** The expectation that ministers take responsibility for their own conduct and that of their department.

Table 7.4 Individual ministerial responsibility and cases where ministers have resigned or been sacked

Responsibility	Cases where ministers have resigned
For personal conduct	Matt Hancock resigned from the role of health secretary in June 2021 after footage of him kissing a close aide surfaced in the press, which meant he had broken Covid-19 social distancing rules.
For personal decisions and actions	Priti Patel resigned from the role of secretary of international development in November 2017 over unsanctioned meetings she had with the Israeli government.
For departmental decisions and actions	Amber Rudd resigned from the role of home secretary in part over the Windrush scandal.
	Gavin Williamson was sacked in a Cabinet reshuffle in September 2021 following a second year of controversy over A-level results.

There have been a number of cases where it seems that individual ministerial responsibility has not been applied:
+ Gavin Williamson remained in post as education secretary despite huge controversy over the 2020 A-level grades during Covid-19. This was especially controversial as Williamson had previously been sacked as defence secretary over a leak from a National Security Council meeting.
+ A number of ministers have been accused of bullying and not resigned, including Priti Patel and Dominic Raab (although the latter eventually did).
+ Boris Johnson and Rishi Sunak were given fixed penalty fines over 'Partygate' but remained in office. Sunak received a second fine over a video in which he was shown to be not wearing a seatbelt in a car.
+ Kwasi Kwarteng did not resign but was sacked by Liz Truss following the economic impact of the 'mini-budget' in September 2022.

> **Exam tip**
>
> When evaluating the power of the role of prime minister, it is important to compare different prime ministers and recognise changes that occur over time. 'Change over time' is an effective way to start to gain AO2 and AO3 marks, as you consider the reasons power changes, and how powerful a prime minister is **today**.

Is individual ministerial responsibility still important?

Yes	No
+ **Ministers** have resigned both for legal and political responsibility. + There is a high expectation of adherence to the Ministerial Code and ministers who fail to do so are often reported on negatively in the press. + Ministers have been sacked for their or their department's conduct, either almost immediately or at a later date.	+ Ministers have often ignored criticisms of their actions and retained their position. + That the prime minister has had to sack ministers suggests that they cannot be relied upon to resign as convention would expect. + The Ministerial Code can be changed and rewritten by the prime minister.

> **Minister** An MP or member of the House of Lords appointed to oversee the work of a government department or part of a government department.

Now test yourself

TESTED ◯

13 Distinguish between political and legal ministerial responsibility.

14 Outline one example where individual ministerial responsibility has been acted upon.

15 Outline one example where individual ministerial responsibility has not been acted upon.

What is collective responsibility?

REVISED ◯

Cabinet collective responsibility should ensure that:
+ once a decision is made by the cabinet, it is given public support by all ministers
+ any discussions on how this decision was reached should remain confidential, meaning disagreements can happen in private between the cabinet but should not happen in public
+ anyone who cannot maintain collective responsibility should resign from their ministerial role

> **Collective responsibility** The expectation that ministers must support decisions publicly made by the cabinet, or resign.
>
> **Payroll vote** MPs who hold a position within the government and are therefore expected to support the government.

Collective responsibility creates a 'payroll vote', which means that anyone holding a role in government is expected to support the government publicly, and vote for its measures in Parliament. It is called the 'payroll vote' as senior and junior ministers get an extra salary for their role. However, private parliamentary secretaries are also included in the 'payroll vote' even though this position is not salaried. This means the 'payroll vote' is usually 140–160 MPs whose vote the government can rely on for any issue.

Does cabinet collective responsibility work?

Yes	No
+ Ministers have resigned when they have been unable to support government policies, e.g. two ministers (Johnson, foreign secretary and Davis, Brexit secretary), one parliamentary under secretary and four private parliamentary secretaries resigned because they did not support the Chequers agreement that laid out the type of future relationship between the UK and EU. + It ensures the executive is a collective body, limiting the power of the prime minister. + It ensures scrutiny of policies put forward at cabinet, e.g. there was disagreement over Johnson's 'living with Covid' policy. + It ensures an appearance of public unity, even when there are 'big beasts' in the cabinet. + It is a flexible policy that can be changed, e.g. collective responsibility was suspended in 2016 to allow ministers to campaign for either side of the Brexit referendum.	+ There have been public disagreements, which suggests the confidentiality aspect of collective responsibility does not work, e.g. Johnson's 'living with Covid' policy ultimately leaked out. + There have been public disagreements following which ministers have not resigned, e.g. there were calls for May to sack Johnson in 2017 after he ran a 'hard Brexit' event in the Foreign Office. + As prime ministers may need to include 'big beasts', they may find it difficult to sack ministers who do not uphold collective responsibility. + It is a flexible policy that can be changed, which undermines its importance. + As a convention, there is little that can be done if a minister ignores cabinet collective responsibility unless the prime minister is willing to sack them, e.g. in 2019 the government's Chief Whip Julian Smith criticised ministers over Brexit negotiations saying that it was the 'worst example of ill-discipline in cabinet in British political history'.

Answers at **www.hoddereducation.co.uk/myrevisionnotesdownloads**

Now test yourself — TESTED ◯

16 Explain what is meant by the 'payroll vote'.

17 Outline the features of cabinet collective responsibility.

18 List two arguments for and two arguments against the importance of cabinet collective responsibility.

Exam tip

You must understand the difference between individual ministerial responsibility and collective responsibility very clearly, and be able to explain each one.

7.3 The prime minister and the cabinet

What factors affect the relationship between the cabinet and the prime minister?

REVISED ◯

The factors that affect the prime minister's relationship with cabinet are similar to those that affect the prime minister's power.

+ **The extent of cabinet unity:** if lots of party factions or 'big beasts' are represented in cabinet this could result in less unity and therefore less willingness of the prime minister to rely on cabinet.

+ **The prime minister's style:** a 'spatial' prime minister may rely more on their SpAds than on cabinet, or on consulting with a few key cabinet members rather than the body as a whole.

+ **The experience of cabinet members:** a cabinet of experienced and trusted ministers may have greater individual freedom than a new cabinet, one with inexperienced ministers or one created by a new prime minister.

+ **National circumstances:** in times of national crisis, showing unity in the cabinet can be reassuring when difficult decisions need to be made. However, at other times, a lack of urgency may mean that divisions begin to emerge in the cabinet.

+ **The prime minister sets the agenda:** this means that the cabinet does not have complete freedom in what its members may wish to discuss at a cabinet meeting.

Is the cabinet important?

Yes	No
+ The executive in the UK is collective, and therefore the cabinet is needed to give authority and legitimacy to decisions.	+ Prerogative powers allow the prime minister to appoint whoever they wish to cabinet, limiting meaningful scrutiny.
+ The cabinet can resolve disputes within government policy confidentially.	+ Prime ministers have relied on small groups of core cabinet members rather than consulting the whole body.
+ The cabinet has the power to remove a prime minister by withdrawing its support.	+ Prime ministers can use their power to control the agenda to limit debates that take place.
+ The cabinet can ensure the views of the whole party are heard, and therefore lend power to the prime minister through party unity and control of the House of Commons.	+ There have been breaches of collective responsibility that undermine the role of the cabinet.
+ The cabinet formulates and refines government policy.	+ Prime ministers can choose to rely more on SpAds.
+ The cabinet helps to manage crises and national circumstances that are unforeseen.	+ Collective responsibility limits the impact discussions held at cabinet might have.

What factors must a prime minister consider when appointing cabinet members?

REVISED ◯

When appointing cabinet members a prime minister must consider:

+ **Party factions:** it is useful if the cabinet represents all the wings of a party.

+ **Experience:** senior ministers will be expected to have had experience in the lower ranks of government to run a government department.

83

+ **'Big beasts':** individuals who are personally popular could undermine the prime minister if left out.
+ **Supporters of the prime minister:** those that share the PM's vision and direction for the country will support their policy agenda.

Government department
A part of the executive, headed by a government minister, that oversees a particular policy area.

Exam tip

When looking at arguments for and against the importance of the cabinet (or any other essay topic) it is useful to see if you can pair arguments up, so that you can directly contrast competing arguments and then evaluate which side is stronger.

Now test yourself

TESTED ◯

19 List the factors a prime minister might consider when choosing their cabinet.
20 Outline two arguments for and two arguments against the importance of the cabinet.
21 Explain two factors that may affect a prime minister's relationship with cabinet.

Case studies

Former prime ministers

Margaret Thatcher, 1979–90

Election history as leader	Key events	Leadership style
+ 1979: 43 seat majority + 1983: 144 seat majority + 1987: 102 seat majority	+ Race riots in 1981 + Falklands War + IRA bombing in Brighton + Miners' strikes + Poll tax protests + Cold War	+ Known as the 'Iron Lady' as a dominant figure within her government with a clear idea of the policies she wanted + Associated with a presidential style of leadership
Cabinet issues	**Achievements**	**Loss of power**
+ Divisions of 'wets' and 'dries' + Key allies, such as Nigel Lawson, left her cabinet which weakened her power + Geoffrey Howe's resignation from cabinet, having been in the cabinet from 1979–90, spelled the end of Thatcher's time in office	+ Only one defeat on an entire bill in the House of Commons (Shops Bill) + Educational reform + Housing Act 1980 + Victory in Falklands conflict + Britain joins the European Exchange Rate Mechanism	+ Unpopularity of the poll tax policy + Challenges from within her party and poor opinion polling led to fear of a 1992 election defeat + Howe's resignation and attack of Thatcher, November 1990 + Convinced by her cabinet to resign in November 1990

Tony Blair, 1997–2008

Election history as leader	Key events	Leadership style
+ 1997: 179 seat majority + 2001: 167 seat majority + 2005: 67 seat majority	+ 9/11 + Iraq War + July 7th bombings in London + Cash for honours scandal + Good Friday Agreement + Handover of Hong Kong + IRA bombings in Soho	+ Blair was a young and charismatic leader with an informal style + Often associated with a presidential style of management + Associated with 'sofa government' rather than cabinet government
Cabinet issues	**Achievements**	**Loss of power**
+ Gordon Brown as chancellor was a challenge to Blair's power + Robin Cook resigned from the cabinet in protest at the Iraq war + Divisions of Blairites vs. Brownites	+ Devolution to Scotland and Wales + House of Lords reform + Constitutional Reform Act + Human Rights Act, 1998 + National minimum wage introduced	+ Blair was accused of misleading Parliament over the Iraq War, and this war eroded his popular support + He announced his intention to step down in 2007, and Gordon Brown took over

David Cameron, 2010–16

Election history as leader	Key events	Leadership style
+ 2010: gained 306 seats. Formed a Coalition with Liberal Democrats who had 57 seats + 2015: 10 seat majority	+ Scottish independence referendum, 2014 + Intervention in Libya in 2011 + Islamic state in Syria (Cameron lost a vote on taking military action in Syria) + Brexit referendum + AV referendum 2011	+ A more casual, and laissez-faire style of leadership + As he was in a coalition, he had to be mindful of the role of his Deputy Prime Minister Nick Clegg. For example, when Cameron could not take PMQs, Clegg stood in
Cabinet issues	**Achievements**	**Loss of power**
+ The coalition meant the cabinet comprised both Conservatives and Liberal Democrats + Relied on the 'Quad' – Cameron, Clegg, Osborne and Alexander rather than the full cabinet	+ Fixed-term Parliaments Act + Succession to the Crown Act + Marriage (Same Sex Couples) Act	+ Having campaigned to remain, Cameron resigned after the UK voted to leave the EU in the Brexit referendum

Boris Johnson, 2019–22

Election history as leader	Key events	Leadership style
+ 2019: 80 seat majority	+ Covid-19 pandemic + Prorogation of Parliament (and the subsequent *Miller* v *PM*, 2019 case in the Supreme Court) + Scotland's push for a second independence referendum (and subsequent Supreme Court case) + Ukraine War + 'Partygate'	+ Johnson was known for his media personality characterised by bullishness and gaffes but a determination to follow his policy + This was seen in the removal of the whip from 21 MPs who voted against him
Cabinet issues	**Achievements**	**Loss of power**
+ Numerous members of cabinet faced allegations over their conduct — Williamson (A-levels), Patel (bullying, Israeli meetings), Hancock (breaking Covid-19 regulations) + While there were a number of 'big beasts' in cabinet that came to challenge Johnson, he initially dominated them	+ The UK leaving the European Union + Coronavirus Act 2020	+ Months of increasing allegations around 'Partygate' + In 2022, a junior minister defended to the press the appointment of Chris Pincher. It was later reported that Johnson had prior knowledge of the allegations against Pincher resulting in mass resignation of ministers

7 The prime minister and the executive

Exam tip

The specification says that you must study at least one prime minister before 1997 and one after. It is important to be able to compare prime ministers and examine the circumstances that made them more or less successful.

Exam tip

When looking at the events that have impacted prime ministers, try to identify the ones that they could control, such as their own policy, versus the ones they could not, such as a national crisis. This will help you to evaluate more accurately whether any strengths or weaknesses can be attributed to the prime minister in question or to other circumstances.

Six weeks of Liz Truss

Following the resignation of Boris Johnson, the summer of 2022 saw a Conservative Party leadership contest to decide the next leader. On 6 September 2022, Liz Truss was elected by 57% of the Conservative Party membership. Just 2 days into her premiership, the queen died. From 9 September until 21 September parliamentary business was suspended as the country entered an official mourning period.

Truss's cabinet appointments had some issues:

+ Foreign Secretary Suella Braverman resigned having sent a government document from a personal e-mail address on 19 October.
+ Chancellor Kwasi Kwarteng was sacked after delivering a 'mini-budget' on 23 September which contained a range of tax cuts which led to a sharp fall in the value of the pound.

The tax cuts in the mini-budget were named by the press as 'Trussonomics', meaning economic policy of low-tax, high growth and a focus on free market economics.

On 19 October 2022, a chaotic vote took place in Parliament on fracking (see Case study in section 6.5, page 76) that led to her resignation the following day. Rishi Sunak, who had lost in the leadership election in the summer of 2022, took over from Liz Truss.

This example demonstrates a range of factors that can affect a prime minister's power, including circumstances, party unity, cabinet and the opposition.

Summary

+ The UK executive is collective and made up of the prime minister and cabinet.
+ Prime ministers have a number of powers that they can exercise alone, but the success of these depends on a range of factors.
+ Collective ministerial responsibility and individual ministerial responsibility apply to ministers, but the extent of this can be debated.
+ The cabinet has a number of roles, and its power and influence varies with each prime minister.

Revision tasks

1 Give three examples of national circumstances that have affected the power of a prime minister and explain the impact that each event had.

2 Outline three arguments that show prime ministers remain the dominant force in UK politics and three that show they do not, giving an example for each.

3 Compare two prime ministers' case studies and identify the key reasons that explain the differences in their power.

Exam practice

1 Evaluate the view that the prime minister remains the dominant force in UK politics. (30 marks)

2 Evaluate the view that the cabinet is no longer an effective body of government. (30 marks)

3 Evaluate the view that national circumstances are the most significant factor for prime ministerial power. (30 marks)

Exam skills

It is crucial that throughout your essays you demonstrate evaluation skills (AO3) — this means you **must** make a decision over what the answer to a question is. This should be evident in your introduction, in each paragraph and in your conclusion. Evaluating arguments is often best done by comparing pairs of arguments — usually one for and one against — and showing which one is more convincing **and why**. This means you must very clearly choose a side, and explain why you believe that side to be more significant than the other. In your conclusion, you should identify the overall pattern or trend and argue for it. For example, in question 3 in the Exam practice box, you should:

+ Show why national circumstances might affect prime ministerial power.
+ Introduce other factors that might affect prime ministerial power **and compare these to national circumstances each time**.
+ Reach an overall conclusion on whether it is national circumstances, or another factor and **justify your decision**.

8 Relations between branches

8.1 Role and composition of the Supreme Court

What is the structure of the Supreme Court?

REVISED ◐

The UK Supreme Court was formed by the Constitutional Reform Act 2005. It was officially opened on 1 October 2009 and took on the role as the highest court in the UK. It replaced the Law Lords in the House of Lords who previously held this role. The court is made up of 12 judges, with the head judge being known as the 'president of the Supreme Court'.

> **Supreme Court** The highest court of the UK legal system.

Despite being the highest court in the UK, its decisions could be overruled by UK Parliament as Parliament is sovereign. It is possible that the Supreme Court could be removed entirely by the UK Parliament, just as Parliament created it. However, the likelihood of either of these things happening is slim.

> **Exam tip**
>
> It is useful to compare what is *possible* to what is *probable* in politics. While it is possible for the Supreme Court to be ignored or removed by Parliament, the acceptance of its role and its rulings means that this seems unlikely. This will help you make more substantiated judgements (AO3).

What is the appointment process for a judge?

REVISED ◐

To become a judge on the Supreme Court:
+ A vacancy must occur first, usually by one of the existing judges deciding to retire or resign.
+ A selection commission is established whenever there is a vacancy.
+ An applicant must have at least 2 years' judicial experience and 15 years' experience practising law.

Table 8.1 gives some examples of the backgrounds of Supreme Court judges in the Court in 2023.

Table 8.1 Three Supreme Court members, 2023

Lord Reed — president of the Supreme Court	+ Senior judge in Scotland for 13 years + Studied law at Edinburgh University + Appointed to the Supreme Court in 2012, president since 2020
Lady Rose	+ Served on Government Legal Service serving as a legal adviser on financial services at the Treasury 1995–2001 + Studied at Cambridge University + Appointed to the Supreme Court in 2021
Lord Kitchin	+ Appointed as a High Court judge in 2005 + Studied natural sciences and law at Cambridge University + Appointed to the Supreme Court in 2018

What is the role of the Supreme Court?

REVISED ◐

According to the UK Supreme Court website:
+ The Supreme Court is the final court of appeal for all United Kingdom civil cases, and criminal cases from England, Wales and Northern Ireland.
+ It hears appeals on arguable points of law of general public importance.
+ It concentrates on cases of the greatest public and constitutional importance.

My Revision Notes: Pearson Edexcel A-level Politics: UK Government and Politics, Political Ideas and Global Politics

+ It maintains and develops the role of the highest court in the United Kingdom as a leader in the common law world.
+ Judges are expected to interpret legislation in line with the intention of Parliament and are also responsible for the development of common law:
  + Statute laws are written laws passed by legislature and government of a country.
  + Common law, also known as 'case law', is law that has been developed in judgements made by judges over hundreds of years.

A key power of the Supreme Court is judicial review.

> **Judicial review** The power of the judiciary to review the actions of other branches of government to determine whether they have breached the law or are incompatible with the Human Rights Act.

Usually cases are heard by a panel of five justices, but some cases can be heard by as few as three judges or as many as 11.

> **Now test yourself** TESTED
>
> 1 Define judicial review.
> 2 List three roles of the UK Supreme Court.
> 3 Outline how the UK Supreme Court was formed.

What is judicial independence?

REVISED

Judicial independence is an important principle for the Supreme Court as it should ensure that it can make decisions on the basis of the rule of law (a key principle of the UK Constitution — see section 5.1) rather than because Parliament or the prime minister and cabinet have pressured it into doing so. It is particularly important as many cases that the Supreme Court may deal with will be regarding the actions of the government itself, and therefore any influence could undermine the legitimacy of the ruling and the Court itself.

> **Judicial independence** The principle that judges should be free of influence from other branches of government when making their decisions.

Judicial independence is upheld by the following:
+ The Supreme Court has been a separate branch of government since 2009.
+ Judges are appointed for life (but with an upper age limit of 75) and cannot be removed by the government.
+ Judicial salaries are protected and set by the Salaries Review Body.
+ The selection commission to appoint judges is independent of the government.

What is judicial neutrality?

REVISED

Judicial neutrality is the principle that when judges reach their decisions, they do so by applying the law without personal or party-political bias. This neutrality should also uphold the rule of law, by applying the law equally to everyone.

> **Judicial neutrality** The principle that judges should not apply political opinion in their decision-making process, and judges should remain outside of party politics.

Is the UK Supreme Court neutral and independent?

	Yes	No
Neutral	+ An independent appointment process. + A requirement for judicial experience. + Judges agree to the principle of impartiality.	+ There is limited variation in the background of judges. + There has been intense media scrutiny of the character of judges, rather than rulings. + Judges are taking a more active role in the political arena.
Independent	+ The Supreme Court has been separated from Parliament. + Life appointments and protection of salaries. + Decisions have been upheld by the government even if the government has lost a case.	+ The government has openly criticised rulings of the Supreme Court. + The Court was created by Parliament, and therefore could be removed (at least in theory). + The Court is required to rule on the actions of government, which is inherently political.

> **Exam tip**
>
> It is crucial that you are able to distinguish between judicial independence and judicial neutrality. These are two concepts with very different definitions and you should treat them separately in your essays.

> **Now test yourself** TESTED ◯
>
> 4 Distinguish between judicial independence and judicial neutrality.
> 5 Outline the ways in which judicial independence is ensured in the UK.
> 6 List the reasons judicial independence and neutrality are threatened in the UK.

What are the key cases that the Supreme Court has decided?

REVISED ◯

Table 8.2 Summary of key Supreme Court cases

Case name	Ruling
Evans v *Attorney General*, 2015	The Supreme Court ruled that memos written by Prince Charles to the government could be released.
Miller v *Brexit Secretary*, 2017	An Act of Parliament was needed to take the UK out of the EU.
Human Rights Commission for Judicial Review, 2018	The Court ruled the Northern Ireland Human Rights Commission could not bring a case about abortion in Northern Ireland as the law was in line with human rights standards.
Miller v *Prime Minister*, 2019	The prime minister's use of the prerogative power to prorogue Parliament was unlawful.
Begum v *Home Secretary*, 2021	The Court ruled against Shamima Begum, allowing the home secretary to remove her British citizenship.
Uber v *Aslam*, 2021	Uber drivers are classed as 'workers' for Uber, and therefore entitled to minimum wage and holiday pay.
Abortion Services (Safe Access Zones) (Northern Ireland) Bill, 2022	The Court declared that 'safe zones' around abortion clinics was compatible with the European Convention on Human Rights.
Elan-Cane v *Home Secretary*, 2022	The Court ruled that the Home Office did not have to offer a 'third gender' option on passports.

> **Exam tip**
>
> Ensure that you understand the difference between 'power' and 'influence'. It is possible for a branch of government to be given a power but lack the ability to carry it out if it is weak. Similarly, it is possible to have influence without have formal power.

Is the UK Supreme Court powerful?

Yes	No
+ The Court's rulings have been upheld. + The Court has an accepted place within UK politics, and now has over 200 applications for cases each year. + With the withdrawal from the EU (and therefore the European Court of Justice), arguably the Court has gained power. + Judicial review allows the Court to declare actions of the government *ultra vires*, and therefore challenges government power. + The media report widely on the Supreme Court, recognising the power that it has. + Judges are increasingly active figures, giving speeches and appearing in the media. + Rulings of **incompatibility** with the Human Rights Act carry an expectation that the government should change the law.	+ Parliament remains sovereign and therefore could ignore the decision of the Court, or even remove it. + The UK remains a part of the Council of Europe and the European Court of Human Rights, so citizens could apply for review here instead. + The Court can only interpret the law of Parliament, and therefore Parliament can just change the law if needed. + The Supreme Court can only act on cases brought to it, rather than seeking out cases it wishes to hear. + As judges are unelected, they lack the legitimacy of Parliament or the executive. + The Supreme Court cannot overturn statute law.

Ultra vires This means that a public body or government has acted beyond the power that it has.

Incompatibility The Court can rule that a law passed by Parliament is incompatible with the Human Rights Act.

Now test yourself

7 Outline three key cases the Supreme Court has ruled on.

8 Define *ultra vires*.

9 Give two arguments for and two against the Supreme Court being seen as a powerful body.

TESTED ⬤

8.2 Parliament and the executive

How effective is parliamentary scrutiny?

REVISED ⬤

The UK political system has 'fused powers'. This means that the executive is drawn from the legislative branch, rather than being separate from it. One of Parliament's three key roles is to scrutinise the executive. This section looks at the methods that Parliament has to do this.

Is Parliament effective at scrutiny?

Yes	No
+ Humble addresses have been used more to force the release of government documents — 16 of the 138 opposition day motions between 2017 and 2022 were humble addresses. + Select committees have been successful — in 2017, David Davis's appearance before the Brexit Select Committee led to promises that Parliament would vote on Brexit *before* the UK left the EU. + The use of urgent questions has increased — Speaker Hoyle granted an urgent question in October 2022 directed at PM Truss following her controversial mini-budget.	+ The government rarely loses votes in the House of Commons — the only votes that Boris Johnson lost between 2019 and 2022 were three opposition day motions (which are not binding) and one humble address. + Select committee reports can be ignored — the UCL Constitution Unit said about 60% of reports are not acted upon. + Prime Minister's Questions is more about political theatre — in February 2016, David Cameron told Jeremy Corbyn to 'put on a proper suit, do up your tie, and sing the national anthem'.

Answers at **www.hoddereducation.co.uk/myrevisionnotesdownloads**

Is the UK now an 'elective dictatorship'?

A phrase popularised by Lord Chancellor Hailsham in 1976, an elective dictatorship refers to the domination of Parliament by the government. It suggests the ineffectiveness of Parliamentary scrutiny (above) but also suggests the power of the government.

> **Exam tip**
>
> Ensure that you answer the question set, not the one you hoped would come up. The debates over the effectiveness of parliamentary scrutiny and an elective dictatorship are similar, but not the same. Understanding this nuanced difference will help you achieve good marks.

Elective dictatorship The domination of Parliament by the government resulting in ineffective checks on government.

Backbench rebellion When backbench MPs of the government's party vote against government policy.

Is the UK an elective dictatorship?

Yes	No
+ The government usually has a majority due to the first-past-the-post voting system.	+ Recent elections have seen lower or non-existent government majorities.
+ Whips ensure that the government should win most votes.	+ The number of **backbench rebellions** has risen in recent years, especially as party divisions have deepened.
+ The 'payroll vote' is usually 140–160 MPs, which goes a long way to guaranteeing government success in Parliament.	+ The House of Lords has become more willing to challenge the government following 1999 reform.
+ The government has majorities on the committees in Parliament.	+ Other bodies have challenged the power of the government, such as the Supreme Court and devolved bodies.
+ The backbench business and opposition days that are scheduled are not binding.	
+ The House of Lords has limited powers to check the government.	

> **Now test yourself**
>
>
> 10 Outline three arguments showing Parliament is effective at scrutiny.
>
> 11 Explain what is meant by the term 'elective dictatorship'.
>
> 12 List three reasons the UK could be considered an elective dictatorship.

The changing relationship between Parliament and the executive

The following factors have changed the relationship between Parliament and the executive:

+ **The majority that the government has.** Using whips and a strong majority, the government could dominate Parliament, but it cannot so easily in coalitions, minority governments or small majorities.
+ **National circumstances.** In the event of national crises, it can be important for Parliament to be seen as united and representing the UK as a whole, for example following 9/11 or the July 7th bombings in London.
+ **Policy issues.** If a policy issue is controversial, it could divide parties into **factions**, which can allow Parliament greater power. For example in 2017 Theresa May faced three defeats in the Commons on Brexit.
+ **Polling.** Popular prime ministers may have more influence over Parliament, being able to control their party and the media. This is

(Party) faction A group within a political party that shares a common ideological belief or set of principles.

91

especially true when elections focus on party leaders. However, weaker prime ministers may find Parliament more willing to challenge them.

+ **Reforms.** There have been a number of reforms to Parliament since 1997 that have affected this relationship. These could be formal reforms, such as the House of Lords Act 1999, or more informal reforms, such as increased use of urgent questions and the humble address.

> **Exam tip**
>
> When assessing the importance of factors that change, it is important to make clear how you reached your judgement. For example, you might say that the key factor influencing the relationship between Parliament and the executive today is national circumstances, but that might change in future.

What future reforms could affect this relationship?

Table 8.3 Assessing the potential impact of different possible reforms

Reform	Possible impact
Reforming the electoral system to a more proportional electoral system	Could reduce the size of a government majority, which would make it more possible for backbench rebellions or the powers of Parliament to be used to scrutinise the government.
Reforming the House of Lords to a fully or partially elected chamber	This would give greater legitimacy to the House of Lords, making it more likely to challenge the government. It could also challenge the Parliament Acts of 1911 and 1949 as the Lords would now have a mandate.
Greater devolution to the regions and nations of the UK	This would reduce the areas over which the government has power, and therefore could reduce the influence of government within the UK or increase the willingness of Parliament to scrutinise these more limited areas.
The formalisation of parliamentary powers/ reduction in prerogative powers, such as declaring war	While Cameron's loss of the vote on military action in Syria suggests Parliament should have a greater role over decisions on military action, if this were formally given to Parliament, it would reduce the power of the government to act alone.
Reform to the monarchy	Linked to the point above, any reform to the UK monarchy, especially if it were abolished, could affect this relationship as it might remove prerogative powers from the prime minister, or it might require a new **head of state** to be found, which could result in direct elections for the prime minister.

> **Head of state** The chief representative of a nation; different to the head of government.

> **Exam tip**
>
> Looking at possible reforms can be useful as it can help to explain that the answer you have reached is based on current circumstances. You must be wary of 'future-gazing' however — this means trying to guess what will happen rather than assessing what has happened.

> **Now test yourself** TESTED
>
> 13 Outline three factors that affect the relationship of Parliament and the executive.
> 14 Outline three possible reforms that could affect the relationship of Parliament and the executive.

Answers at **www.hoddereducation.co.uk/myrevisionnotesdownloads**

8.3 The structure of the European Union (EU)

The European Union is a political and economic union of 27 European countries which aims to promote peace, protect freedoms of citizens, protect the environment, and establish an internal market and monetary union.

THE EUROPEAN UNION

EUROPEAN COMMISSION	COUNCIL OF MINISTERS	EUROPEAN COUNCIL	EUROPEAN PARLIAMENT	EUROPEAN COURT OF JUSTICE
(voice of common interest)	**(voice of the member states)**	**(setting the strategy)**	**(the people's voice)**	**(upholding EU law)**
Function: executive arm of the EU. Proposes legislation and policies, and represents the EU in external negotiations.	**Function:** coordinates member states' policies and refines the EU's foreign policy.	**Function:** high-level policy making to set the EU's strategy and budget.	**Function:** shares legislative power with council, exercises democratic supervision of EU institutions, shares authority with Council over EU budget.	**Function:** gives legal judgement on cases brought before it.
Structure: one commissioner from each member state, and is headed by a president.	**Structure:** relevant ministers of member states. Presidency rotating every 6 months.	**Structure:** head of state or government from each member state, the President of the European Council and the President of the European Commission meet twice every 6 months to define the political agenda of the EU.	**Structure:** 751 members of the European Parliament (MEPs), directly elected by EU citizens.	**Structure:** one judge from each member state.

Figure 8.1 Government of the European Union

Source: Global Challenges Foundation

> **Exam tip**
>
> You do not need an extensive understanding of the structure of the EU, but it can help you to understand how Brexit came about and how the relationship between the UK and the EU continues to evolve today.

> **European Union** A political and economic union of European member states.

What are the 'four freedoms'?

REVISED ●

The cornerstones of the EU single market are the four freedoms:

1 **Free movement of people:** allowing workers and citizens to move between the member countries with ease.
2 **Free movement of goods:** allowing trade without custom barriers or tariffs.
3 **Free movement of money:** allowing payments to move between member states easily.
4 **Free movement of services:** allowing companies to operate easily throughout member countries.

> **Four freedoms** The EU principle of the free movement of goods, services, capital and people.

The UK and Brexit

In 2006, David Cameron said the Conservative Party should 'stop banging on about Europe' at his first conference speech as party leader. However, by 2013, he outlined plans to hold an in–out referendum on UK membership of the EU. His speech covered the balance of power between the EU and the member states as a reason, but he was also facing pressure from euro-sceptics in his party and from the rise of UKIP. This pledge was then put into the Conservative Party manifesto for the 2015 election. When the Conservative Party won a majority in that election, a referendum was set for 2016.

Figure 8.2 outlines the events leading up to the UK's exit from the EU after the referendum.

2016	Brexit referendum, with 52% of voters voting that the UK should leave the EU
January 2017	*Miller* v *Brexit Secretary* was decided in the Supreme Court
March 2017	Article 50 invoked, letting the EU know the UK planned to leave
June 2017	General election resulting in confidence and supply agreement between Conservatives and DUP
2018 –19	The Conservative government loses three votes in Parliament on the Brexit deal
2019	General election following another defeat of Brexit legislation; Conservatives win with a substantial majority
31 January 2020	UK formally leaves the EU

Figure 8.2 Timeline of events leading up to the UK's withdrawal from the EU

> **Now test yourself** TESTED ○
>
> **15** Outline the role of the European Court of Justice.
>
> **16** List the 'four freedoms of the EU'.
>
> **17** Outline why the Conservative Party included a referendum on EU membership in its 2015 manifesto.

What impact has leaving the EU had on the UK?

+ The result of the referendum in 2016 led to difficulties passing Brexit legislation through Parliament, ultimately resulting in two snap elections (2017 and 2019) and two prime ministers resigning (Cameron and May).
+ The Withdrawal Agreement of 2018 included the retention of lots of current EU law in UK statute law. This was then to be reviewed by government departments determining whether to keep these laws or not. The Retained EU Law (Revocation and Reform) Bill 2022–23 would overhaul the retained EU law.

> **Retained law** Law from the EU that the UK has retained in statute law.

+ Many parties in the 2019 election pledged a second referendum on EU membership for the UK. However, the Conservative Party won with a majority.
+ An EU–UK trade agreement came into force in 2021, providing for free trade and cooperation in a range of policy areas.
+ There have been controversies over the Northern Ireland Protocol and the possible use of Article 16 (see the Case study in section 5.4). This has further exposed factions in the Conservative Party.
+ The final cases involving the UK are being heard in the European Court of Justice in 2023; these cases began before the UK left the EU. After that, the European Court of Justice will not have jurisdiction over the UK.

What is the difference between the EU and the Council of Europe?

Table 8.4 Differences between the EU and the Council of Europe

The EU	The Council of Europe
The European Economic Community (EEC), which would become the European Union (EU), was set up in 1958.	Set up in 1949 to uphold human rights and democracy after the Second World War.
27 member states.	46 member states.
Has some legal sovereignty over member states therefore cannot be ignored.	Does not have legal sovereignty over member states therefore can be ignored.
Its main court is the European Court of Justice (ECJ).	Its main court is the European Court of Human Rights (ECtHR).
Guarantees the rights of EU citizens through the EU Charter of Fundamental Rights.	Tries to protect human rights through the European Convention on Human Rights (ECHR) (integrated into UK law as the Human Rights Act 1998).
Example of its role and impact	**Example of its role and impact**
Thierry Delvigne v *Commune de Lesparre Médoc*, 2015 ✦ Convicted murderer Thierry Delvigne challenged the French government in the ECJ over not being allowed to vote as a prisoner. ✦ It was claimed this violated the EU Charter of Fundamental Rights. ✦ The European Court of Justice decided against Delvigne, saying that the punishment was proportionate. ✦ Had the ECJ ruled in favour of Delvigne, the UK would have been bound by this decision.	*Hirst* v *UK*, 2005 ✦ John Hirst was a prisoner convicted of manslaughter who challenged the UK government in the ECtHR over not being allowed to vote as a prisoner. ✦ It was claimed that this violated the European Convention on Human Rights. ✦ The European Court of Human Rights ruled in favour of Hirst, saying the UK's ban on prisoners not having a vote should be overturned. ✦ The UK ignored the ECtHR ruling. ✦ A compromise was accepted by the ECtHR in 2017 giving around 100 prisoners the right to vote.

Now test yourself

TESTED

18 Give three ways in which Brexit has affected the UK.

19 Outline the difference between the European Union and the Council of Europe.

20 Define 'retained law'.

Exam tip

You must be absolutely clear that although the UK left the European Union, it remains a member of the Council of Europe and is therefore subject to the European Court of Human Rights.

8.4 Sovereignty

What is the difference between political and legal sovereignty?

Table 8.5 Political and legal sovereignty

Legal sovereignty	Political sovereignty
✦ Where power lies in a political system according to the laws or constitution of that country ✦ Where power lies in theory ✦ Also known as *de jure* sovereignty	✦ Where power is actually exercised in a political system ✦ Where power lies in reality ✦ Also known as *de facto* sovereignty

Legal sovereignty The legal right of an entity to exercise power in a political system.

Political sovereignty The political ability of an entity to exercise power in a political system.

95

In the UK, Parliament is deemed to be legally sovereign. As the UK is a unitary state, all political power resides in Parliament. However, challenges have arisen to this.

> **Exam tip**
>
> Remember that the House of Lords is a part of Parliament. It cannot therefore be considered a challenge to parliamentary sovereignty.

What are the main challenges to parliamentary sovereignty in the UK?

REVISED

Table 8.6 Challenges to parliamentary sovereignty

Challenge	How parliamentary sovereignty has been challenged	How Parliament has remained sovereign
The Supreme Court	The government lost twice over Brexit in the Supreme Court in 2017 and 2019.	The Supreme Court upheld the home secretary's decision to remove citizenship from Shamima Begum.
Devolved assemblies	Scotland has used its power to enact different policies to the UK on tuition fees and prescription charges.	The Supreme Court ruled that the Scottish government did not have a right to call a second referendum on Scottish independence.
The use of referendums	The expectation of the use of referendums has led to calls for their wider use, undermining the power of Parliament to make these decisions. Examples include referendums on Brexit, Scottish independence and the alternative vote.	Referendums are called by Parliament only and therefore many requests have been denied. The Supreme Court upheld this power of Parliament.
The EU	Despite leaving the EU, it has remained a challenge to ensure the position of Northern Ireland within the union due to the Northern Ireland Protocol.	Retained law is being challenged and removed by the 2022–23 bill going through Parliament.
The government	The government's dominance of Parliament means that it can overcome parliamentary sovereignty and force legislation through, using its majority in the House of Commons and the limits on the House of Lords, such as the Hunting Act 2004. The repeal of the Fixed-term Parliaments Act again gives power to the prime minister to call elections.	Recent governments have had smaller majorities and faced a range of challenges by Parliament trying to reclaim its sovereignty, such as the use of urgent questions and the humble address.
The ECtHR	The government plan to fly asylum seekers to Rwanda was successfully challenged by the ECtHR in 2022, delaying the implementation of this plan.	Parliament can make any law it wishes, and reaction to the ECtHR has included suggestions of a British Bill of Rights, removing the power of the ECtHR, or even leaving the ECtHR.
The Human Rights Act	Linked to the ECtHR, the Human Rights Act and declarations of incompatibility can limit the law that Parliament can make.	Parliament can change legislation or ignore 'incompatibility' declarations as has been seen with various anti-terrorism Acts allowing for detention without trial.

> **Now test yourself** TESTED
>
> 21 Outline what is meant by *de facto* and *de jure* sovereignty.
>
> 22 Explain why the House of Lords is not a challenge to parliamentary sovereignty.
>
> 23 List three ways in which parliamentary sovereignty can be challenged, and give an example for each.

Case study

Shamima Begum

+ In 2015, at the age of 15, Shamima Begum left the UK and flew to Istanbul and on to Syria where she joined ISIS.
+ In 2019, she was found in a refugee camp and said she wanted to return to the UK.
+ In February 2019, the then Home Secretary Sajid Javid passed an order removing UK citizenship from Begum.
+ Under UK law, citizenship cannot be removed from a person if it leaves them stateless. However, it was claimed that Begum was entitled to Bangladeshi citizenship.
+ In 2020, the UK Court of Appeal ruled that Begum could return to the UK to fight the loss of citizenship.
+ In 2021, the UK Supreme Court overturned the ruling of the Court of Appeal.

+ In 2023, the Special Immigration Appeals Committee rejected Begum's appeal regarding the loss of her citizenship, to which Home Secretary Suella Braverman posted a Tweet that said:

> My priority is, and always will be, the safety and security of the UK. I am pleased with the decision from the court today, who have agreed with the government's position on every appeal ground.

This is a useful example of the importance of the relationships between branches of government in the UK, including the role of the Supreme Court, the prime minister and cabinet and Parliament, and how each of these can affect the rights of UK Citizens.

Summary

+ The UK Supreme Court has a key power of judicial review and is guided by principles of judicial neutrality and judicial independence.
+ The Supreme Court has played an influential role in a number of key cases, underlining its power.
+ Although the UK has left the EU, the EU has had and continues to have an impact on UK politics.
+ The EU and the Council of Europe are different entities, and the UK remains a member of the latter.
+ The location of sovereignty in the UK is legally in Parliament but it has a number of challenges to it politically.

Revision tasks

1 For three key court cases from the UK Supreme Court, copy and complete the table below.

Case	Ruling	How it shows the impact of the Supreme Court	How it shows the limitations of the Supreme Court

2 Explain the difference between the European Court of Justice and the European Court of Human Rights and give an example of a ruling from both courts.

3 List five challenges to parliamentary sovereignty in the UK, and for each one give one example to support that it is a challenge and one to oppose that it is a challenge.

Exam practice

1 Evaluate the view that the challenges to parliamentary sovereignty mean that the UK is no longer a unitary state. (30 marks)
2 Evaluate the view that the power of the Supreme Court cannot be justified in the UK's democracy. (30 marks)
3 Evaluate the view that the UK is increasingly an 'elective dictatorship'. (30 marks)

Exam skills

Source questions

The questions you will face in Paper 1 and Paper 2 will be source questions. There is a choice of two in each paper. The source should be used to identify the arguments for the essay that you have chosen. For example, in question 1 in the Exam practice box, if you had a source but it did not include reference to the Supreme Court as a challenge to parliamentary sovereignty, you should not use it in your essay. Instead, you should:
+ Highlight the arguments the source makes that are relevant to your question.
+ Sort them into arguments for and arguments against the question.
+ Try, if you can, to pair up for and against arguments.
+ Use these pairs as the basis for the paragraphs that you will write.

You do not need to write about source reliability and provenance.

My Revision Notes: Pearson Edexcel A-level Politics: UK Government and Politics, Political Ideas and Global Politics

9 Liberalism

9.1 Core ideas and principles

What is individualism?

As a core belief of liberalism, individualists:
+ value the individual and protection of individual rights more than a collective group
+ believe that individuals are not a resource, but rather are valuable in their own right
+ think that individuals have equal worth
+ believe in showing tolerance and respecting the beliefs of others even if individuals disagree

Egoistical individualism says that individuals are self-reliant, so society is just a collection of individuals, while developmental individualism says that individual freedom is more closely linked to the formation of a society and a state that can help the more disadvantaged.

> **Egoistical individualism** Individual freedom is linked to self-reliance and self-interest of individuals.
>
> **Developmental individualism** Individual freedom is linked to a society in which individuals can achieve their aspirations.

> **Exam tip**
>
> It is important to remember that the question stem is always 'to what extent' for ideologies. Therefore, when looking at a difference, like egoistical and developmental individualism, it is not enough to point it out. You must also show how deep that division is.

Individualism is closely associated with:

Strands	Thinkers
+ Classical liberals — egoistical individualism + Modern liberals — developmental individualism	+ John Stuart Mill + John Rawls

What is freedom/liberty?

Freedom/liberty is a core belief of liberalism:
+ Individuals have freedom as a natural right.
+ Authoritarian governments are not legitimate and instead a social contract should be formed where individuals consent to be ruled and can withdraw their consent.
+ There should be a limited government that does not restrict individual freedom unless one individual is impinging on the freedom of another. This is 'negative freedom'.
+ 'Positive freedom' is the idea that individuals should be able to act on their own free will to achieve their goals, but that some state intervention may be necessary to achieve this.

> **Negative freedom** Where individuals are free from constraints or limitations.

Freedom/liberty is closely associated with:

Strands	Thinkers
+ Classical liberals — negative freedom + Modern liberals — positive freedom	+ John Locke + John Stuart Mill

What is the state?

Beliefs about the state within liberalism:

+ The state is a 'necessary evil' — humans need the state as they are self-seeking and so it can prevent exploitation, but the self-seeking nature of humans means they may use the power of the state for their own interests.
+ A minimal state is needed — a limited government, that has checks and balances on the power that it has.
+ There should be a clear understanding of what the rights of citizens are within this state.
+ The state should only have a limited role in the economy.
+ Some liberals are more comfortable with the 'enabling state' that plays a larger role to promote equality and defend the vulnerable.

The state is closely associated with:

Strands
+ Classical liberals — minimal state
+ Modern liberals — enabling state

Thinkers
+ John Stuart Mill
+ John Rawls
+ Betty Friedan

> **Minimal state** Where role of the state is limited in order to protect individual freedom.

> **Now test yourself**
>
> 1 Explain what is meant by the phrase 'necessary evil'.
> 2 Distinguish between egoistical individualism and developmental individualism.
> 3 Distinguish between positive freedom and negative freedom.
>
> TESTED

What is rationalism?

Rationalism is a core belief of liberalism:

+ Human beings are rational individuals, capable of reason rather than needing authority to guide them.
+ Individuals should therefore make their own decisions based on the best outcome for them, without the influence of external forces.
+ Individuals take responsibility for their decisions.

Rationalism is closely associated with:

Strands
+ Classical and modern liberalism

Thinker
+ John Locke

> **Exam tip**
>
> You will not be asked to compare ideologies. Therefore, try to avoid drawing comparisons, for example between the liberal view on rationality and the conservative view on rationality. You must compare *within* an ideology, not between them.

What is equality/social justice?

Equality/social justice is a core belief of liberalism:

+ Foundational equality, where all individuals are born with equal rights. Modern liberals have broadened this to include rights of women and minority groups.
+ Equality of opportunity, where all individuals have the same chance of success, rather than equality of outcome.
+ Formal equality, where all individuals have the same political and legal rights in society.
+ A belief in meritocracy, where the ability and effort of individuals determine their place in society.

Modern liberals have placed a greater emphasis on social justice, with the state having a greater role in preventing extreme inequality.

Equality/social justice is closely associated with:

Strands
+ Classical and modern liberals

Thinkers
+ John Locke
+ John Rawls

> **Equality of opportunity** All individuals have the same opportunity to succeed in life.
>
> **Formal equality** All individuals have the same political and legal rights in society.

What is liberal democracy?

Liberal democracy is a core belief of liberalism:

+ a limited government, which does not have unlimited power
+ government by consent of the governed, usually through free and fair elections
+ protection of rights and tolerance of a range of views
+ a social contract, where the consent of the governed can be removed

Liberal democracy is closely associated with:

Strands	Thinkers
+ Classical and modern liberals	+ John Locke + John Stuart Mill

> **Limited government** A government whose power is restricted by checks and balances and often through the separation of powers.

Now test yourself

TESTED ◯

4 Explain what is meant by 'limited government'.
5 Distinguish between foundational equality and formal equality.
6 Define the term 'equality of opportunity'.

9.2 Differing views and tensions

What is classical liberalism?

Classical liberalism has its roots in the seventeenth century, as part of the Enlightenment, which rejected traditional sources of authority and looked for an improvement in rights and opportunities. Classical liberals tend to believe:

+ in egoistical individualism — that people are self-seeking and society is therefore a collection of individuals
+ that the authority of government must be limited and exercised in accordance with the law
+ in the necessity for some government, as without the law individual rights could be infringed upon by other individuals
+ that a social contract exists, in which individuals consent to be governed by the state but could withdraw that consent
+ in foundational equality, in which all individuals are born with the same natural rights
+ that individuals have negative rights, where the only restrictions on individuals should come if their actions are interfering with the rights of others
+ in equality of opportunity, where everyone has the same opportunity to succeed but the outcomes will be different as individuals are inherently different
+ in a meritocracy, where individuals' place in society is determined by their effort and ability
+ in laissez-faire capitalism, where the government has a minimal role in economic intervention

> **Foundational equality** All humans are born with the same rights and these cannot be removed. These are also known as 'natural rights'.

> **Exam tip**
>
> You must show agreement and disagreement in your essays. As there are only two strands in liberalism, it can be easy just to focus on the differences, but you must also discuss what modern and classical liberals agree about and the extent to which they do.

What is modern liberalism?

Modern liberalism has its roots in the nineteenth century and a reaction to mass industrialisation under laissez-faire capitalism, which was causing increasing inequality. They tend to believe in:

+ developmental individualism, where individual freedoms are linked to the creation of a society which can help individuals to maintain and develop their freedoms

- **positive freedom** where a slightly more interventionalist state is necessary in order to allow individuals to use their freedom to attain their aspirations — this is linked to a greater belief in a more 'organic society', where there is a societal good rather than just individual interests
- greater state intervention in the economy, such as Keynesian economics, to ensure greater economic stability and equality
- a development in foundational equality to include women and minority groups, as these individuals are rational too
- an **enabling state**, which has greater intervention to help narrow extreme inequality and overcome disadvantages faced by some individuals
- democracy and universal enfranchisement as long as this is under a limited government and a state in which the rights of individuals and groups are protected

> **Positive freedom** The principle that freedom is linked to the opportunity to fulfil an individual's potential.
>
> **Enabling state** A state that helps individuals to achieve their potential and which is therefore often a larger state.

How do liberals agree and disagree on the four themes?

	General areas of agreement	Areas of disagreement
Human nature	+ An optimistic view of human nature. + Humans are rational and capable of reason and therefore able to solve problems. + Humans will act in a self-seeking way and are self-serving, but as they are rational they can understand other perspectives. + Humans will seek to plan their own destiny, rather than rely on authority. + Humans are born equal and with equal rights.	+ Human self-interest can lead to the infringing of the rights of others. Classical liberals suggest this is the only time the state should interfere in individual freedoms (negative freedom). Modern liberals argue that to achieve their self-interested goals, an enabling state is needed. + Classical liberals believe that human rationality results in egoistical individualism, whereas modern liberals argue for developmental individualism.
Society	+ Belief in a natural society that gives 'natural rights' to individuals. + Society is a collection of individuals, all with guaranteed rights. + There should be tolerance within society, provided the belief is not damaging. + Society should allow individuals to reach their potential. + Foundational and formal equality should be given to all individuals.	+ Classical liberals are more comfortable with **meritocracy** and a minimalist welfare state to prevent dependency or limits on freedom, whereas modern liberals see that disadvantaged groups need support to achieve their potential, arguing for greater social justice in society, tackled by the state. + Classical liberals argue in a natural society there will be natural laws that are followed. Modern liberals argue that this leads to the oppression of groups such as women and societal reform is therefore needed.
State	+ A **mechanistic view** of the state, in which the state is created to serve the interests of individuals. + Some level of state is needed in order to ensure equality under the law and prevent individuals impinging on the rights of others. + There should be a social contract, in which the consent of the governed can be given and taken away. + The state is a necessary evil. + Traditional authority and hierarchy is a hindrance to individual freedom. + General agreement on democracy and a limited government, with a shared concern over 'tyranny of the majority'.	+ Modern liberals argue for an enabling state, whereas classical liberals argue for a minimal state, sometimes called the 'night watchman state'. + Classical liberals acknowledge that equality of opportunity will lead to different outcomes, whereas modern liberals argue the state should have greater intervention to prevent excessive inequality of outcome. + Classical liberals argue the state should maintain order to allow capitalism to grow, whereas modern liberals argue for improving the life of the most vulnerable through a greater, although not complete, welfare state.

→

101

	General areas of agreement	Areas of disagreement
Economy	+ Property is a natural right. + General support of capitalism and limited government intervention in economic management.	+ Classical liberals believe in **laissez-faire capitalism** whereas modern liberals believe in **Keynesianism** to prevent instability. + Classical liberals argue state intervention leads to a culture of dependency but modern liberals argue a lack of state intervention can lead to exploitation. + Classical liberals see tax as an infringement whereas modern liberals are more comfortable with it to achieve positive freedom.

Meritocracy A society in which success and organisation are based on the ability and effort of individuals.

Mechanistic view A perception that the state is created to serve the interests of individuals.

Laissez-faire capitalism An economic system that has minimal government intervention, instead allowing the market to regulate itself.

Keynesianism An economic system in which the government has a greater role in order to achieve stability and full employment.

Exam tip

As there are 8 AO3 marks available, you are expected to judge the depth of agreement or disagreement. Words like 'superficial' or 'fundamental' can be helpful in showing your judgement.

Now test yourself

TESTED

7 Explain what is meant by the phrase 'social contract'.

8 Distinguish between Keynesian economics and laissez-faire economics.

9 Explain why equality of opportunity may lead to different outcomes for different individuals.

10 Identify two areas of agreement within liberalism on the role of the state.

11 Identify two areas of disagreement within liberalism on the economy.

12 Outline how liberals disagree about meritocracy.

9.3 Key thinkers

What do the key thinkers believe?

REVISED

John Locke

Key text: *Two Treatises of Government* (1690)

Key beliefs:

+ Social contract theory — government was based on the consent of the governed, which could be given and taken away, in return for protection of rights. This was based on the rationality of humans.
+ Limited government — government should have checks and balances on its power, based on consent of the governed.
+ Rejection of the traditional, hierarchical state, especially the 'divine right' of monarchies.

Key quotes/ideas:

+ On human nature: 'Reason must be our last judge and guide in everything'
+ On authority: 'It is evident that absolute monarchy… is indeed inconsistent with civil society'
+ On the state: '… where there is no law, there is no freedom'
+ On the state: government should protect 'life, liberty and estate'
+ On society: natural law meant humans should not harm 'the life, the liberty, health, limb, or goods of another'

Social contract theory Government is based on consent of the governed in exchange for a protection of freedoms, but consent can be removed if the government fails to protect these freedoms.

Mary Wollstonecraft

Key text: *A Vindication of the Rights of Women* (1792)

Key beliefs:

+ Reason — women are rational beings who can act independently and are capable of reason.
+ Formal equality — all individuals have the same political and legal rights and this includes women as they are rational individuals. Women should therefore be allowed the same civil rights as men, including education.
+ Women should be able to have a career in order to ensure that they are economically free and not dependent on men.

Key /ideas:

+ On the rights of women: 'I do not wish them to have power over men; but over themselves.'
+ On education: 'Strengthen the female mind by enlarging it, and there will be an end to blind obedience'
+ On equality and rationality: 'My own sex, I hope, will excuse me, if I treat them like rational creatures, instead of flattering their fascinating graces, and viewing them as if they were in a state of perpetual childhood, unable to stand alone'
+ On freedom and equality: described women as 'slaves… in a political and civil sense'

John Stuart Mill

Key text: *On Liberty* (1859)

Key beliefs:

+ Harm principle — individuals should be free to do as they wish, as long as their actions do not result in harm of others.
+ Tolerance — there should be an acceptance of differing views and beliefs, even if an individual does not agree with them.
+ Human actions are either 'self-regarding' or 'other-regarding'. Self-regarding actions affect the individual acting, whereas other-regarding actions affect other people.

Key /ideas:

+ On freedom: 'The only freedom which deserves the name, is that of pursuing our own good in our own way, so long as we do not attempt to deprive others of theirs, or impede their effort to obtain it.'
+ On the state: 'The only purpose for which power can be rightfully exercised over any member of a civilised community against his will, is to prevent harm to others'
+ On freedom: 'The human faculties of perception, judgment, discriminative feeling, mental activity, and even moral preference, are exercised only in making a choice. He who does anything because it is the custom, makes no choice'

John Rawls

Key text: *A Theory of Justice* (1971)

Key beliefs:

+ Theory of justice — that there must be social justice within society and society must guarantee every individual a life worth living.
+ The veil of ignorance — a philosophical question by Rawls designed to show that redistribution of wealth was in line with liberal values. It suggested that when people were asked to agree on what society they wanted, they did so without knowing what kind of person they might be in the new society (e.g. they could be a man or a woman, black or white, etc.).
+ Individuals within society should not be able to succeed at the expense of others (distributive justice); there should be a greater role of the state in narrowing excessive inequality.

Exam tip

It can be useful to quickly jot down the name of all the key thinkers for the ideology essay you are answering as soon as you get into the exam and then tick them off as you use them.

Harm principle The theory that individuals should be free to do anything provided it does not cause harm to other individuals.

Tolerance Respecting the beliefs of others, even if individuals disagree with them.

Now test yourself

13 Outline Locke's view on consent of the governed.

14 Outline Wollstonecraft's view on formal equality.

15 Outline Mill's view on the harm principle.

TESTED ○

103

Key quotes/ideas:

+ On social justice: Rawls argued for 'distributive justice'
+ On social justice: 'It may be expedient but it is not just that some should have less in order that others may prosper'
+ On freedom: 'Each person is to have an equal right to the most extensive basic liberty compatible with a similar liberty for others'
+ On equality: 'In a just society the liberties of equal citizenship are taken as settled; the rights secured by justice are not subject to political bargaining or to the calculus of social interests'
+ On the state and social justice: 'The natural distribution is neither just nor unjust; nor is it unjust that persons are born into society at some particular position. These are simply natural facts. What is just and unjust is the way that institutions deal with these facts'

Exam tip

The two key thinkers you use in your essay *must* come from the correct part of your specification. So, for liberalism, you *must* use two thinkers from the ones in this chapter.

Betty Friedan

Key text: *The Feminine Mystique* (1963)

Key beliefs:

+ Legal equality — women are equally capable as men and therefore laws oppressing women should be removed to provide equality under the law.
+ Equal opportunity — women are being held back from equality due to the belief that only certain jobs are 'acceptable' for women to undertake.
+ The cause of this inequality is cultural patriarchal values rather than the role of the state, such as expecting women to fulfil domestic roles.

Key /ideas:

+ On freedom: 'Who knows what women can be when they are finally free to be themselves'
+ On equality: 'A girl should not expect special privilege because of her sex but neither should she adjust to prejudice and discrimination.'
+ On equality: 'In almost every professional field, in business and in the arts and sciences, women are still treated as second-class citizens'
+ On equality: 'The feminist revolution had to be fought because women quite simply were stopped at a state of evolution far short of their human capacity'
+ On equality: 'Why should women accept this picture of a half-life, instead of a share in the whole of human destiny?'

How do liberals disagree on the four themes?		
	Classical liberalism	**Modern liberalism**
Human nature	+ Negative freedoms + Humans are all born with the same equal, natural rights + Egoistical individualism	+ Positive freedoms + Humans are all born with the *potential* for the same equal, natural rights + Developmental individualism
Society	+ Society came before the state + Society is a collection of individuals + Greater belief in meritocracy	+ Natural society led to the oppression of women and minority groups + Greater belief in the need for some intervention in society and welfare
State	+ Minimal state/night watchman state + Negative freedoms + Early classical liberals had concerns over the extent of democracy	+ Enabling state + Positive freedoms + Belief in democracy and extension of the franchise
Economy	+ Laissez-faire economics + Low tax	+ Keynesian economics + Comfortable with more tax to allow for an enabling state

Answers at **www.hoddereducation.co.uk/myrevisionnotesdownloads**

Now test yourself

TESTED ◯

16 Outline Rawls's view on the veil of ignorance.

17 Outline Friedan's view on legal equality.

Summary

✚ Core beliefs of liberalism are individualism, freedom/liberty, the state, rationalism, equality/social justice and liberal democracy.

✚ There are competing strands within liberalism of classical liberals and modern liberals.

✚ The key thinkers for liberalism are Locke, Wollstonecraft, Mill, Rawls and Friedan.

Revision tasks

1 Outline the meaning of five core beliefs of liberalism.

2 Distinguish between the views of classical liberals and modern liberals.

3 Copy and complete the table below.

Key thinker (name)	How the key thinker could link to the four themes (human nature, the state, society and the economy)	How the key thinker could link to the core beliefs of liberalism

Exam skills

Using thinkers

In your exam, you must *use* thinkers in your essays. This means you must show how their specific beliefs relate to the argument you are making. You should never write sentences such as: 'Classical liberals, like John Locke, believe in a minimal state…'. This is because this sentence describes a generic belief of principles rather than the actual thinking of John Locke.

The key beliefs of each thinker can be found in the bullet points above. You should use them like this:

```
Classical liberals strongly believe in a minimal
state. While they agree the state is necessary for
some protections, Locke argued this extended only to
the protection of life, freedom and property…
```

Thinkers should be used like you use contemporary examples in your 30-mark essays.

Exam practice

1 To what extent do classical and modern liberals agree about equality? (24 marks)

2 To what extent is there disagreement within liberalism about the role of the state? (24 marks)

10 Conservatism

10.1 Core ideas and principles

Conservatism is an ideology that seeks to conserve key principles and society. However, it is not just about keeping everything the same. Rather it is about 'changing to conserve' — the idea that to maintain the principles and beliefs of a society, some small evolutionary change is necessary to ensure the principles still work.

What is pragmatism?

REVISED ○

As a core belief of conservatism, pragmatists:
+ value practical experience over ideological or abstract thinking — this is known as 'empiricism'
+ believe that 'changing to conserve', or slow incremental change, is better than revolutionary change
+ argue that small change allows essential principles and institutions of society to be preserved
+ believe that humans are not rational or able to understand complex reality, therefore simple, practical strategies are better than abstract ideas

Pragmatism is closely associated with:

Strands
+ Traditional conservatives
+ One-nation conservatives

Thinkers
+ Burke
+ Oakeshott

Exam tip

It is important to recognise that conservatives do not want to 'conserve' or prevent change entirely. They recognise that some change is necessary in order to protect the hierarchy of society, but believe this change should be made cautiously.

What is tradition?

REVISED ○

Tradition is a core belief of conservatism:
+ Traditions are the practices, customs, institutions and principles that have developed over time and create stability.
+ Tradition provides a sense of belonging, identity and a way of making sense of the complex world.
+ The practices and institutions developed over time have shown themselves to work, therefore change should be incremental, and only if it improves on the current practices.
+ Abandoning traditions can have far-reaching and damaging consequences.

Tradition is closely associated with:

Strands
+ Traditional conservatives
+ One-nation conservatives

Thinkers
+ Burke
+ Oakeshott

What is human imperfection?

REVISED ○

As a core belief of conservatism, humans:
+ are morally imperfect, naturally motivated by selfish desires
+ are intellectually imperfect, with little capacity for rational understanding, especially of abstract thought
+ are psychologically imperfect, needing tradition and social order for comfort
+ would therefore seek a social contract, trading some individual freedom for law-and-order and protections offered by the state

Human imperfection is closely associated with:

Strands
+ Traditional conservatives
+ One-nation conservatives

Thinkers
+ Hobbes
+ Burke
+ Oakeshott

> **Human imperfection**
> Humans are naturally flawed and therefore not able to make good decisions for themselves.

Now test yourself   TESTED ◯

1 Explain what is meant by 'empiricism'.

2 Define 'human imperfection'.

3 Outline why tradition is important for conservatives.

What is the organic state?   REVISED ◯

As a core belief of conservatism, the organic state:

+ is not created, but grows in a slow, evolutionary manner where everything is connected
+ is made up of many parts, with the state and society being more important than these individual parts
+ includes traditional institutions that provide authority to humans, who naturally seek structure
+ includes a natural hierarchy as humans have different abilities
+ includes *noblesse oblige*, or paternalism
+ sees individual rights as given by the state as only the state can maintain them

> **Authority** The idea that there is a hierarchy and those in higher positions are best placed to make decisions for the good of society.
>
> **Hierarchy** A natural order to society arranged in fixed tiers that is not necessarily based on the ability of the individual.

Organic state is closely associated with:

Strands
+ Traditional conservatives
+ One-nation conservatives
+ Neo-conservatism

Thinkers
+ Hobbes
+ Burke
+ Oakeshott

What is paternalism?   REVISED ◯

As a core belief of conservatism, paternalists believe that:

+ society is inherently unequal and hierarchical, with a natural order and organic state
+ within this natural order, the elite in society are the natural leaders
+ the elite have a responsibility to help the less fortunate
+ if the state does not deal with societal problems, the traditional hierarchy and organic state will be at risk
+ this is sometimes called '*noblesse oblige*'

> *Noblesse oblige* The responsibility of those with power and wealth to help the less fortunate.

Paternalism is closely associated with:

Strands
+ Traditional conservatives
+ One-nation conservatives
+ Neo-conservatives

Thinkers
+ Hobbes
+ Burke
+ Oakeshott

What is libertarianism?   REVISED ◯

As a core belief of conservatism, libertarianism is:

+ a belief in individual freedom and liberty
+ a belief in laissez-faire economics, free from state intervention
+ a belief in a small government with limited intervention
+ somewhat in conflict with paternalism, seeing it as a challenge to individual freedom

107

Libertarianism is closely associated with:

Strands
+ Traditional conservatives
+ Neo-liberal conservatives

Thinkers
+ Burke
+ Rand
+ Nozick

Exam tip

When you are writing about the four themes — human nature, the state, the economy and society — remember that some of the beliefs outlined here will be applicable to more than one theme.

Now test yourself   TESTED ◯

4   Define the 'organic state'.
5   Outline the meaning of paternalism for conservatives.
6   Explain why paternalism and libertarianism conflict.

10.2 Differing views and tensions

What do traditional conservatives believe?   REVISED ◯

Traditional conservatism can be seen as a reaction to the French revolution and removal of the French monarchy in the eighteen century. Traditional conservatives tend to believe that:

+ there is a hierarchy to the organic state, which is naturally unequal
+ society is a living organism in which all the parts are interconnected
+ the elite are best placed to rule over this society but have an obligation to the less fortunate
+ a laissez-faire approach to economic intervention and society is best
+ pragmatism in any change is crucial — change should be evolutionary and incremental
+ humans are imperfect

> **Laissez-faire** Describes a government that has minimal intervention in the economy and running of the state.

Traditional conservatism is closely associated with the work of Thomas Burke.

What do one-nation conservatives believe?   REVISED ◯

One-nation conservatism came about as a reaction to mass industrialisation, which led to calls for social change and a risk of calls for revolutionary change in the nineteenth century. One-nation conservatives tend to believe in:

+ maintaining the traditional hierarchy and institutions of society to provide stability and tradition
+ a form of nationalism where all classes are part of 'the nation'
+ some social reforms for the working classes such as voting rights and societal improvements — this would ensure social order and contentment, which would protect the hierarchy and traditions of society

Later, this would include a greater role (but not an unlimited one) for the state in economic management, known as 'Keynesian economics', and a greater focus on the welfare state to provide minimum standards of living and therefore protect the structure of society.

One-nation conservatism is closely associated with Prime Minister Benjamin Disraeli who tried to retain but update some of the key ideas of Thomas Burke. It is also associated with the policies of Prime Minister Harold Macmillan.

> **Exam tip**
>
> Your essays for ideologies should be driven by strands not thinkers. This means you should evaluate the agreements and disagreements between *strands* and use thinkers only to support your argument.

108

What does the New Right believe?

The New Right emerged in the 1970s as Keynesian economic policies were beginning to fail, with economies showing low growth, high inflation and high unemployment. It combines two strands — neo-liberalism and neo-conservatism (Table 10.1).

Table 10.1 Neo-liberal and neo-conservative beliefs

Neo-liberal beliefs	Neo-conservative beliefs
+ Society is atomistic, made up of individuals whose rights are more important than society. + There is no state obligation to the less fortunate and no social contract. + Human are capable of rational thought; they are not imperfect. + A dislike of the role of the state, favouring individual liberty and a minimalist government. + An organic society limits the ability of humans from reaching their full potential. + State welfare makes individuals dependent on the state. + The economy should be a free-market with little government intervention.	+ Update and modernise traditional conservatism. + Maintain the organic society, uphold law and order and prevent social fragmentation. + Recognise the need for paternalism in a welfare state but argue for a smaller welfare state to overcome dependency. + Reverse the permissive attitudes of the 1960s and replace them with traditional values such as heterosexual marriage and promotion of traditional family values. This is **anti-permissiveness**. + Belief in human imperfection, that humans are not naturally moral or hard working.

Anti-permissiveness Rejecting permissiveness where people make their own moral choices and these choices are not objectively 'right' or 'wrong'.

Now test yourself

 TESTED

7 List three beliefs of traditional conservatives.

8 List three beliefs of one-nation conservatives.

9 Distinguish between neo-liberals and neo-conservatives.

Exam tip

When analysing 'agreement' within an ideology, you do not have to find areas where everyone agrees entirely. Instead, you may argue that two or more strands agree on something, even if another strand does not.

Radical Drastic and extensive change in society, politics or the economy.

Change to conserve Society should adapt incrementally to current circumstances in order to prevent revolutionary change.

Now test yourself

 TESTED

10 Identify two areas of agreement within conservatism on human nature.

11 Identify two areas of disagreement within conservatism on society.

12 Outline how conservatives disagree about private property.

How do conservatives agree and disagree on the four themes?

	General areas of agreement	Areas of disagreement
Human nature	+ Most conservatives have a negative view of human nature. + Human are imperfect and not rational, excepting neo-liberals. + There is a hierarchical nature to society, driven by human imperfection. + General agreement that humans need pragmatism over abstract ideologies.	+ Neo-liberals broadly reject human imperfection and believe humans can be rational. + There is variation between all the strands of conservatism on how negative their view of human imperfection is.
Society	+ Society is an organic state made up of interconnecting principles and evolves slowly. + Change should be incremental and not radical. + Humans need the order and structure of society, including traditions. + There is a natural hierarchy in society as humans are naturally unequal. + There is an expectation of paternalism.	+ Neo-liberals argue for an atomistic society rather than an organic one. + The New Right has an issue with paternalism and the extent of the welfare state, creating dependence rather than a meritocracy. + Neo-conservatives champion traditional family values, whereas neo-liberals champion individual freedom.
State	+ The ruling class is best placed to rule and has a paternalistic obligation. + Taxation can be used to fund paternalistic state intervention. + The state should allow and defend private property ownership. + Changes to the state or by the state should be incremental, allowing a 'change to conserve' model.	+ One-nation conservatives are more comfortable with a slightly larger state and more state intervention than traditional and New Right conservatives. + New Right conservatives do not believe the state gives individuals rights. + New Right conservatives believe the state limits individual freedom. + New Right conservatives argue for a minimalist state.
Economy	+ The state should defend private property ownership. + Minimal state intervention in the economy. + Belief in capitalism and free market economics. + General agreement on the role of taxation being used to fund government intervention.	+ The role and imposition of tax. Neo-liberals especially see tax as problematic, whereas one-nation conservatives are more sympathetic to it. + One-nation conservatives are more comfortable with state intervention in the economy than other conservatives. + Neo-liberals advocate for a very minimalistic state to allow for individual atomism, whereas most conservatives argue for an organic state. + Disagreement on the role of private property — most conservatives argue it gives individuals a stake in society whereas neo-liberals argue it reduces dependency on the state. + Disagreement over the level of deregulation and intervention in the economy.

10.3 Key thinkers

What do the key thinkers believe?

REVISED ○

Thomas Hobbes

Key text: *Leviathan* (1651)

Key beliefs:
+ Order in society will balance the need for human freedom.
+ Humans are needy and vulnerable and therefore need societal structure.
+ Humans will give up some freedoms in return for security from a strong central state.

Answers at **www.hoddereducation.co.uk/myrevisionnotesdownloads**

Key quotes/ideas:

✦ On human nature: 'Humans are driven by a perpetual and restless desire of power'

✦ On human selfishness, material gratification and distrust: it is the human 'state of nature'

✦ On society: life without order of the state is 'solitary, poor, nasty, brutish and short'

✦ On rationality: 'The passions of men are commonly more potent than their reason'

Edmund Burke

Key text: *Reflections on the Revolution in France* (1790)

Key beliefs:

✦ Change should be incremental and evolutionary and done only to conserve the practices and ideals of society ('change to conserve').

✦ Tradition and empiricism — traditions should be respected and passed down through generations and any change should be based on empirical evidence not abstract theory.

✦ Paternalism — the ruling class had an obligation to the rest of society.

Key quotes/ideas:

✦ On the importance of tradition as a guide for humans: 'wisdom without reflection'

✦ On society: '[Society] is a partnership not only between those who are living, but between those who are living, those who are dead and those who are to be born'

✦ On the organic society: 'little platoons'

✦ On hierarchy: he believed in 'true natural aristocracy' rule

✦ On the state: 'A state without the means of some change is without the means of its conservation'

✦ On society: 'All men have equal rights but not to equal things'

✦ On change: 'Politics ought to be adjusted not to human reasonings but to human nature'

> **Tradition** The customs and practices that are passed down from one generation to the next, often based on lived experience and what works effectively.
>
> **Empiricism** Knowledge comes from lived experience and not from abstract theories.

Michael Oakeshott

Key texts: *Rationalism in Politics* (1962); *On Human Conduct* (1975)

Key beliefs:

✦ Human imperfection — humans are imperfect and unable to comprehend the world around them and society is unpredictable.

✦ Pragmatism — change should be made on the basis of real-world evidence, not abstract ideas.

✦ Humans should accept the traditions of society as they have been shown to work.

Key quotes/ideas:

✦ On humans: 'fallible but not terrible'

✦ On belief that implementing abstract ideas leads to unexpected consequences: 'the politics of scepticism'

✦ On tradition: 'To be a conservative… is to prefer the tried to the untried'

✦ On tradition: 'What has stood the test of time should not be cast away lightly'

✦ On change: 'To be a conservative… is to prefer the familiar to the unknown'

✦ On the state: it exists to 'prevent the bad rather than create the good'

> **Exam tip**
>
> You must use two thinkers in your essays in order to be able to score more than 9/24. *Using* a key thinker involves more than just putting their name into your essay. Instead you must outline what they specifically think and how that links to the argument you are making.

> **Now test yourself**
>
> 13 Outline Hobbes's view on human nature.
>
> 14 Outline Burke's view on change.
>
> 15 Outline Oakeshott's view on pragmatism.
>
> TESTED

Ayn Rand

Key texts: *Atlas Shrugged* (1957); *The Virtue of Selfishness* (1964)

Key beliefs:

✦ Objectivism — humans are rational and acting in a self-interested way is rational.

111

+ Freedom — support for a capitalist economy largely free of government intervention.
+ Individuals' rights are more important than society as a whole and governments can limit these freedoms so the state should be minimalist, providing only order and security.

Key quotes/ideas:
+ On human nature: 'virtue of selfishness'
+ On society: 'atomistic individualism'
+ On society: '… man must be the beneficiary of his own moral actions'

Robert Nozick
Key texts: *Anarchy, State and Utopia* (1974)

Key beliefs:
+ Libertarianism — a belief in individual freedom that means individuals cannot be used as a resource against their will.
+ Self-ownership — individuals own their own abilities, labour and bodies.
+ Growth of government is a threat to the freedoms of individuals.
+ Some formal authority is needed in order to enforce law and order but the state should have minimal interference in the lives of individuals.

Key quotes/ideas:
+ On human nature: humans are 'pack animals'
+ On society: 'There are only individual people, different individual people, with their own lives'
+ On tax: 'Taxation of earnings is on a par with forced labour'
+ On the state: '… the state's claim to legitimacy induces its citizens to believe they have some duty to obey its edicts, pay its taxes, fight its battles, and so on…'
+ On the role of the state: '… limited to the narrow functions of force, theft, enforcement of contracts, and so on'
+ On the welfare state: '…enrich some persons at the expense of others'

> **Atomism** Belief that society is made up of individuals who act in self-interested ways.
>
> **Libertarianism** A philosophy in which individual freedom is achieved through minimal state intervention in the lives of citizens or the economy.

> **Exam tip**
>
> You do not need to memorise lots of quotes from thinkers, but you can use small quotes in your essays if it helps you to explain what a thinker believes.

What does each strand of conservatism believe about the four themes?

	Traditional conservatives	One-nation conservatives	Neo-conservatives	Neo-liberals
Human nature	+ A pessimistic view of human nature + Humans are not rational	—	+ Humans can act rationally	+ Humans are rational
Society	+ Incremental not revolutionary reform, only to protect key principles of society + There is a natural hierarchy + Organic society	+ Provision of social welfare would protect the societal hierarchy	+ Emphasise traditional family values in an organic society	+ Individuals are more important than society + Society is atomistic
State	+ Respect tradition + Act pragmatically + Defend traditional institutions + Rule by a natural aristocracy + A paternalistic responsibility	+ A paternalistic duty including social welfare provision + Running a managed economy + Provision of some, limited reform	+ A smaller provision of welfare + A smaller government focusing on law and order	+ A smaller government + Very small welfare state, if at all
Economy	+ Laissez-faire approach to economic management	+ Greater government intervention + Keynesian economics	+ Free market economy + Low tax + Minimal state intervention	+ Free market economy + Low tax + Minimal state intervention

Answers at **www.hoddereducation.co.uk/myrevisionnotesdownloads**

Now test yourself

16 Outline Rand's view on society.

17 Outline Nozick's view on tax and the welfare state.

Summary

✦ Core beliefs of conservatism are pragmatism, tradition, human imperfection, organic society, paternalism and libertarianism.

✦ There are competing strands with differing views within conservatism — traditional conservatives, one-nation conservatives and the New Right (made up of neo-conservatives and neo-liberals).

✦ The key thinkers for conservatism are Hobbes, Burke, Oakeshott, Rand and Nozick.

Revision tasks

1 Outline the meaning of five core beliefs of conservatism.

2 Distinguish between the views of traditional conservatives, one-nation conservatives, and New Right conservatives.

3 Copy and complete the table below.

Key thinker (name)	How the key thinker could link to the four themes (human nature, the state, society and the economy)	How the key thinker could link to the core beliefs of conservatism

Exam skills

24-mark structure

A 24-mark essay is awarded marks on three assessment objectives (AO): AO1, AO2 and AO3. Each AO is worth 8 marks.

Your essay must have an introduction, usually two paragraphs and a conclusion that answers the question directly. Usually, each paragraph should be about a *factor*. For example, in question 2 in the Exam practice box, you could write paragraphs on:

✦ rationality — how far conservatives agree that humans are rational

✦ self-interest — how far conservatives agree that this determines how humans act

Exam practice

1 To what extent do conservatives agree about the role of the state in the economy? (24 marks)

2 To what extent do conservatives agree about human imperfection? (24 marks)

11 Socialism

11.1 Core ideas and principles

What is collectivism?

REVISED ●

Collectivism is a core belief of socialism:
+ Humans achieve more through collective effort than individual effort, including political, social and economic aims.
+ Humans prefer to work and live together than alone, united through fraternity.
+ Wasting energy should be avoided, using people's skills and abilities more efficiently and effectively as a group.
+ Society can only be improved through collective action.
+ The interests of a group should therefore be more important than the interests of the individual.
+ Common ownership is advocated to allow all individuals to take part in and benefit from production.

Later socialists attach less importance to common ownership, allowing for some capitalism and to avoid a centralised state suppressing freedom.

Collectivism is closely associated with:

> **Fraternity** The bonds that naturally exist between humans sharing the same basic nature and outlook.
>
> **Common ownership** The ownership of the means of production by all those involved in the process, to benefit the whole of society.

Strands
+ Revolutionary socialists — collective ownership
+ Social democracy and the third way — some acceptance of capitalism

Thinkers
+ Marx and Engels
+ Webb

What is common humanity?

REVISED ●

Common humanity is a core belief of socialism:
+ Humans naturally want to work together more than they want to compete with one another.
+ Humans are sociable and rational and can be influenced by moral considerations as well as more selfish, material desires.
+ Human behaviour is decided within the framework of a society, so individuals must be viewed as part of society.
+ Like collectivism, understanding a shared humanity means that society can benefit from efficient and effective use of individuals' abilities.
+ Capitalism encourages competition between people, which results in conflict, especially when unchecked.
+ Later socialists are more forgiving of some aspects of capitalism, if material motivation can be paired with moral motivation of people.

Common humanity is closely associated with:

Strands
+ Revolutionary socialists — opposed to capitalism
+ Social democracy and third way — capitalism can be harnessed for a greater human good

Thinkers
+ Marx and Engels
+ Crosland
+ Giddens

What is equality?

REVISED ●

Socialists believe that inequality is a result of capitalism rather than due to differences between individuals. There are different types of equality:
+ **Absolute equality:** all individuals should receive the same outcomes provided their efforts were their best.
+ **Equality of outcome:** what each individual gains in society should be similar.

Answers at **www.hoddereducation.co.uk/myrevisionnotesdownloads**

- **Equality of opportunity:** all individuals should have an equal chance to succeed, but whether they do will depend on the ability and effort they put in. Some socialists are sceptical of this, however, as humans do not all have the same abilities, therefore the same opportunity will not afford the same outcome.
- **Equality of welfare:** all individuals should have a minimum standard of living.

Equality is closely associated with:

Strands
+ Revolutionary socialists — absolute equality
+ Social democracy — equality of opportunity/welfare
+ Third way — equality of opportunity

Thinkers
+ Marx and Engels
+ Webb
+ Crosland

Now test yourself   TESTED ◯

1 Explain what is meant by 'collectivism'.
2 Distinguish between equality of outcome and equality of opportunity.
3 Outline why equality is important for socialists.

What is social class?   REVISED ◯

Social class is a core belief of socialism:
- Social class is a result of capitalism, which creates social hierarchies, division and exploits workers.
- Social class action has therefore been the cause of change in history, fighting for the rights of those within a class.
- There is a commitment to improve the lives and conditions of the working class, but with a belief that the class system will not last forever.

Socialists' attachment to social class and a resulting class consciousness was closely influenced by industrialisation in the nineteenth century. With deindustrialisation, the connection of socialists to social class has weakened.

Social class is closely associated with:

Strands
+ Revolutionary socialists — favouring class revolution
+ Social democracy and the third way — a more flexible approach to combatting social class

Thinkers
+ Marx and Engels
+ Crosland
+ Giddens

Class consciousness
Social class is central to the ideas of socialism and the exploited class must adopt a revolutionary class consciousness to overthrow the exploiters.

What is workers' control?   REVISED ◯

Workers' control is a core belief of socialism:
- There should be ownership by the workers of the places in which they work, either partly or totally.
- Workers are key in the methods of production and therefore should have at least some control over the work.
- Capitalism exploits workers, especially if it is completely unchecked, so allowing workers' control over the means of production allows them to gain more from the production.

Capitalism An economic model in which wealth and the means of production are privately owned and goods are produced for the profit of the owners.

Workers' control is closely associated with:

Strand		Thinkers
+ Revolutionary socialists		+ Marx and Engels

Now test yourself   TESTED ◯

4 Explain what is meant by 'workers' control'.
5 Explain why socialists object to capitalism.
6 Outline the meaning of 'class consciousness'.

11.2 Differing views and tensions

What is revolutionary socialism?   REVISED ◯

Revolutionary socialism emerged in the nineteenth century, especially in response to mass industrialisation. Revolutionary socialists believed:

+ that workers were unable to influence the political and economic system that exploited them
+ that the institutions of power were firmly entrenched and could not be reformed effectively
+ that revolution was necessary, overthrowing the ruling class with workers taking over the means of production
+ that capitalism had corrupted the positive natural tendencies of humans for common humanity and fraternity
+ in the 'dialectic', whereby progress would be achieved through the clash of two opposing ideals, usually the current values of society and a challenging set of values — this clash would result in a new society and ultimately the state would wither away

> **Dialectic** Where two opposing sets of values — often the exploiters and the exploited — clash to create a new society, over and over again creating new stages of history.

While Marx and Engels saw no need for democracy once the state had withered away, Luxemburg argued for elections.

What is social democracy?   REVISED ◯

Social democracy emerged after the Second World War, arguing for reform of capitalism rather than revolution. It is a form of evolutionary socialism. Evolutionary socialists tend to believe that:

+ the inequalities produced by capitalism need to be remedied with a fairer distribution of wealth to achieve social justice, rather than common ownership
+ this could be achieved with greater state intervention through a mixed economy and Keynesian economics
+ capitalism can be reformed through the use of a welfare state to redistribute wealth
+ this could be afforded through economic growth and the resulting increase in taxation

> **Evolutionary socialism** A gradual, reformist approach to achieve socialism via legal and political means.

These ideals were challenged during the economic downturns of the 1970s and 1980s when demand on welfare increased and taxation incomes fell.

What is the third way?

The third way emerged in the late twentieth century, as work had become less industrialised and the world was more globalised. It is also a form of 'evolutionary socialism'. The third way tends to believe:

✛ that there is an acceptance of the free-market, rather than heavy state intervention

✛ that there is a focus on social inclusion based on equality of opportunity — this means that the state should invest in key areas such as infrastructure and education to allow everyone a chance to succeed and to contribute to the wealth of the nation

✛ that rights that are given to individuals are balanced with the responsibilities they owe to society

✛ in the benefits of a meritocratic system, where individuals can amass wealth provided it contributes to the overall progress of the nation

✛ that there should be a more limited welfare state that is targeted at the most vulnerable but can expect these groups to work towards their own betterment as well

> **Cooperation** Humans working collectively together for the benefit of all.
>
> **Keynesian economics** An economic system in which the government has a greater role in order to achieve stability and full employment.

How do socialists agree and disagree on the four themes?

	General areas of agreement	Areas of disagreement
Human nature	✛ There is an optimistic view of human nature in which humans are fundamentally cooperative, rational, social, moral, and want to work and act collectively. ✛ Human nature is a result of society rather than innate, therefore human nature is malleable. ✛ There is a belief in common humanity.	✛ The optimistic view of revolutionary socialists means that humans want to work together for the common good, where more modern socialists accept the need also for material gain. ✛ Revolutionary socialists believe that capitalism has corrupted human nature, whereas social democrats and the third way see a reformed capitalism as a workable solution.
Society	✛ Humans need society in order to fulfil their potential. ✛ Society shapes human nature and understanding. ✛ Humans naturally tend toward society and collective understanding, including fraternity. ✛ There is a shared belief in equality and the need therefore to reform capitalism. ✛ Society should be based on **cooperation**.	✛ Revolutionary socialists see class conflict as inevitable, whereas social democrats and third way socialists are more flexible in their approach to class. ✛ Revolutionary socialists saw revolution as a necessity, whereas evolutionary socialists argued that reform was possible, creating gradual improvements.
State	✛ There is a role for the state in managing the economy and inequality, at least in the short term. ✛ The state is needed to promote the values of socialism.	✛ There is substantial disagreement about the type of equality that is preferable, with revolutionary socialists arguing for absolute equality and equality of outcome, and third way socialists and social democrats arguing for equality of opportunity and equality of welfare. ✛ Revolutionary socialists argue that the state is naturally exploitative, whereas the third way and social democrats see a role for the state in overcoming inequality. ✛ Revolutionary socialists argued the state would wither away whereas third way and social democrats argue for reform of the state.
Economy	✛ Competition (especially under capitalism) can create division and inequality. ✛ The economy should work to benefit all within it, not just some.	✛ Revolutionary socialists argued for a centralised state organising production but social democrats and third way socialists prefer a degree of capitalism. ✛ The third way argue for a smaller welfare state than social democrats. ✛ Social democrats argue for a mixed economy based on **Keynesian economics**, whereas third way socialists argue for greater deregulation to create tax for welfare.

Now test yourself

TESTED

7 List three beliefs of revolutionary socialists.

8 List three beliefs of social democracy.

9 Distinguish between Keynesian economics and free-market capitalism.

Exam tip

Try to avoid a structure where you have one paragraph of agreement and one paragraph of disagreement. Often this structure will mean you are not judging the *extent* of agreement or disagreement and therefore hinder your AO3 evaluation skills. Instead, try to find two separate factors for which you can discuss agreement and disagreement.

Now test yourself

TESTED

10 Identify two areas of agreement within socialism on the economy.

11 Identify two areas of disagreement within socialism on the role of the state.

12 Outline how socialists disagree over the issue of welfare.

11.3 Key thinkers

What do the key thinkers believe?

REVISED

Karl Marx and Friedrich Engels

Key texts: *The Communist Manifesto* (1848), *Das Kapital* (1867)

Key beliefs:

+ Social class — a belief in:
  + historical materialism, where the method of material production influences the nature and organisation of society
  + dialectic change, where two opposing sets of values — often the exploiters and the exploited — clash to create a new society, over and over again, creating new stages of history
  + class consciousness, where social class is central to the ideas of socialism, and the exploited class must adopt a revolutionary class consciousness to overthrow the exploiters
+ Humans as social beings — human nature is determined by society and common humanity is only possible under socialism.
+ They advocated a form of communism commonly referred to as 'Marxism'.

Key quotes/ideas:

+ On human nature: that society and capitalism had created a 'false consciousness'
+ On revolution: it was 'historically inevitable'
+ On capitalism: it created 'the seeds of its own destruction' by creating a resentful workforce
+ On the state: the liberal state was 'merely a committee' from which the ruling elite could control power
+ On the state under socialism: 'The state is not "abolished", it withers away'
+ On equality: 'from each according to his ability, to each according to his needs'

> **Historical materialism** Where the method of material production influences the nature and organisation of society.
>
> **Communism** An economic (and political) system in which the means of production are held in common ownership, society is classless and wealth is equally distributed.
>
> **Marxism** An ideological strand of socialism based on the work of Marx and Engels in which capitalism will ultimately be replaced by communism.

Beatrice Webb

Key text: *The Minority Report of the Poor Law Commission* (1909)

Key beliefs:

+ 'The inevitability of gradualness' — gradual reform in an age of expanding democracy would achieve greater equality for working classes.
+ The expansion of the state — the growth of the state to provide amenities and welfare and ultimately socialism was necessary, not the overthrow of the state.

Key quotes/ideas:

+ On society and equality: she argued there should be a 'national minimum of civilised life'
+ On revolution: they were 'chaotic, inefficient and counter-productive'
+ On common ownership: she favoured 'cooperative federalism' with customers having ownership and decision-making power over businesses and their profits
+ On the state: it would 'silently change its character… from police power, to housekeeping on a national scale'
+ On capitalism: it was the cause of 'crippling poverty and demeaning inequality'
+ On the state: it should provide 'a sufficient nourishment and training when young, a living-wage when able-bodied, treatment when sick, and modest but secure livelihood when disabled or aged'

> **Exam tip**
>
> While you must use two key thinkers from this chapter to be able to gain more than 9/24 marks, this does not prevent you from using thinkers from other chapters if they are relevant *in addition* to these two. For example, the idea of a 'reserve army of labour' comes from Marx, but is often discussed in feminism. This use must **only** be in addition to the key thinkers from the relevant topic.

> **Now test yourself**   TESTED ◯
>
> **13** Define 'historical materialism'.
> **14** Outline the view of Marx and Engels on human nature.
> **15** Outline Webb's view on the state.

Rosa Luxemburg

Key text: *The Accumulation of Capital* (1913)

Key beliefs:

+ Evolutionary socialism, or revisionism, was not possible, as the nature of capitalism was exploitation and therefore socialism could not be brought about by gradual reform.
+ The struggle of the working classes (the proletariat) for reform and democracy would create the necessary conditions for mass strikes and ultimately create a socialist revolution.

Key quotes/ideas:

+ On the state: 'Without general elections, without unrestricted freedom of the press and assembly, without a free struggle of opinion, life dies in every institution'
+ On freedom: 'Freedom is how free your opponent is'

> **Revisionism** The attempt to redefine socialism to a less radical, more evolutionary movement.
> **Social justice** The distribution of wealth in society to limit inequality.

Anthony Crosland

Key text: *The Future of Socialism* (1956)

Key beliefs:

+ The inherent contradictions in capitalism had been reduced in modern capitalism and therefore these contradictions could no longer be used to create social change.
+ State-managed capitalism can create social justice and greater equality through a mixed economy, universal benefits and full employment.

Key quotes/ideas:

+ On capitalism: 'the evolutionary and revolutionary philosophies of progress have proved false'

119

+ On equality and class: '... equality of opportunity and social mobility... are not enough. They need to be combined with measures... to equalise the distribution of rewards and privileges so as to diminish the degree of class stratification'
+ On collective ownership: it would make a socialist state a 'dull functional nightmare'
+ On social justice: 'I came to hate and loathe social injustice because I dislike the class structure of our society, because I could not tolerate the indefensible differences of status and income that disfigure our society'

Anthony Giddens

Key text: *The Third Way: The Renewal of Social Democracy* (1998)

Key beliefs:

+ an acceptance of greater free-market capitalism largely free of state intervention
+ a focus on equality of opportunity over equality, and responsibility and community instead of class conflict
+ in the 'third way', drawing on key strengths of social democracy and free-market capitalism

Key quotes/ideas:

+ On the state: 'Investment in education is an imperative of government today, a key basis of the "redistribution of possibilities"'
+ On the economy: he argued for 'communitarianism', pairing free-market individualism with responsibility towards community and others
+ On welfare: he argued for 'positive welfare', helping individuals to help themselves, rather than simply giving out welfare
+ On the economy and the state: a belief in a 'social investment state', investing economic profits in social infrastructure

> **Exam tip**
>
> Do not fall into the trap of just comparing thinkers — you must compare strands. Some thinkers may be applicable to more than one strand of an ideology and some strands may not have any key thinkers at all listed in the specification. Therefore, always compare strands, not thinkers.

> **Now test yourself**
>
> 16 Outline Luxembourg's view on evolutionary socialism.
>
> 17 Outline Crosland's view on social justice.
>
> 18 Outline Gidden's view on the economy.
>
> TESTED

How do socialists disagree on the four themes?			
	Revolutionary socialism	**Social democracy**	**Third Way**
Human nature	+ An optimistic view of human nature + Capitalism has corrupted human nature	+ An optimistic view of human nature but understanding of the need for material gain	+ An optimistic view of human nature but understanding of the need for material gain
Society	+ Common humanity + Dialectic understanding + Historical materialism + Class conflict was inevitable	+ Inequalities needed to be remedied + Gradual improvements in society were possible	+ Social inclusion based on equality of opportunity + Rights of individuals are balanced with responsibilities to society
State	+ The state would 'wither away' and die + Revolution was needed as workers could not influence the state and it could not be effectively reformed + A focus on absolute equality and equality of outcome	+ Responsible for a fairer distribution of wealth and social justice + A focus on equality of opportunity and equality of welfare	+ Responsible for investment in social infrastructure + A focus on equality of opportunity and equality of welfare
Economy	+ Centralised state planning + Common ownership of the means of production + No private property	+ Capitalism reformed to produce a welfare state, high employment and universal benefits + Acceptance of private property + Keynesian economics	+ Free-market capitalism with tax used to fund social infrastructure + Acceptance of private property + A more limited, targeted welfare state, that encourages the cooperation of those involved

Answers at **www.hoddereducation.co.uk/myrevisionnotesdownloads**

Summary

+ Core beliefs of socialism are collectivism, common humanity, equality, social class and workers' control.
+ There are competing strands with differing views within socialism — revolutionary socialists, social democrats and third way socialists.
+ The key thinkers for socialism are Marx and Engels, Webb, Luxemburg, Crosland and Giddens.

Revision tasks

1 Outline the meaning of five core beliefs of socialism.
2 Distinguish between the views of revolutionary socialists, social democrats and the third way.
3 Copy and complete the table below.

Key thinker (name)	How the key thinker could link to the four themes (human nature, the state, society and the economy)	How the key thinker could link to the core beliefs of socialism

Exam skills

Comparing strands and reaching a judgement

Your essays for ideologies must be strand driven — this means you should be comparing **strands not thinkers**. So, although each of your paragraphs should focus on a particular *factor*, you should compare the areas in which the strands agree and/or disagree. For example, in question 2 in the Exam practice box:

+ Revolutionary socialists disagree with evolutionary socialists on the existence of the state.
+ But within evolutionary socialism, social democrats and third way socialists disagree over the state's role in economic management.

It is fine to find agreement between only some, but not all, strands — this is still an area of agreement. You **must** show both agreement and disagreement in your essay before reaching a judgement on the extent of agreement. To do this, think of 'extent' as a sliding scale from 0% to 100% — having written about the levels of both agreement and disagreement, where would you place the answer to the question overall on this scale, and why?

Exam practice

1 To what extent do socialists agree about equality?   (24 marks)
2 To what extent is socialism a coherent theory?   (24 marks)

121

12 Anarchism

12.1 Core ideas and principles

What is the rejection of the state?

REVISED

The rejection of the state is a core belief of anarchism:

+ The state comprises the government, authority and power.
+ The state is oppressive and rules with the threat of violence to back it up.
+ Democracy is a fraud, designed to make individuals believe they have power within the state.
+ The state restricts the freedom of rational individuals, especially through the removal of choice over their actions.
+ The state is commanding, controlling and corrupting.
+ All of this means that the state cannot be justified and must be resisted and rejected.

Rejection of the state is closely associated with:

Strands	Thinkers
+ Individualist anarchists + Collectivist anarchists	+ Bakunin — 'propaganda by deed' + Stirner — insurrection + Proudhon — new institutions

State The sovereign body that exerts power over humans under its controlled area.

Government The system and institutions of rule, which anarchists consider are based on deceit and violence.

Authority The right to power, which anarchists see as commanding, controlling and corrupting.

Power The means by which the state enforces its authority, such as police, military and law.

What is liberty?

REVISED

Liberty is a core belief of anarchism:

+ Liberty can only be achieved with freedom from the state.
+ Liberty is desirable as individuals are rational.
+ Individualist anarchists suggest liberty is necessary for personal good, whereas collectivist anarchists argue it is necessary for the common good.

Liberty is closely associated with:

Strands	Thinkers
+ Individualist anarchists — personal good + Collectivist anarchists — common good	+ Bakunun + Stirner + Proudhon

What is meant by 'anarchy is order'?

REVISED

'Anarchy is order' is a core belief of anarchism:

+ While anarchists reject the state, there would be order without a state.
+ The anarchist social order might include a decentralised community of self-governing, voluntary communities leading to a peaceful, stable but stateless society.
+ There is no common understanding of what an anarchists' society would look like in reality, with thinkers putting forward different ideas.

'Anarchy is order' is closely associated with:

Strands	Thinkers
+ Individualist anarchists + Collectivist anarchists	+ Stirner + Proudhon + Kropotkin

Exam tip

Some thinkers can be used for more than one strand of an ideology, depending on their beliefs and their quotes. The beliefs of thinkers may not be associated with just one strand of an ideology, so you **must** compare strands.

Now test yourself

TESTED

1 List the three things that make up the state.
2 Explain what is meant by 'anarchy is order'.
3 Give three reasons why the state should be resisted for anarchists.

Answers at **www.hoddereducation.co.uk/myrevisionnotesdownloads**

What is meant by 'economic freedom'?

REVISED

As a core belief of anarchism, economic freedom means:
+ Anarchists broadly oppose capitalism.
+ Anarchists broadly oppose private property within the current capitalist models, as it causes inequality and exploitation.
+ There should not be state intervention in the economic system as regulation makes solidarity impossible.

Solidarity Sympathy, cooperation and harmony between individuals, therefore not requiring state regulation.

Collectivist anarchists argue that property could be mutually owned, whereas anarcho-capitalists argue all aspects of infrastructure could be left to a free market as rational individuals will make the best choices for this provision.

Economic freedom is closely associated with:

Strands
+ Individualist anarchists — a market free of state intervention
+ Collectivist anarchists — abolish private property

Thinkers
+ Proudhon
+ Kropotkin
+ Bakunin

What is meant by 'utopian'?

REVISED

As a core belief of anarchism, 'utopian' means:
+ A utopia is an ideal society of peace and liberty.
+ For anarchists, the rational and optimistic nature of humans makes this possible.
+ There is disagreement within the strands of anarchism of what this utopia looks like — collectivist anarchists would remove capitalism while anarcho-capitalists would have entirely free-market capitalism.
+ There has been criticism made of the realistic chance of a utopian society being formed, but anarchists argue that no ideal other form of society has been formed (such as a liberal society).

Exam tip

Often the core beliefs outlined in these chapters can be used as factors to be discussed in a paragraph. Sometimes, however, a question may ask about the extent of agreement in one of these core beliefs. You need to find both agreement and disagreement.

'Utopian' is closely associated with:

Strands
+ Individualist anarchists — a natural creation of order out of freedom from the state
+ Collectivist anarchists — a utopia developed from altruism

Thinkers
+ Kropotkin

Altruism Concern for the welfare of others based on social solidarity.

Now test yourself

TESTED

4 Explain what is meant by 'utopia'.
5 Explain why anarchists oppose private property.
6 Explain one criticism of the anarchist view of utopia.

12.2 Differing views and tensions

What is collectivist anarchism?

REVISED

Collectivist anarchists believe that humans tend towards natural cooperation, working together to achieve goals for the common good. Therefore, there should be common ownership; this strand has links to socialism. There are several strands within collective anarchism:
+ **Anarcho-communism**
    + Advocates for a stateless society with a Marxist view of communism.
    + This would include small communities with voluntary membership that trade between one another and have direct democracy within each community.

Direct democracy Citizens making law and policy directly, rather than through an elected government.

+ Opposes private property, instead having common ownership and equality of wealth production.
+ **Mutualism**
  + Although this is similar to anarcho-communism, mutualism values goods by the labour it took to produce them rather than a market value.
  + Links individualist and collectivist anarchism, rejecting exploitative profit and instead trading equitably.
  + Opposes mass private property but allows limited private property based on use.
+ **Anarcho-syndicalism**
  + Sees trade unions as the vehicle for change and the basis of society.
  + Argues for direct action such as not paying tax or rent, leading to a general strike and then a revolution.

> **Syndicalism** A revolutionary movement with trade unions at its heart, using direct action to lead to revolution.

What is individualist anarchism?

REVISED

Individualist anarchists believe humans do not naturally tend towards cooperation but towards individualism. They argue society can limit individual freedoms and remove individual sovereignty. There are two key strands of individualist anarchism:

+ **Egoism**
  + Individuals are naturally selfish, but in this selfishness recognise the need to avoid conflict.
  + Individuals should have autonomy to act as they see fit, without limit or restriction.
  + Ultimately a union of egoists will form, resulting in harmony.
  + Rejects private property but allows individuals to keep the product of their work.
+ **Anarcho-capitalism**
  + Advocates for total free-market capitalism, free of state intervention.
  + All state-provided services would also be provided by the free market.
  + Individuals may succeed or fail within this system and therefore it does not advocate for equality.

> **Autonomy** Freedom to act without restriction from the state or other people.

> **Exam tip**
>
> When comparing strands, it may be difficult to find areas that they agree on entirely. Instead, you may be able to find points that the strands agree on in principle, or an issue that they agree is an issue, although they disagree on how to tackle it.

> **Now test yourself** TESTED
>
> 7 Distinguish between anarcho-communists and anarcho-syndicalists.
> 8 List two beliefs of individualist anarchists.
> 9 List two beliefs of collectivist anarchists.

How do anarchists agree and disagree on the four themes?

	General areas of agreement	Areas of disagreement
Human nature	+ Anarchists have an optimistic view of human nature as rational and full of potential. + People are broadly self-interested and will therefore act in their best interests. + Every individual is entitled to their own freedom.	+ Individualist anarchists see the state as preventing rational humans exercising individual liberty. Collectivist anarchists argue that it prevents cooperative liberty. + Individualist anarchists have a less positive view of human nature, being more selfish, compared to the cooperative view of collectivist anarchists. + There is disagreement between key thinkers on whether individuals are born basically good (Proudhon) or born without a specific nature (Bakunin).
Society	+ Individuals need society for development. + There is a broad agreement in 'utopia'.	+ Individualist anarchists argue humans are not naturally cooperative, whereas collectivist anarchists argue that they are. + There are differences within collective anarchism on the type of state that should prevail. + Individualist anarchists argue that ordered society suppresses freedom, whereas collectivist anarchists do not.

Answers at **www.hoddereducation.co.uk/myrevisionnotesdownloads**

	General areas of agreement	Areas of disagreement
State	+ The state should be rejected as it is unnecessary and suppresses liberty. + The state is commanding, controlling and corrupting. + There is agreement between some strands that the state should be overthrown through revolutionary action.	+ Anarchists disagree on how to reject the state — through **direct action**, **insurrection**, violence, revolution or gradual change.
Economy	+ The economy should be free of state interference as the state defends economic inequality. + The economy should be based on the liberty of the people to act as they wish within it.	+ Collectivist anarchists argue for common ownership to foster **mutualism**, egoists argue individuals should act as they rationally see best and anarcho-capitalists argue a free market will allow individuals to make decisions to best suit them. + Collectivist anarchists argue capitalism creates exploitation, whereas anarcho-capitalists argue it is state intervention in capitalism which is the problem. + Collectivist anarchists argue state socialism is still an authority that restricts liberty, whereas anarcho-capitalists argue that state ownership attacks property rights.

Direct action Action taken by an individual, both non-violent and violent, beyond the traditional political framework of that individual.

Insurrection Individuals elevating themselves beyond state institutions, so that the institutions decay and die away.

Mutualism Exchange of goods equitably between producers organised individually or in small-scale private property.

Exam tip

There is overlap between some of these themes — for example human nature and society often overlap, as do the state and economy. However, you must ensure that whichever box you are choosing arguments from directly addresses the question you have been asked in an exam.

Now test yourself

TESTED ○

10 Identify two areas of agreement between anarchists on human nature.

11 Identify two areas of disagreement within anarchism on the economy.

12 Identify two areas of disagreement within anarchism on society.

12.3 Key thinkers

What do the key thinkers believe?

REVISED ○

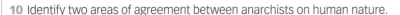

Max Stirner

Key text: *The Ego and His Own* (1845)

Key beliefs:

+ The self-interested and rational individual — humans are rational and self-interested and should act in their own interest.
+ Union of egoists — through revolution, a new society of self-interested individuals will be able to create harmony.

Key quotes/ideas:

+ On the state: '… we two, the State and I, are enemies'
+ On the state: 'I am free in no state'
+ On society: 'We have only one relation to each other, that of useability, of utility, of use'

125

Pierre-Joseph Proudhon

Key text: *What is Property?* (1840)

Key beliefs:

+ Private property — opposition to private property as it limits freedom and should be replaced with mutualism.
+ Rejection and overthrow of the state but through peaceful means.

Key quotes/ideas:

+ On the state: 'To be governed is to be watched over, inspected, spied on, directed, legislated, regimented, closed in, indoctrinated, preached at, controlled, assessed, evaluated, censored, commanded; all by creatures that have neither the right, nor wisdom, nor virtue'
+ On the economy: 'Property is theft'
+ On the economy: '… the right to own without the need to occupy'

Mikhail Bakunin

Key text: *God and the State* (1871)

Key beliefs:

+ Human sociability — humans are naturally sociable and cooperative; abolish private property and replace it with collectivisation.
+ Propaganda by deed — direct action was needed to create a general strike and then revolution.

Key quotes/ideas:

+ On the state: 'Every command slaps liberty in the face'
+ On human nature: 'The best of men, the most intelligent, unselfish, generous and pure, will always inevitably be corrupted in this pursuit'
+ On society: it is 'the tree of freedom and liberty is its fruit'

> **Collectivisation** Abolish private property and replace it with common ownership.
>
> **Mutual aid** Humans are successful when they work cooperatively rather than compete as individuals.

Peter Kropotkin

Key text: *Mutual Aid: A Factor of Evolution* (1902)

Key beliefs:

+ Mutual aid — allows humans to grow and flourish.
+ Revolution — was needed to abolish the state and private property resulting in utopia.

Key quote/idea:

+ On society: 'No ruling authorities… No government of man by man; no crystallisation and immobility'

Emma Goldman

Key text: *Living My Life* (1931)

Key beliefs:

+ The state is a cold monster, which should be rejected as immoral.
+ Revolution is necessity as the state is naturally corrupting and therefore cannot be reformed.

Key quotes/ideas:

+ On the state and society: anarchism stands for 'liberation from the shackles and restraint of government. It stands for a social order based on the free grouping of individuals'
+ On the state: 'It is a machine that crushes you in order to sustain the ruling class, your masters'

> **Exam tip**
>
> Quotes from key thinkers should be used as examples to support the arguments you have made. Do not open a paragraph with a thinker or their quotes.

Now test yourself	TESTED ◯

13 Outline Stirner's view of human nature.

14 Outline Proudhon's view of the state.

15 Outline Bakunin's view on revolution.

Answers at **www.hoddereducation.co.uk/myrevisionnotesdownloads**

How do anarchists disagree on the four themes?

	Collectivist anarchists	Individualist anarchists
Human nature	+ Humans are naturally sociable, altruistic and cooperative	+ Humans are naturally selfish + Rational humans will work together for their own interest
Society	+ Should be organised as voluntary communities for mutual benefit + Working for the common good	+ Society restricts liberty + Fear individuality will become subject to the collective will + A union of egoists + Working for individual benefit resulting in harmony
State	+ Creates greed and exploitation + Some revolution may be needed, but also peaceful means can remove the state	+ The coercive nature of the state restricts liberty + The need for mostly peaceful methods to overthrow the state
Economy	+ Mutually beneficial trading + Common ownership + Abolition of private property excepting limited 'use'	+ For some, total free-market economy + The market would provide services that the state once did

Summary

+ Core beliefs of anarchism are rejection of the state, liberty, anarchy is order, economic freedom and utopia.
+ There are competing strands with differing views within anarchism — collectivist anarchism (including anarcho-communism, mutualism and anarcho-syndicalism) and individualist anarchism (including anarcho-capitalism and egoism).
+ The key thinkers for anarchism are Stirner, Proudhon, Bakunin, Kropotkin, Goldman.

Revision tasks

1 Outline the meaning of five core beliefs of anarchism.
2 Distinguish between the views of collectivist and individualist anarchists.
3 Copy and complete the table below.

Key thinker (name)	How the key thinker could link to the four themes (human nature, the state, society and the economy)	How the key thinker could link to the core beliefs of anarchism

Exam skills

Timing and planning

Exam timing is crucial. There is no point taking 'just a couple of extra minutes' on one question as it will leave you short on another. Your timings should be:

+ 12 marks = 15 minutes maximum
+ 24 marks = 30 minutes maximum
+ 30 marks = 45 minutes maximum

To make **effective** use of your time, you should **always** plan your answers for 24- and 30-mark questions — you

do have time. The best advice is not to write anything for about 30–60 seconds, so you can read the question and ensure you are answering the exact question set. Then take another 30–60 seconds to plan your essay — this could just be identifying the factors you plan to write about in each paragraph. A plan should be no longer than 20 words and should help you to ensure your essay is coherent and addresses the question set.

Exam practice

1 To what extent do anarchists agree about the state? (24 marks)
2 To what extent do anarchists disagree about human nature? (24 marks)

My Revision Notes: Pearson Edexcel A-level Politics: UK Government and Politics, Political Ideas and Global Politics

13 Ecologism

13.1 Core ideas and principles

What is ecology?

REVISED ○

Ecology is a core belief of ecologism:
+ The idea that all living things are interdependent.
+ Because of this interdependence, there is no hierarchy of living things, with each dependent on the other (ecocentrism) and certainly humans are not above other living things (anthropocentrism).
+ High levels of biodiversity are needed to ensure stability in the natural world.
+ Anthropocentrism has depleted resources and polluted the natural world.

Ecology is closely associated with:

Strands
+ Deep green ecologism
+ Shallow green ecologism

Thinkers
+ Leopold
+ Carson

What is holism?

REVISED ○

Holism is a core belief of ecologism:
+ All aspects of nature are interconnected and can only be understood as such.
+ A wide biodiversity is necessary to preserve and protect the natural ecosystem.
+ It challenges the mechanistic world view that nature could be studied as independent parts without interconnectivity.
+ This supports the view that the whole of nature is greater than the sum of its parts.
+ Parts of nature cannot be repaired or replaced in isolation, like in a machine.

Holism is closely associated with:

Strand
+ Deep green ecologism

Thinkers
+ Merchant
+ Schumacher

Biodiversity A wide diversity of species within nature helps to ensure balance and stability of nature.

Mechanistic world view Nature is like a machine made of constituent parts, which can be understood, repaired and replaced in isolation.

What is environmental ethics?

REVISED ○

Environmental ethics is a core belief of ecologism:
+ Human morality only applies to humans and is therefore anthropocentric.
+ An environmental moral code for humans in relation to nature should be developed, including:
  + The need to protect nature for future generations — humans have a moral obligation to those not yet born to protect and preserve the environment.
  + The need to protect animal rights — humans have a duty to question animal cruelty, e.g. animal experimentation, as they too can feel pain.
  + The need for moral responsibility to the whole of nature, not just living things — a responsibility to protect the land, soil and water as well as living organisms.

Answers at **www.hoddereducation.co.uk/myrevisionnotesdownloads**

Environmental ethics is closely associated with:

Strand
+ Deep green ecologism

Thinker
+ Leopold

Exam tip

Some thinkers can be used for more than one strand of an ideology, depending on their beliefs and their quotes. The beliefs of thinkers may not be associated with only one strand of an ideology, so you **must** compare strands.

Now test yourself   TESTED ○

1   Explain what is meant by 'holism'.
2   List the three points that should be included in environmental ethics.
3   Define a 'mechanistic world view'.

What is environmental consciousness?   REVISED ●

Environmental consciousness is a core belief of ecologism:
+   A radical change is needed in human consciousness to see humans as deeply connected to nature.
+   This is different to creating a new moral code (like environmental ethics) but changing the entire mindset of humans.
+   This change would remove the need for a separate environmental ethics; instead concern for the natural world would be part of the human consciousness.
+   This would lead to better protection of the natural world as a matter of course.

Environmental consciousness is closely associated with:

> **Environmental consciousness** A human consciousness in which people identify innately with the environment, as part of it not master of it.

Strand
+ Deep green ecologism

Thinker
+ Bookchin (critic of environmental consciousness)

What is post-materialism and anti-consumerism?   REVISED ●

Post-materialism and anti-consumerism are core beliefs of ecologism:
+   opposing materialism and the valuing of material goods over spiritual or moral values
+   challenging the view that materialism leads to happiness, which has been driven through the creation of false needs (e.g. through advertising)
+   understanding that materialism leads to ecological problems through resources depletion
+   challenging the view that consumption is good for the economy and therefore desirable

Post-materialism and anti-consumerism are closely associated with:

Strands
+ Shallow green ecologism
+ Deep green ecologism

Thinker
+ Schumacher

What is sustainability?

Sustainability is a core belief of ecologism:

+ It refers to the ability of the earth and its ecosystem to sustain health and balance over time.
+ The idea that current levels of growth, industrialisation and consumerism are unsustainable and could create an ecosystem that cannot be sustained over time.
+ Change is therefore required to achieve sustainability, including biodiversity, preservation of natural resources and the ecosystem, managerialism (including, for example, pollution control) and green capitalism.

> **Industrialisation** Large-scale production and wealth accumulation with continuous, unlimited growth to satisfy consumerism.

Sustainability is closely associated with:

Strands
+ Deep green ecologism and social ecologism — strong support for sustainability and radical change + Shallow green ecologism— green capitalism

Thinkers
+ Schumacher + Leopold

Exam tip

Often the core beliefs outlined in these chapters can be used as factors to be discussed in a paragraph. Sometimes, however, a question may ask about the extent of agreement in one of these core beliefs. You need to find both agreement and disagreement.

Now test yourself

4 Explain what is meant by 'environmental consciousness'.
5 Define 'sustainability'.
6 Outline why materialism should be opposed.

13.2 Ecologism: differing views and tensions

What is deep green ecologism?

Deep green ecologists tend to believe:
+ in the protection of nature for the sake of nature
+ that humans are just one species on the planet and anthropocentric thinking devastates the ecosystem
+ in holism — all ecological issues are interconnected and interdependent, therefore no issue can be solved in isolation
+ that the balance of nature must be maintained, rather than maintained to sustain human goals
+ that a biocentric/ecocentric view is needed
+ that radical change is needed in the consciousness and understanding of humans regarding their place in the ecosystem and its interconnected nature, creating environmental consciousness
+ that humans should value quality over quantity in terms of consumerism
+ that the link between happiness and consumption, the mechanistic world view and the unlimited industrialisation and economic growth goals, should be broken
+ that economic reform is too limited to achieve strong sustainability

> **Anthropocentric** A view with humans at the centre of it and nature as a tool for humans to use for their own ends.
>
> **Ecocentric** A nature-centred rather than human-centred view of the world.
>
> **Consumerism** The consumption of goods as a means to happiness.

There is disagreement within deep green ecology over what a deep green society would look like.

What is shallow green ecologism?

REVISED

Shallow green ecologists tend to believe:
+ in the protection of nature for the sake of humans
+ that all things are interconnected and therefore human intervention should be limited to avoid unforeseen consequences
+ that environmental issues can be solved independently of one another
+ that humanity's impact should be reduced to protect the environment for the sake of future generations
+ that more environmentally protective methods of production (green capitalism) and managerialism should be developed
+ in reform over radical change, especially of human consciousness
+ in 'enlightened anthropocentrism' where humans recognise their roles as stewards of nature and reformed political and economic structures support this outlook

> **Green capitalism** A capitalist free-market delivering more environmentally sustainable methods of production.

What is social ecology?

REVISED

Social ecology is made up of three strands, which argue that existing hierarchies have resulted in environmental damage and changing these structures is necessary to protect the environment.

Table 13.1 The three strands of social ecology

Eco-socialism	Eco-anarchism	Eco-feminism
+ Capitalism is the root cause of environmental issues. + Unlimited growth is unsustainable. + Capitalism causes nature to be seen as a commodity, rather than having its own value. + Green capitalism is flawed. + Capitalism should be overthrown.	+ Domination is the cause of environmental issues, often of humans by humans. + The state, capitalism and hierarchy must be overthrown to protect nature. + A new society of small communities with environmental ethics and an interconnected relationship with nature would protect nature.	+ The domination of nature by men is similar to the domination of women by men. + Overthrow the mechanistic world view. + A post-patriarchal society with a less gendered view of nature would allow a greater interconnected view of nature regardless of gender.

> **Exam tip**
>
> When comparing strands, it may be difficult to find areas that they agree on entirely. Instead, you may be able to find points they agree on as a principle, or an issue that the strands agree is an issue, but disagree on how to tackle it.

> **Now test yourself**
>
> TESTED
>
> 7 List three beliefs of deep green ecologists.
> 8 List three beliefs of shallow green ecologists.
> 9 Distinguish between eco-socialism, eco-anarchism and eco-feminism.

How do ecologists agree and disagree on the four themes?

	General areas of agreement	Areas of disagreement
Human nature	+ Humans have held an anthropocentric view, driven by a mechanistic world view and consumerism. + Development of at least environmental ethics is necessary. + There is an obligation to protect nature. + A change in ethical frameworks is needed.	+ Shallow green ecologists argue for 'enlightened anthropocentrism', whereas deep green ecologists argue for 'environmental consciousness'. + Social ecologists argue that social structures need to be changed before a radical change in consciousness can come about.
Society	+ Society has been driven to 'false needs' through advertising, leading to materialism and consumerism. + A post-material world is needed. + Materialism and consumerism are getting worse.	+ Social ecologists argue for radical change to society, whereas shallow green ecologists are more reformist. + Shallow green ecologists argue for the protection of nature for future societies, rather than for nature in its own right as deep green ecologists argue. + Social ecologists argue for the overthrow of current social hierarchies to protect nature.
State	+ There is some agreement between deep green and social ecologists that the state is part of the problem and that revolutionary change is needed to remove and realign the state with nature.	+ Shallow green ecologists see state intervention as a solution, whereas deep green ecologists and social ecologists see the state as part of the problem. + Deep green ecologists argue for **decentralised** small societies with local decision making, whereas shallow green ecologists argue for reformed societal institutions. + Within shallow green ecology, some argue for weak sustainability from the state, while others argue for green capitalism and managerialism.
Economy	+ Unlimited growth is a barrier to ecologism and so requires **limits to growth**. + Consumerism needs to be reformed in order to achieve greater sustainability. + **Sustainability** is needed. + The mechanistic world view is not applicable to nature and fails to understand the interconnectivity of the environment.	+ Shallow green ecologists argue for green capitalism and managerialism while deep green ecologists would overthrow capitalism, as would eco-socialists and eco-anarchists. + The theory of environmental consciousness from deep green ecologists is challenged by some shallow green ecologists as unworkable. + Deep green ecologists believe in strong sustainability and shallow green ecologists in weak sustainability.

Sustainability The ability of the environment to maintain health over time.

Limits to growth Nature comprises of finite resources which require a need for limits to economic growth.

Decentralisation The process by which society is broken up into smaller societies that are more self-sufficient and therefore more sustainable and dependent on the natural world.

Exam tip

There is overlap between some of these themes — for example human nature and society often overlap, as do the state and economy. However, you must ensure that whichever box you are choosing arguments from directly addresses the question you have been asked in an exam.

Now test yourself

TESTED

10 Identify two areas of agreement between ecologists on human nature.

11 Identify two areas of disagreement within ecologism on the economy.

12 Distinguish between weak sustainability and strong sustainability.

Answers at **www.hoddereducation.co.uk/myrevisionnotesdownloads**

What do the key thinkers believe?

Aldo Leopold

Key text: *A Sand Country Almanac* (1949)

Key beliefs:
+ The land ethic — the environment as a whole has a right to life. This is biocentric equality where all of the environment has equal worth.
+ Conservation fails — conservation is based on the current economy, rather than looking beyond the economy to change the relationship between humans and the environment.

> **Biocentric equality** All living livings are equal to one another.

Key quotes/ideas:
+ On human nature: they have 'hammered the artefact called civilisation' out of nature
+ On the environment: it includes 'soils, waters, plants and animals, or collectively: the land'
+ On human nature: it needs 'a new kind of people' to protect nature
+ On human nature: 'We abuse the land because we regard it as a commodity belonging to us'

Rachel Carson

Key text: *The Silent Spring* (1962)

Key beliefs:
+ The state and society have poisoned nature and damaged sustainability and a better, more balanced relationship between man and the environment is needed.
+ Nature should be seen holistically as having intrinsic value, rather than existing for the convenience of man.

Key quotes/ideas:
+ On the environment: 'In nature, nothing exists alone'

E. F. Schumacher

Key text: *Small is Beautiful* (1973)

Key beliefs:
+ Buddhist economics — the maximum quality of life comes from minimal consumption.
+ Traditional economics is flawed — based on the principles of maximum, unlimited growth and consumerism. A new economics is needed.

> **Buddhist economics** A view of economics where human needs should be met to achieve maximum quality of life from minimal consumption.

Key quotes/ideas:
+ On the economy: 'Infinite growth in material consumption in a finite world is an impossibility'
+ On the economy: 'enoughness', focusing on wellbeing over consumption
+ On materialism: it 'does not fit into this world, because it contains within itself no limiting principle'

Murray Bookchin

Key text: *The Ecology of Freedom* (1982)

Key beliefs:
+ Social structures of oppression are the causes of environmental crises and therefore should be overthrown.
+ Lessons from ecology should be learnt and applied to future societal developments.

Key quotes/ideas:

✚ On society and the state: 'As long as hierarchy persists… the project of dominating nature will continue to exist and inevitably lead our planet to ecological extinction'

✚ On society: he argued for 'ecotopia'

✚ On deep green thinkers: 'eco-la-la' was his critical response to environmental consciousness

Carolyn Merchant

Key text: *The Death of Nature* (1980)

Key beliefs:

✚ Gender oppression — the death of nature is linked to the patriarchy, which therefore should be overthrown to create a new relationship with nature regardless of gender.

✚ Mechanistic world view — fails to see nature as holistic and leads to the exploitation of nature.

Key quotes/ideas:

✚ On capitalism: 'All of this is part of a "progressive" narrative that technology can be used to interact with and dominate and control nature'

Exam tip

Quotes from key thinkers should be used as examples to support the arguments you have made. Do not open a paragraph with a thinker or their quotes.

Now test yourself   TESTED

13 Outline Leopold's view of human nature.

14 Outline Schumacher's view of the economy.

15 Outline Bookchin's view on society.

How do ecologists disagree on the four themes?

	Deep green ecologists	Shallow green ecologists	Social ecologists
Human nature	✚ Need an environmental consciousness and ecocentric view ✚ False needs created by consumerism and materialism	✚ Need enlightened anthropocentrism	✚ Argue for the need for radical social change to change human nature
Society	✚ Holism ✚ Decentralised societies ✚ Nature with intrinsic value ✚ Environmental consciousness ✚ Equality of man within nature	✚ Intergenerational equality ✚ Awareness and minimising of environmental impact ✚ Environmental ethics ✚ Greater acceptance of mechanistic world view ✚ Stewardship of man within nature	✚ Argue for the need for radical social change to overthrow hierarchies that cause oppression
State	✚ Remove the state ✚ Decentralised societies ✚ Revolutionary	✚ State intervention in managerialism ✚ Reformist	✚ Remove the state ✚ Revolutionary
Economy	✚ Replace capitalism ✚ Strong sustainability ✚ Revolutionary	✚ Green capitalism ✚ Weak sustainability ✚ Reformist	✚ Replace capitalism ✚ Revolutionary

Summary

✤ Core beliefs of ecologism are ecology, holism, environmental ethics, environmental consciousness, post-materialism and anti-consumerism, and sustainability.
✤ There are competing strands with differing views within ecology — deep green ecologists, shallow green ecologists and social ecology (including eco-socialism, eco-anarchism and eco-feminism).
✤ The key thinkers for nationalism are Leopold, Carson, Schumacher, Bookchin and Merchant.

Revision tasks

1 Outline the meaning of five core beliefs of ecologism.

2 Distinguish between the views of deep green ecologists, shallow green ecologists and social ecologists.

3 Copy and complete the table below.

Key thinker (name)	How the key thinker could link to the four themes (human nature, the state, society and the economy)	How the key thinker could link to the core beliefs of ecologism

Exam skills

Timing and planning

Exam timing is crucial. There is no point taking 'just a couple of extra minutes' on one question as it will leave you short on another. Your timings should be:

✤ 12 marks = 15 minutes maximum
✤ 24 marks = 30 minutes maximum
✤ 30 marks = 45 minutes maximum

To make **effective** use of your time, you should **always** plan your answers for 24- and 30-mark questions — you **do** have time. The best advice is not to write anything for about 30–60 seconds, so you can read the question and ensure you are answering the exact question set. Then take another 30–60 seconds to plan your essay — this could just be identifying the factors you plan to write about in each paragraph. A plan should be no longer than 20 words and should help you to ensure your essay is coherent and addresses the question set.

Exam practice

1 To what extent is ecologism a coherent theory? (24 marks)

2 To what extent do ecologists agree over sustainability? (24 marks)

14 Feminism

14.1 Core ideas and principles

What is sex and gender?

REVISED ⬤

Differentiation between sex and gender is a core belief of feminism:
+ Feminism makes a key differentiation between 'sex' and 'gender'.
+ Most feminists would assert that sex is biological and is something you are born with — male and female.
+ Gender is cultural and forms stereotypes of ideal expectations for men and women — masculine and feminine.
+ Sex does not change over history but gender does as cultural expectations change.
+ Most feminists agree that the nature of being a 'woman' is determined by society, not by biology.

Sex and gender are closely associated with:

Strands
+ Socialist feminists — 'feminine' is determined by capitalism
+ Radical and postmodern feminists — 'feminine' stereotypes are imposed on women

Thinkers
+ de Beauvoir
+ Perkins Gilman
+ Rowbotham
+ Millett

What is the patriarchy?

REVISED ⬤

Patriarchy is a core belief of feminism:
+ A social and political system created by men for the benefit of men, oppressing women.
+ Sylvia Walby argued there were six areas of the patriarchy in society — the state (legal), the household (housework and childcare), violence (abuse), paid work (the pay gap), sexuality (a negative view of women enjoying sex/sexuality) and culture (advertising and expectations).
+ The extent of the patriarchy and the solutions for it differ between the strands of feminism.

Patriarchy is closely associated with:

Strands
+ Liberal feminists — reform of the state
+ Socialist feminists — reform of capitalism
+ Radical feminists — extensive reform

Thinkers
+ de Beauvoir
+ Rowbotham
+ Millett

> **Exam tip**
>
> Some thinkers can be used for more than one strand of an ideology, depending on their beliefs and their quotes. The beliefs of thinkers may not be associated with just one strand of an ideology, so you **must** compare strands.

What is 'the personal is political'?

REVISED ⬤

'The personal is political' is a core belief of feminism:
+ There is a distinction between the public sphere (society outside the family home) and the private sphere (inside the family home).
+ All relationships between men and women, public and private, are based on an inequality of power.
+ In the public sphere, women deserve equal pay, representation, etc., provided for by legislation from the state.
+ In the private sphere, constructs of the marriage and family oppress woman.

> **Public sphere** The area of society in which relationships are public, i.e. those outside the family home.
>
> **Private sphere** The area of society in which relationships are private, i.e. those inside the family home.

'The personal is political' is closely associated with:

Strands	Thinkers
+ Radical feminists — the family is a construct + Liberal feminists — the private sphere should be free of state interference	+ Perkins Gilman + Rowbotham + Millett

> **Now test yourself**
> TESTED
>
> 1 Distinguish between sex and gender.
> 2 Distinguish between the public sphere and the private sphere.
> 3 List Walby's six structures of the patriarchy.

What are equality feminism and difference feminism?

REVISED

As core beliefs of feminism, equality feminism and difference feminism mean:

Equality feminism	Difference feminism
+ Differences between sexes are broadly irrelevant. + There are not inherently 'male' and 'female' traits. + Differences in society between men and women are from society (nurture) rather than nature. + Most feminists are equality feminists.	+ Differences between men and women are fundamentally a result of sex, known as '**essentialism**'. + This means men and women have different outlooks and approach things differently. + These differences are due to nature, not society (nurture). + Few feminists are difference feminists. + A form of difference feminism is '**cultural feminism**'.

> **Equality feminism** Equality feminists argue that men and women are fundamentally the same.
>
> **Difference feminism** Difference feminists argue that men and women are fundamentally different.
>
> **Essentialism** Biology creates differences in the characters of men and women.
>
> **Cultural feminism** A form of difference feminism that looks to promote 'women's values' over male ones.

Equality feminism and difference feminism are closely associated with:

Strand	Thinker
+ Most of all the strands are 'equality feminists'	+ de Beauvoir

What is intersectionality?

REVISED

Intersectionality is now a core belief of feminism:
+ Minority groups such as 'women of colour' were largely excluded from early ideologies of feminism.

> **Intersectionality** A challenge to the idea that being a woman alone is the biggest cause of oppression; women have overlapping characteristics as well as gender, e.g. race, class and age, that cause differences in experience and oppression.

+ Minority women often suffer greater oppression as they are oppressed for multiple characteristics.
+ There are overlapping spheres of oppression for women that, in addition to their sex, can include class, race, sexuality or disability.

> **Exam tip**
>
> Often the core beliefs outlined in these chapters can be used as factors to be discussed in a paragraph. Sometimes, however, a question may ask about the extent of agreement in one of these core beliefs. You need to find both agreement and disagreement.

Intersectionality is closely associated with:

Strand	Thinker
+ Postmodern feminists	+ hooks

What are the waves of feminism?

+ **First wave (1800s–1940s):** focus on gaining legal and political rights for women.
+ **Second wave (1960s–1980s):** focus on the roles expected of women and challenging them.
+ **Third wave (1990s–2000s):** focus on intersectionality.
+ **Fourth wave (2010s onwards):** focus on the everyday experiences of women and challenging misogyny.

> **Waves of feminism** The time periods during which feminism was targeting different goals or outcomes.

> **Now test yourself** TESTED
>
> 4 Distinguish between equality feminisim and difference feminism.
> 5 Explain what is meant by 'intersectionality'.
> 6 Outline the four waves of feminism.

14.2 Differing views and tensions

What is liberal feminism?

Liberal feminists tend to believe:
+ that all humans are of equal value and deserve the same rights
+ in foundational equality and equality of opportunity for women
+ in equality of legal, economic and political rights for women
+ in equality in the public sphere
+ in individualism — the idea that women are rational, capable and autonomous individuals therefore deserving of gender equality
+ in reform of society and the state to achieve equality, rather than revolution
+ that the patriarchy is not entrenched and is a modern phenomenon

> **Equality of opportunity** All individuals should have the same opportunities to succeed in society.
>
> **Legal equality** The law applying equally to everyone, including women.
>
> **Gender equality** Treating everyone in society the same, regardless of their gender.

What is socialist feminism?

REVISED ○

Socialist feminists tend to believe that:
+ inequality stems from capitalism and therefore reform or revolution of this economic system is necessary
+ capitalism places women in a position of a 'reserve army of labour'
+ capitalism oppresses women by creating an environment where they are expected to do mostly domestic work in order to allow for the employment of men in the free-market
+ women need economic liberation to be free and achieve equality
+ social constructs like marriage ensure women are economically dependent on men and therefore need reform/revolution

What is radical feminism?

REVISED ○

Radical feminists tend to believe that:
+ society is entirely patriarchal, which creates inequality between the sexes
+ society is therefore in need of radical reform that changes the structure of society
+ 'the personal is political' and the patriarchy exists in the public and private spheres and in all relationships between men and women
+ the patriarchy is deep-seated and historical and therefore cannot be overcome through reform

Some (few) radical feminists are 'difference feminists'.

What is postmodern feminism?

REVISED ○

Postmodern feminists tend to believe:
+ that the patriarchy is different for women of different characteristics — race, class etc.
+ that 'women' are different to one another with very different experiences (do not confuse this with 'difference feminism')
+ in intersectionality
+ that there is no fixed definition of a 'woman'; this can be defined by individuals

Postmodern feminists have conflicting views over protests against misogyny, especially about whether protests such as Femen and SlutWalk demonstrate women's freedoms or uphold patriarchal views.

> **Exam tip**
>
> When comparing strands, it may be difficult to find areas that they agree on entirely. Instead, you may be able to find points the strands agree on as a principle, or an issue that they agree is an issue, but disagree on how to tackle it.

Now test yourself

TESTED ○

7 List three beliefs of liberal feminists.
8 List three beliefs of socialist feminists.
9 List three beliefs of radical feminists.

How do feminists agree and disagree on the four themes?

	General areas of agreement	Areas of disagreement
Human nature	+ Women are rational, capable and therefore deserving of foundational equality. + Sex is something you are born with. + There is a difference between sex and gender. + There are no inherent differences between men and women.	+ Difference feminists believe that there is a difference between men and women. + There are differing views on how engrained the patriarchy is in consciousness, with liberals arguing it is more recent and radicals arguing it is historically engrained.
Society	+ **Gender stereotypes** are created by society. + The patriarchy is evident in the public sphere and pervades every aspect of society and culture. + The patriarchy is a society designed by men for the benefit of men. + Society creates roles and expectations for women. + Women are seen as 'other'. + Women are conditioned to accept certain roles within society.	+ Liberal feminists believe that equality should be more limited to the public sphere, whereas radicals believe 'the personal is political'. + Liberal feminists believe **reform** of society through legal means is possible, socialist feminists believe reform or revolution of capitalism is necessary for societal reform, and radical feminists believe reform is not possible and revolution is needed. + Postmodernists believe intersectionality is key to understanding and reforming society.
State	+ The state underpins the patriarchy, furthering the oppression of women.	+ Socialist feminists see the state as the agent of capitalism. + Liberal feminists believe the state can be reformed and itself be an agent of reform. + Radical feminists believe that the patriarchy is rooted in the state, which therefore cannot be effectively reformed. + Feminists disagree over whether the role of the state should be in the public or private sphere.
Economy	+ Women are oppressed within the economic system, providing free labour at home and seen as a '**reserve army of labour**' for the capitalist, free-market economic model. + Women's work is undervalued, both at home (where domestic work is unpaid) and in the workplace (where a pay gap exists). + Women are expected to fulfil certain stereotypical jobs within the capitalist system. + Women's economic dependence on men limits their freedom and equality.	+ Socialist feminists argue that capitalism is the root of the patriarchy and therefore is the biggest factor in need of reform or revolution. + Postmodern feminists include intersectionality in this discussion, citing race and class as overlapping factors of economic **discrimination**.

Gender stereotypes The expectations of the roles and behaviours that society has of men and women.

Reserve army of labour Women amount to a spare workforce called to the workplace only when needed.

Reformist Seeking gradual, peaceful change to society, often through legal means and existing institutions.

Discrimination Where one group experiences less favourable treatment than another group.

Exam tip

There is overlap between some of these themes — for example human nature and society often overlap, as do the state and economy. However, you must ensure that whichever box you are choosing arguments from directly addresses the question you have been asked in an exam.

Answers at **www.hoddereducation.co.uk/myrevisionnotesdownloads**

Now test yourself

TESTED ◯

10 Identify two areas of agreement between feminists on human nature.

11 Identify two areas of disagreement within feminism on society.

12 Explain why all feminists believe capitalism causes oppression.

14.3 Key thinkers

What do the key thinkers believe?

REVISED ◯

Charlotte Perkins Gilman

Key text: *The Yellow Wallpaper* (1892)

Key beliefs:

+ Sex and domestic violence — women depend on their sexuality to survive as they are not economically independent, and therefore need to use their body to please their husbands to survive.
+ Societal pressure — society conditions young girls into stereotypical roles such as motherhood through the toys and clothes that are marketed to them to reinforce these attitudes.

Key quotes/ideas:

+ On society: 'A house does not need a wife any more than it needs a husband'
+ On the economy: 'The labor of women in the house, certainly, enables men to produce more wealth than they otherwise could; and in this way women are economic factors in society. But so are horses'

Simone de Beauvoir

Key text: *The Second Sex* (1949)

Key beliefs:

+ Sex vs. gender — that sex and gender are different, one biological, one cultural.
+ 'Otherness' — that women are defined in opposition to what men are, where men are the 'norm' and women are 'other'.

Key quotes/ideas:

+ On society: 'One is not born, but rather becomes, a woman'

> **Otherness** The idea that women are defined in opposition to men, where men are the 'norm' and women are 'other'.

Kate Millett

Key text: *Sexual Politics* (1970)

Key beliefs:

+ Family — the traditional family was the biggest cause of oppression and needed revolution to achieve equality.
+ Women in art and literature — how women are typically portrayed is degrading and reinforces stereotypes and expectations of women.

Key quotes/ideas:

+ On society: 'The complete destruction of traditional marriage and the nuclear family is the "revolutionary or utopian" goal of feminism'

Sheila Rowbotham

Key text: *Women's Consciousness, Man's World* (1973)

Key beliefs:

+ Capitalism is the key cause of inequality, forcing women into family roles to survive and making them economically dependent on the family and marriage.
+ The family as an institution is a cause of oppression for women in capitalism.

141

Key quotes/ideas:

✛ On the patriarchy: 'Men will often admit other women are oppressed, but not you'

✛ On the economy: 'Clearly society has a tremendous stake in insisting on a woman's natural fitness for the career of mother; the alternatives are too expensive'

Exam tip

Quotes from key thinkers should be used as examples to support the arguments you have made. Do not open a paragraph with a thinker or their quotes.

bell hooks

Key text: *Ain't I a Woman: Black Women and Feminism* (1981)

Key beliefs:

✛ Women of colour have different concerns and experiences of oppression.

✛ **Intersectionality** — mainstream feminism focussed on white, middle-class women rather than the overlapping characteristics, which also cause oppression.

Key quotes/ideas:

✛ On intersectionality:

   ✛ '… we must assume responsibility for eliminating all the forces that divide women'

   ✛ 'We despaired as we witness the appropriation of feminist ideology by elitist, racist white women'

✛ On the patriarchy: 'We all knew firsthand that we had been socialized as females by patriarchal thinking to see ourselves as inferior to men'

Now test yourself

TESTED

13 Outline de Beauvoir's view of 'otherness'.

14 Outline Millett's view on the family.

15 Outline Perkins Gilman's view on society.

How do feminists disagree on the four themes?

	Liberal feminists	Socialist feminists	Radical feminists	Postmodern feminists
Human nature	✛ Sex is not the same as gender	✛ Sex is not the same as gender	✛ Sex is not the same as gender	✛ Sex is not the same as gender
Society	✛ Legal and **political equality** ✛ Forces women into certain roles	✛ Women's roles are determined by capitalism	✛ 'The personal is political'	✛ Intersectionality
State	✛ Can be reformed and can ensure legal and political equality ✛ Should act in the public sphere	✛ Ensures oppression through capitalism	✛ Cannot be reformed as patriarchy is deep rooted	✛ Intersectionality
Economy	✛ Women are oppressed by the economy	✛ Is in need of reform to achieve equality for women	✛ Reform of capitalism would be part of wider reforms to society	✛ Intersectionality

---

Political equality The equal rights of women to vote and protest.

Answers at **www.hoddereducation.co.uk/myrevisionnotesdownloads**

Summary

+ Core beliefs of feminism are sex and gender, patriarchy, 'the personal is political', equality feminism and difference feminism, and intersectionality.
+ There are competing strands with differing views within socialism — liberal feminists, socialist feminists, radical feminists and postmodern feminists.
+ The key thinkers for feminism are Perkins Gilman, de Beauvoir, Millett, Rowbotham and hooks.

Revision tasks

1 Outline the meaning of five core beliefs of feminism.

2 Distinguish between the views of liberal, socialist, radical and post-modern feminists.

3 Copy and complete the table below.

Key thinker (name)	How the key thinker could link to the four themes (human nature, the state, society and the economy)	How the key thinker could link to the core beliefs of feminism

Exam skills

Timing and planning

Exam timing is crucial. There is no point taking 'just a couple of extra minutes' on one question as it will leave you short on another. Your timings should be:

+ 12 marks = 15 minutes maximum
+ 24 marks = 30 minutes maximum
+ 30 marks = 45 minutes maximum

To make **effective** use of your time, you should **always** plan your answers for 24- and 30-mark questions — you **do** have time. The best advice is not to write anything for about 30–60 seconds, so you can read the question and ensure you are answering the exact question set. Then take another 30–60 seconds to plan your essay — this could just be identifying the factors you plan to write about in each paragraph. A plan should be no longer than 20 words and should help you to ensure your essay is coherent and addresses the question set.

Exam practice

1 To what extent do feminists agree that 'the personal is political'? (24 marks)

2 To what extent do feminists disagree about the role of the state? (24 marks)

15 Multiculturalism

15.1 Core ideas and principles

What is the politics of recognition?

The politics of recognition is a core belief of multiculturalism:

+ Cultural differences are positive and should be celebrated.
+ Recognition of cultural identity is important for individuals as it shapes self-understanding — individuals understand the world through the cultural norms in which they grew up.
+ A lack of recognition can reduce the self-worth of individuals or impact their willingness to participate in the community and in politics.
+ Minority groups have been historically disadvantaged, and recognition of this and cultural differences is necessary to achieve formal equality.
+ The state should be responsible for ensuring formal equality and removing discrimination so that minority groups can achieve equal dignity and equal recognition:
    + Equal dignity: an understanding of the equal intrinsic value that every individual in society has, creating equal political and legal rights for everyone.
    + Equal recognition: the recognition of minority cultures and values in laws alongside the majority cultures and values, to avoid cultural oppression.
+ Too much emphasis is placed on the identity of the individual rather than on the identity of groups.

Formal equality When all individuals in society have the same political and legal rights.

Culture The shared values, customs and beliefs of a group.

The politics of recognition is closely associated with:

Strands	Thinkers
+ Liberal multiculturalism + Pluralist multiculturalism	+ Kymlicka + Taylor

What is culture and identity?

As a core belief of multiculturalism, culture and identity means:

+ Identity is the sense of self individuals have about who they are and what makes them who they are.
+ 'Identity politics' suggests that the political actions individuals take are intrinsically linked to who they perceive themselves to be.
+ The cultural community with which individuals identify may not be a geographic one — it may be based on aspects such as religion, social class, race, ethnicity and gender.
+ Identity politics has been associated with a more radical political action, where the oppression of a minority group or culture requires a response from that group.
+ Identity politics can have a more positive influence, allowing minority groups to redefine their oppression, finding a sense of pride in their cultural identity and overcoming discrimination.
+ 'Communitarianism' is a challenge to the liberal view that society is made up of individual, autonomous actors, suggesting instead individuals see themselves as part of communities, which themselves contain variations of identity.

Identity politics The acceptance of a sense of identity by a minority group is an act of political liberation against oppression.

This belief is criticised for causing and encouraging division within society rather than encouraging understanding between different groups and communities.

Answers at **www.hoddereducation.co.uk/myrevisionnotesdownloads**

Culture and identity is closely associated with:

Strand	Thinkers
+ Pluralist multiculturalists	+ Taylor + Parekh

Exam tip

Some thinkers can be used for more than one strand of an ideology, depending on their beliefs and their quotes. The beliefs of thinkers may not be associated with just one strand of an ideology, so you **must** compare strands.

Now test yourself   TESTED ○

1 Distinguish between equal dignity and equal representation.
2 Explain what is meant by 'communitarianism'.
3 Explain what is meant by 'identity politics'.

What are minority rights?   REVISED ○

Minority rights are a core belief of multiculturalism:
+ A belief that minority groups should have differentiated rights granted to them based on their collective identity, provided these do not conflict with the rights of the majority within society.
+ This will help to counter the expectations of minority groups conforming to the culture, norms and values of the majority group in society.
+ This is not the same as a liberal belief in equal rights, as this suggests that minority groups may need different rights than those granted to the majority of a society.
+ The granting of differentiated rights will allow minority groups to integrate into society and allow for multicultural integration.
+ Three types of groups' rights were identified:
    + Representation: counteracting historic discrimination with positive discrimination.
    + Polyethnic: immigrant groups are assisted by the state in maintaining their cultural identity.
    + Self-government: for minorities or indigenous groups to govern themselves if they have been historically oppressed and seek self-government.
+ This has been criticised:
    + The rights of individuals in a liberal society may clash with the rights minority groups desire.
    + Positive discrimination is itself a form of discrimination.
    + Minority groups can be isolated and divisions in society can be encouraged.

Multicultural integration
Integration being different for different groups allowing for a sense of belonging to the whole group as well as minority groups/cultures.

Positive discrimination
Giving one group preferential treatment on the basis of historical oppression.

Minority rights are closely associated with:

Strands	Thinkers
+ All strands	+ Kymlicka + Taylor

What is diversity?

Diversity is a core belief of multiculturalism:

+ Due to the growth of globalisation and international migration, societies are becoming increasingly diverse.
+ This diversity should be celebrated, showing the inclusion of different cultures and races within the political, economic and cultural framework of a society is possible.
+ Diversity should be encouraged, as it recognises the importance of individual 'identity'.
+ 'Shallow diversity' suggests that the cultures and values of minority groups should be tolerated but there should be an expectation of conformity to the national law and culture.
+ 'Deep diversity' suggests that the cultures and values of minority groups should be accommodated within national law and culture, allowing them to coexist.
+ This has been criticised as undermining the need for a strong national culture and identity which creates societal unity and creating instead segregation.

> **Segregation** The separation of cultural groups based on their beliefs.

Diversity is closely associated with:

Strands
+ All strands

Thinkers
+ Kymlicka and Modood — shallow diversity
+ Parekh and Taylor — deep diversity

Exam tip

Often the core beliefs outlined in these chapters can be used as factors to be discussed in a paragraph. Sometimes, however, a question may ask about the extent of agreement in one of these core beliefs. You need to find both agreement and disagreement.

Now test yourself

TESTED

4 Distinguish between shallow diversity and deep diversity.
5 List the three types of group differentiated rights.
6 Give two reasons why minority rights have been criticised.

15.2 Differing views and tensions

What is liberal multiculturalism?

Liberal multiculturalists tend to believe in the general concepts of liberalism:

+ **The neutral state:** the state does not promote one set of values over another and should remain 'neutral' in the treatment it gives to different cultures and beliefs.
+ **Pluralism:** cultural diversity should be encouraged, supported and celebrated by the state.
+ **Tolerance:** actions and beliefs of minority groups should be tolerated provided they do not cause harm to other groups.
+ **Liberal democracy:** the state should provide equal dignity and equal recognition through formal equality and the outlawing of discrimination and the expectation of individualist integration.

> **Individualist integration** Everyone being treated on an individual basis when being integrated into a state, being given equal individual rights rather than rights based on difference.

What is pluralist multiculturalism?

Pluralist multiculturalists tend to believe:
+ that diversity has intrinsic value
+ that imposing liberal values on other cultures and value systems is not possible; instead recognition and respect of all cultures and values is needed
+ in 'value pluralism', which recognises that values often conflict with one another in a way which cannot be resolved, so liberal values are not superior to other values
+ in 'universalism', which means that certain values are universally applicable to societies
+ in 'deep diversity', where all cultures are equal and recognising this is necessary to encourage minorities to engage in the political system
+ in the inclusion and recognition of other cultures, which means that the national culture needs constant review

> **Universalism** Some values are universally applicable regardless of culture, history or other differences.

What is cosmopolitan multiculturalism?

Cosmopolitan multiculturalists tend to believe:
+ that people are understood as individuals and cultural differences will ultimately fade away — this challenges the view that individuals are best understood as part of their culture (communitarianism)
+ in a globalised and multicultural world; individuals can choose what culture/s they belong to, sometimes criticised as a 'pick and mix' approach
+ that individuals can belong to numerous cultures, which may overlap with one another and is not predicated on active involvement in that community
+ that diversity is positive, allowing individuals to learn and develop, mixing cultures and creating new cultures, and promoting global citizenship, creating cosmopolitan integration.

> **Cosmopolitan integration** The widest freedoms for all cultures to mix and learn from other cultures.

What is the conservative criticism of multiculturalism?

There have been a number of criticisms levelled at multiculturalism from conservatives:
+ A pessimistic view of human nature means that humans should rely on tradition, and diversity threatens these traditions and the resulting societal stability.
+ The equal value of minority cultures will undermine the majority culture and values, which will lead to resentment and division.
+ There can be no diversity within unity, so assimilation should be encouraged.
+ The necessity for state intervention to protect minorities increases the power of the state.

> **Exam tip**
>
> When comparing strands, it may be difficult to find areas that they agree on entirely. Instead, you may be able to find point that strands agree on as a principle, or an issue that they agree is an issue, but disagree on how to tackle it.

> **Now test yourself**
>
> 7 List three beliefs of liberal multiculturalists.
> 8 List three beliefs of pluralist multiculturalists.
> 9 List three beliefs of cosmopolitan multiculturalists.

How do multiculturalists agree and disagree on the four themes?

	General areas of agreement	Areas of disagreement
Human nature	+ Human nature is intrinsically linked to culture, and humans can only understand the world through this lens. + Humans are not individuals, but part of broader cultures. + Humans identify with cultures and this forms parts of their self-identification. + Human nature is not fixed, but is shaped by culture. + Humans need their identity to be recognised and respected.	+ Liberal multiculturalists and cosmopolitan multiculturalists place greater importance on the role of the individual in their actions, compared to pluralist multiculturalists who suggest action is determined by community.
Society	+ Society is not atomistic, but intrinsically contains its own cultures and values. + Cultural communities may not be bound by geographic borders. + **Diversity** within society is positive.	+ Those who believe in shallow diversity expect a level of conformity from minority groups that deep diversity proponents do not. + Cosmopolitan multiculturalists see cultural differences fading away as people become global citizens, compared to pluralist multiculturalists who would encourage the protection of such differences. + There is disagreement over value pluralism compared to shallow diversity. + Liberal multiculturalists place a greater emphasis on **tolerance**, compared to pluralist multiculturalists who argue for societal reordering to achieve equality.
State	+ The state should promote and protect cultural diversity and ensure tolerance. + The state should encourage cultural integration, rather than individualist integration which expects the dominant culture to prevail.	+ Liberal multiculturalists argue the state should provide for equal dignity and equal recognition but conservative criticisms have been levelled at this. + There is disagreement over whether the state should provide equal rights or group differentiated rights.
Economy	+ Economic policy should respect diversity of communities.	+ There is disagreement over economic subsidy of group differentiated rights rather than equal rights. + Liberal multiculturalists argue for greater economic freedom, where pluralist multiculturalists argue some protectionism may be necessary for minority groups.

Diversity Different races and cultures that exist within a state creating differences that should be celebrated.

Tolerance Acceptance of a wide range of values and customs.

Exam tip

There is overlap between some of these themes — for example human nature and society often overlap, as do the state and economy. However, you must ensure that whichever box you are choosing arguments from directly addresses the question you have been asked in an exam.

Now test yourself   TESTED ◯

10 Identify two areas of agreement between multiculturalists on human nature.

11 Identify two areas of disagreement within multiculturalism on society.

12 Explain why all multiculturalists believe that culture is important.

Answers at **www.hoddereducation.co.uk/myrevisionnotesdownloads**

15.3 Key thinkers

What do the key thinkers believe?

Isaiah Berlin

Key text: *Two Concepts of Liberty* (1958)

Key beliefs:
+ Value pluralism — there are key values that are universal but it is not for the state to determine which of these principles is more or less important than others.
+ Liberty — only a liberal society, which protects freedom, can value pluralism.

Key quotes/ideas:
+ On human nature: '… human nature generates values which, though equally sacred, equally ultimate, exclude one another, without there being any possibility of establishing an objective hierarchical relation among them'

> **Value pluralism** No one right or set of values is more or less important than any other.

Charles Taylor

Key text: *Multiculturalism and the Politics of Recognition* (1994)

Key beliefs:
+ Equal dignity — all individuals should be afforded the same rights and protections.
+ Equal recognition — all individuals should be recognised for their uniqueness, which may result in differentiated rights to protect minority values and cultures.

Key quotes/ideas:
+ On human nature: 'Non-recognition or misrecognition can inflict harm'
+ On society: 'It is impossible to understand ourselves and others… without understanding the communities in which we function'
+ On society: '… dominant groups tend to entrench their hegemony by inculcating an image of inferiority in the subjugated'

Bhikhu Parekh

Key text: *Rethinking Multiculturalism* (2000)

Key beliefs:
+ Rejection of universalist liberalism — the individual can only be understood as embedded within their culture.
+ Justification for deep diversity — diversity strengthens society through exposure to other cultures and all cultures are worthy of respect.
+ Deep diversity.

Key quotes/ideas:
+ On society: 'The norms governing respective claims, including the principles of justice, cannot be derived from one culture alone but through an open and equal dialogue between them'
+ On society: '… a community of citizens and a community of communities'

Tariq Modood

Key text: *Multiculturalism* (2007)

Key beliefs:
+ Strong cultural identities are inherently good and necessary for society to ensure citizens have both rights and a sense of belonging.
+ Integration — all forms of this (assimilation, individualist, multiculturalist, cosmopolitan) may be valid but it must be individual/community choice, not state imposed.

> **Assimilation** The expectation of minority groups adopting the values and traditions of the majority group.

Key quotes/ideas:

+ On equality: it is 'adapt[ing] public attitudes and arrangements so that the heritage they represent is encouraged rather than contemptuously expect[ing] them to wither away'
+ On society: 'A sense of belonging to one's country is necessary to make a success of a multicultural society'

Will Kymlicka

Key text: *Multicultural citizen* (1995)

Key beliefs:

+ Group differentiated rights — different groups may need different rights, including those of self-representation, polyethnic rights and representative rights.
+ Justification for these rights — the provision of them will allow minority groups to take a full and active part in civic engagement.
+ Shallow diversity.

Key quotes/ideas:

+ On the state: 'The state does not oppose the freedom of people to express their particular cultural concerns, but nor does it nurture such expression'
+ On society: 'If a culture is not generally respected, then the dignity and self-respect of its members will also be threatened'

> **Exam tip**
>
> Quotes from key thinkers should be used as examples to support the arguments you have made. Do not open a paragraph with a thinker or their quotes.

Now test yourself TESTED ◯

13 Outline Berlin's view of 'value pluralism'.

14 Outline Kymlicka's view on rights.

15 Outline Parekh's view on diversity.

How do multiculturalists disagree on the four themes?

	Liberal multiculturalism	Pluralist multiculturalism	Cosmopolitan multiculturalism	The conservative criticism
Human nature	+ Individuals seek freedom and autonomy but from a place of cultural understanding	+ Individuals can only be understood as part of their community	+ Individuals value choice and can pick between cultures	+ A pessimistic view of human nature which undermines self-determinism
Society	+ Shallow diversity + Tolerance	+ Deep diversity + Value pluralism + Universalism	+ Becoming global citizens + Society may not be geographically defined	+ Society is closely linked to national traditions
State	+ Provision of formal equality + Tolerance + The neutrality of the state	+ Provision of **group differentiated rights** + Value pluralism	+ Support of cultural integration	+ Will lead to a large/powerful state
Economy	+ Free-market capitalism with movement of goods and services in a communitarian model	+ Economic support of group differentiated rights may be needed + Capitalism may clash with equality	+ Multicultural societies are a product of global, free-market capitalism	+ Free-market capitalism with little state intervention

Group differentiated rights Rights being given uniquely to groups including self-government, polyethnic rights and representation rights.

Summary

✚ Core beliefs of multiculturalism are the politics of recognition, culture and identity, minority rights and diversity.
✚ There are competing strands with differing views within multiculturalism — liberal multiculturalism, pluralist multiculturalism, cosmopolitan multiculturalism and the conservative criticism.
✚ The key thinkers for multiculturalism are Berlin, Taylor, Parekh, Modood and Kymlicka.

Revision tasks

1 Outline the meaning of five core beliefs of multiculturalism.

2 Distinguish between the views of liberal, pluralist and cosmopolitan multiculturalists.

3 Copy and complete the table below.

Key thinker (name)	How the key thinker could link to the four themes (human nature, the state, society and the economy)	How the key thinker could link to the core beliefs of multiculturalism

Exam skills

Timing and planning

Exam timing is crucial. There is no point taking 'just a couple of extra minutes' on one question as it will leave you short on another. Your timings should be:

✚ 12 marks = 15 minutes maximum
✚ 24 marks = 30 minutes maximum
✚ 30 marks = 45 minutes maximum

To make **effective** use of your time, you should **always** plan your answers for 24- and 30-mark questions — you **do** have time. The best advice is not to write anything for about 30-60 seconds, so you can read the question and ensure you are answering the exact question set. Then take another 30–60 seconds to plan your essay — this could just be identifying the factors you plan to write about in each paragraph. A plan should be no longer than 20 words and should help you to ensure your essay is coherent and addresses the question set.

Exam practice

1 To what extent do multiculturalists agree about the role of the state? (24 marks)

2 To what extent is multiculturalism a coherent theory? (24 marks)

16 Nationalism

16.1 Core ideas and principles

What are nations?

Nationhood (the status of being a nation) is a core belief of nationalism:
+ At its heart, a nation is 'a people', or a community of people who share a common identity or understanding of their community.
+ Beyond this, however, there is no agreed understanding of what constitutes a 'nation'.
+ Nationhood is defined by those within it, which can lead to conflict, for example if one area of a recognised country claims to be a 'nation'.
+ The connection between the people could be:
    + a common language, which often expresses a common history or culture
    + geographical borders, which could be historically drawn or physical geographic boundaries, within which people share a common culture or experience
    + a common or shared ethnicity or religion, which creates a community that might not share a geographic area

Nationhood is closely associated with:

Strands	Thinkers
+ All strands have different ideas about what makes a nation	+ All thinkers have different ideas about what makes a nation

Ethnicity The sense of belonging to a social group that shares common characteristics such as culture, religion or language.

What is self-determination?

Self-determination is a core belief of nationalism:
+ The ability of the people who form a nation to decide how that nation is governed.
+ The belief that a nation should be able to make these decisions as its people know what is best for their nation.
+ This can lead to conflict between groups that identify as nations and fighting for self-determination against other nations.

Self-determination is closely associated with:

Strands	Thinker
+ Liberal nationalism + Anti-/postcolonial nationalism	+ Rousseau

What is the nation-state?

As a core belief of nationalism, the nation-state means:
+ An area with clear geographic boundaries that has self-determination for that area, often seen as a sovereign territory.
+ It is a product of self-determination, and usually organised as a 'country' under one central government (although the nation rules its own state and runs its own economy, it is not universally supported by the majority of nationalists).

The nation-state is closely associated with:

Strand
✛ Liberal nationalism

Thinker
✛ Rousseau, in terms of the 'general will'

Exam tip

Some thinkers can be used for more than one strand of an ideology, depending on their beliefs and their quotes. The beliefs of thinkers may not be associated with just one strand of an ideology, so you **must** compare strands.

Now test yourself   TESTED ⚪

1 Distinguish between the nation and the nation-state.
2 Define 'self-determination'.
3 List the common characteristics that could define a 'nation'.

What is culturalism?   REVISED ⚪

Culturalism is a core belief of nationalism:
✛ People within a nation or nation-state have a strong emotional and cultural tie to their nation.
✛ People have a unique cultural identity, or Volksgeist, based on their history and shared experiences.
✛ This can exist within the boundaries of a nation or a nation-state.
✛ To be a member of a nation therefore takes time, as people need to have the same shared experience and culture as those in the nation to make them a true member of that nation.
✛ Therefore, according to cultural nationalism, a person cannot just opt into a nation.
✛ Culturalism is linked to patriotism.
✛ Culturalism has been associated with a darker side of nationalism, which has resulted in racism.

> *Volksgeist* The unique identity of a nation based on the culture of that nation.

Culturalism is closely associated with:

Strands
✛ Conservative nationalism
✛ Expansionist nationalism

Thinker
✛ von Herder

What is racialism?   REVISED ⚪

Racialism is a belief held by a small group of nationalists:
✛ Racialists believe in creating nations on the basis of people who share the same biological factors.
✛ A belief that the human race is a collection of different races.
✛ A belief that each race shares unique characteristics, abilities or qualities.
✛ There is a close tie between culture and race.
✛ It should not be confused with racism, which argues that one race is superior to another.

Racialism is closely associated with:

Strands
✛ Conservative nationalism
✛ Expansionist nationalism

Thinkers
✛ Maurras
✛ Garvey

153

What is internationalism?

REVISED

Internationalism is a core belief for some forms of nationalism:

Liberal internationalism	Socialist internationalism
+ Self-determination for all nations. + Places importance on international cooperation. + Nations should be free to act as they wish provided they are not causing harm to other nations.	+ Workers' interests are more important than the national boundaries that divide them. + Workers should unite across national boundaries, and ultimately work together to overthrow capitalism.

Liberal internationalism Nations should cooperate and create mutual dependence to avoid international conflict.

Socialist internationalism Class divisions cut across geographical boundaries and are a more significant source of identity.

Internationalism is closely associated with:

Strand	Thinker
+ Liberal nationalism	+ Mazzini

Exam tip

Often the core beliefs outlined in these chapters can be used as factors to be discussed in a paragraph. Sometimes, however, a question may ask about the extent of agreement in one of these core beliefs. You need to find both agreement and disagreement.

Now test yourself

TESTED

4 Distinguish between liberal internationalism and socialist internationalism.
5 Explain what is meant by 'Volksgeist'.
6 Define 'racialism'.

16.2 Differing views and tensions

What is liberal nationalism?

REVISED

Liberal nationalists tend to believe in:
+ civic nationalism, in which a state is legitimate as its citizens actively participate in the state
+ self-determination for any nation that wants it, making it rational
+ inclusivity, where people who want to join a state can by adhering to its values
+ liberal internationalism or cooperation between nations for the benefit of all nationals involved
+ tolerance and multiculturalism (diversity)

Civic nationalism Nationalism, which is based on the active participation of citizens in supporting the values of society.

Rational The result of logical reasoning and decision-making.

What is conservative nationalism?

Conservative nationalists tend to believe in:
+ binding together the current nation using common traditions and practices
+ exclusivity, where the traditions and culture are unique to that nation and cannot easily be opted into
+ the need to adopt the practices of a nation in order to join it, and give up your own
+ culturalism — an emotional tie to the nation, such as patriotism, making it more irrational
+ monoculturalism, preserving the traditions of a nation rather than introducing new ones

What is anti-/postcolonialism?

Anti-/postcolonial nationalists tend to believe in:
+ self-determination, making it rational
+ inclusivity and civic nationalism

Anti-colonial nationalists tend to believe in liberal nationalism, looking to free themselves from colonial rule and gain self-determination.

Postcolonial nationalists, freed from colonial rule, often do not seek to replicate the systems of their oppressors, which is often liberal democracy.

What is expansionist nationalism?

Expansionist nationalists tend to believe in:
+ chauvinism, where one nation is considered superior to another, rejecting the right to self-determination by all nations
+ racialism and therefore exclusivity
+ imperialism/colonialism, expanding their nation over the 'inferior' nations
+ the importance of history and traditions, making it more irrational

> **Chauvinistic nationalism** Nationalism that believes one nation is superior to another.
>
> **Imperialism/colonialism** The control of one country by another.

Exam tip

When comparing strands, it may be difficult to find areas that they agree on entirely. Instead, you may be able to find points strands agree on as a principle, or an issue that they agree is an issue, but disagree on how to tackle it.

Now test yourself TESTED

7 Distinguish between anti-colonial and postcolonial nationalism.
8 List three beliefs of liberal nationalists.
9 List three beliefs of conservative nationalists.

155

How do nationalists agree and disagree on the four themes?

	General areas of agreement	Areas of disagreement
Human nature	+ The world is understood through being a series of nations. + Nation is a self-defined term. + People have a strong sense of national identity, which can be based on many things (language, religion, culture, ethnicity, geography).	+ Liberal nationalists and anti-/postcolonial nationalists tend to have a more rational view of human nature, where conservative and expansionist nationalists have a more irrational view of human nature. + For nationalists who believe in racialism, this suggests race is intrinsically linked to human nature.
Society	+ There are shared histories and traditions that help to shape nations. This is a form of culturalism.	+ More **regressive** nationalists argue for exclusive societies, whereas **progressive** nationalists argue for inclusive societies. + For progressive nationalists who believe in self-determination and civic nationalism, society taking part is key to legitimising the state.
State	+ An acceptance that the nation-state is the basis for the state and nationhood. + There are aspects of civic nationalism, for example even in liberal democracies an expectation of passing citizenship tests can be seen.	+ Liberal internationalists seek cooperation between states, whereas socialist internationalists seek cooperation of working classes beyond borders. + More progressive nationalists (liberal and anti-/postcolonial) argue for self-determination where more regressive nationalists do not, with conservative nationalists fearing it and expansionist nationalists disagreeing with it. + Integral nationalism is an intense form of patriotism in which the individual is subsumed in favour of the interests of the nation.
Economy	+ There are limited links between nationalism and the preferred economic system. + Nationalism has seen a range of economic models used in different countries. + Each nation should have control over the economic model it chooses.	+ Socialist internationalism does advocate workers uniting across borders to overthrow capitalism. + More regressive nationalists may favour protectionism while progressive nationalists may favour international cooperation and trade.

What are the features of the types of nationalism?

	Progressive	Inclusive	Self-determination	Rational	Multicultural	Civic
Liberal	✓	✓	✓	✓	✓	✓
Conservative	✗	✗	✗	✗	✗	✗
Anti-/ postcolonial	✓	✓	✓	✓	✓	✓
Expansionist	✗	✗	✗	✗	✗	✗

Exam tip

There is overlap between some of these themes — for example human nature and society often overlap, as do the state and economy. However, you must ensure that whichever box you are choosing arguments from directly addresses the question you have been asked in an exam.

Regressive Nationalism that looks to the past as the ideal of society and looks to move society back to this.

Progressive Nationalism that looks towards improving society by moving it forwards.

Now test yourself TESTED

10 Identify two areas of agreement within nationalism on the state.

11 Identify two areas of disagreement within nationalism on society.

12 Explain why all nationalists have some belief in culturalism.

Answers at **www.hoddereducation.co.uk/myrevisionnotesdownloads**

16.3 Key thinkers

What do the key thinkers believe?

Jean-Jacques Rousseau
Key text: *The Social Contract* (1762)

Key beliefs:
+ General will — that government should be based on the will of the people within a nation, enforcing their will not guiding it.
+ Civic nationalism — a state or government is legitimate as it is based on the participation of its citizens.

Key quotes/ideas:
+ On society: 'I prefer liberty with danger than peace with slavery'.
+ On the state: 'You are undone if you once forget that the fruits of the earth belong to us all, and the earth itself to nobody.'

Johann Gottfried von Herder
Key text: *Treatise on the Origin of Language* (1772)

Key beliefs:
+ Cultural nationalism — each nation has its own unique character and culture which should be respected.
+ *Volk* – meaning 'people', suggesting that 'people' are the basis for a national cultural identity.

Key quotes/ideas:
+ On society: 'Each nation contains its centre of happiness within itself'
+ On the state: 'The most noble end of government is to become dispensable, so that everyone must govern himself'

Giuseppe Mazzini
Key text: *The Duties of Man* (1860)

Key beliefs:
+ Nationhood — human freedoms could only be guaranteed through the nation-state.
+ 'Action' — rejecting rationalism, instead expecting 'thought and action'.

Key quotes/ideas:
+ On the state: 'The Country is the idea which rises upon that foundation; it is the sentiment of love, the sense of fellowship which binds together all the sons of that territory.'
+ On 'action': 'Slumber not in the tents of your fathers. The world is advancing'

Charles Maurras
Key text: *A French Awakening* (1943)

Key beliefs:
+ Integral nationalism — citizens should thoroughly commit to their nation, putting the nation above self.
+ Militarism — a belief in a strong military to ensure, linked to expansionist nationalism.

Key quotes/ideas:
+ On the state and human nature: 'For monarchy to work, one man must be wise. For democracy to work, a majority of the people must be wise. Which is more likely?'

> **Integral nationalism**
> Intense form of patriotism that subsumes the individual in favour of the interests of the nation.

Marcus Garvey

Key text: *The Philosophy and Opinions of Marcus Garvey* (1986)

Key beliefs:

+ Black pride — black people should be proud of their heritage, culture and norms, rather than replacing them with white culture. This is a form of black nationalism.
+ Pan-Africanism — African people anywhere in the world were united as part of one common people and should overcome cultural and ethnic difference to create strong societies in Africa.

Black nationalism The idea that Black people worldwide are part of 'one people'. It is a reaction to white oppression in the twentieth century.

Key quotes/ideas:

+ On race: 'Up, you mighty race, accomplish what you will'
+ On society: 'A people without the knowledge of their past history, origin and culture is like a tree without roots'

Exam tip

Quotes from key thinkers should be used as examples to support the arguments you have made. Do not open a paragraph with a thinker or their quotes.

Now test yourself TESTED ◯

13 Outline Rousseau's view on civic nationalism.

14 Outline Maurras's view on integral nationalism.

15 Outline Garvey's view on pan-Africanism.

How do nationalists disagree on the four themes?

	Disagreement
Rational vs. irrational	+ Rational nationalists see the state as a logical way of organising people and the nation as serving the state. + Irrational nationalism (or romantic nationalism) sees the state as something with historic traditions and emotional attachment.
Progressive vs. regressive	+ Progressive nationalists seek to improve society, often through national aims and international cooperation. + Regressive nationalists value traditional values and institutions, looking often to return to past ideals.
Inclusive vs. exclusive	+ **Inclusive nationalists** see the nation as something anyone can join if they wish to. + **Exclusive nationalists** argue shared traditions and history create nations, so people cannot just opt into a nation. This can be linked to racialism and culturalism.
Self-determination vs. expansionism	+ Nationalists who believe in self-determination do so for their own nation but also for others too. + Expansionist nationalists believe in the superiority of their state and the right to expand it over other states (colonisation).
Multiculturalism vs. monoculturalism	+ Multicultural nationalists embrace diversity and do not see race as important to citizenship. + Monocultural nationalists seek to have one culture, including traditions, dominate society.
Nationalism vs. internationalism	+ Internationalism looks for cooperation across national borders in supranational organisations. + Nationalism sees individual countries as more important than international cooperation.

Inclusive nationalism Nationalism that believes that anyone can join a nation by choosing to.

Exclusive nationalism A belief that to be a part of a nation, an individual should share the history, language etc. of that nation.

Summary

✦ Core beliefs of nationalism are nations, self-determination, nation-states, culturalism, racialism and internationalism.
✦ There are competing strands with differing views within nationalism — liberal nationalists, conservative nationalists, anti-/postcolonial nationalists and expansionist nationalists.
✦ The key thinkers for nationalism are Rousseau, von Herder, Mazzini, Maurras and Garvey.

Revision tasks

1 Outline the meaning of five core beliefs of nationalism.

2 Distinguish between the views of liberal, conservative, anti-/postcolonial, and expansionist nationalists.

3 Copy and complete the table below.

Key thinker (name)	How the key thinker could link to the four themes (human nature, the state, society and the economy)	How the key thinker could link to the core beliefs of nationalism

Exam skills

Timing and planning

Exam timing is crucial. There is no point taking 'just a couple of extra minutes' on one question as it will leave you short on another. Your timings should be:
✦ 12 marks = 15 minutes maximum
✦ 24 marks = 30 minutes maximum
✦ 30 marks = 45 minutes maximum

To make **effective** use of your time, you should **always** plan your answers for 24- and 30-mark questions — you **do** have time. The best advice is not to write anything for about 30–60 seconds, so you can read the question and ensure you are answering the exact question set. Then take another 30–60 seconds to plan your essay — this could just be identifying the factors you plan to write about in each paragraph. A plan should be no longer than 20 words and should help you to ensure your essay is coherent and addresses the question set.

Exam practice

1 To what extent do nationalists agree about self-determination? (24 marks)

2 To what extent is nationalism a coherent theory? (24 marks)

My Revision Notes: Pearson Edexcel A-level Politics: UK Government and Politics, Political Ideas and Global Politics

17 Comparative theories

17.1 Main ideas of realism

States as key actors in global politics and the balance of power (state sovereignty)

REVISED

According to the theory of realism, nation states constantly seek power and prestige. Since they are 'power maximisers', war and conflict will always define global relations because nation states are predatory and power-hungry.

This dark view of national ambitions connects to philosopher Thomas Hobbes' negative view of humanity in *Leviathan* (1651), in which he argued that humans have 'a perpetual and restless desire of power after power, that ceaseth only in death'.

Since nation states are sovereign, there is no greater authority to command their obedience. Therefore, realists argue that the sovereignty of nation states is the key factor defining global relations. Consequently, there can be no justification for interfering in the sovereign affairs of a nation state. Often defined as Westphalian state sovereignty, this refers to the Peace of Westphalia (1648), which ended the Thirty Years War (1618–48) on the principle that Catholic and Protestant states should accept their religious differences and respect each other's sovereignty.

The significance of the nation state and sovereignty is covered fully in Chapter 18.

The realists' commitment to sovereignty makes them sceptical of institutions of global and regional governance which limit the sovereignty of member states. For realists, the key actors in international relations will always be nation states.

> **Realism** A theory of international relations based on the principle that nation states are self-seeking and power-hungry. Since according to realism there is no authority greater than the nation state, nation states must prioritise their own survival in a hostile world order.

International anarchy and its implications

REVISED

Since nation states always seek the best outcomes for themselves in terms of status and influence (state egoism) and institutions of global governance lack the authority to maintain global order, international relations tend towards conflict between nation states, or international anarchy.

However, despite there being 'no night watchman' (John Mearsheimer) able to impose order, this does not mean that nation states will always be in a constant state of Hobbesian conflict. Realists argue that relative stability can be achieved by:

✦ Nation states respecting each other's sovereignty.
✦ The strengthening of military power and alliances to deter potential aggression. A nation state with a strong military and reliable allies will be so powerful that other powers will not risk conflict with it.
✦ If nation states can provide these sorts of powerful incentives against attack, a favourable balance of power can be established in which nation states will decide to respect each other's borders.

> **International anarchy** Realists argue that there is no authority greater than the nation capable of imposing order, so nation states will pursue their individual interests, leading to a state of global anarchy.

The security dilemma and the inevitability of war

However, warfare is an inevitable part of global relations. This is partly because the realist emphasis on defence and deterrent raises the security dilemma—the problem that, by increasing spending on defence and building alliances, other nation states are pressurised to do the same, as they in turn feel threatened. This can provoke dangerous arms races in which competing nation states regard each other with increasing fear and suspicion. For example, according to many historians, the First World War (1914–18) was caused by a massive arms build-up by the European great powers, which created so much tension that it eventually provoked conflict.

> **Security dilemma** The problem that, when nation states maximise their power to deter aggression, this threatens other nation states, which then increase their own military spending, leading to distrust and arms races. Therefore, actions designed to make a state safer make it less safe.

> **Now test yourself** TESTED
>
> 1 Define 'anarchy'.
> 2 What is meant by 'the balance of power'?
> 3 What is the security dilemma?

17.2 Main ideas of liberalism

Significance of morality and optimism on human nature

Liberals approach international relations in a more cooperative and optimistic way than realists. Whereas realism's emphasis on self-interest and conflict is very Hobbesian, liberalism focuses on philosopher John Locke's belief in human rationality. Consequently, liberals argue that nation states can cooperate rather than compete in institutions of global governance like the United Nations (UN) and the World Trade Organization (WTO).

> **Liberalism** A theory of international relations founded on the principles that nation states are cooperative and so can work together in institutions of global governance, and that free trade, democracy, the rule of law and human rights are essential in international relations.
>
> **Global governance** When sovereign nation states work together and with non-state actors in international/intergovernmental organisations (IGOs) (such as the UN) to address collective problems.

Human rights, the rule of law, democracy and free trade are also central to liberalism. Since Locke argued that all human beings are born with natural rights, liberals regard the protection and advancement of human rights and the rule of law as core issues in global relations.

In addition, liberals believe that democracy should be encouraged. This is based on the philosopher Immanuel Kant's perpetual peace theory that, since republics are accountable to their citizens, they will avoid war as it is not in their best interests.

Liberals encourage free trade on the basis that making nation states economically reliant on each other makes conflict irrational and self-defeating. As the nineteenth-century French liberal economist Frédéric Bastiat stated, 'When goods do not cross borders, armies will.'

Complex interdependence

Liberals argue that, by nation states developing as many shared connections and values as possible, the possibility of conflict is reduced. The political scientists Robert Keohane and Joseph Nye refer to this as a 'complex model of interdependence' in which nation states become so tightly linked that war between them becomes unthinkable because it would be so damaging to their collective interests.

Complex interdependence A liberal term sometimes known as the 'cobweb model of international relations', in which the close relationships that nation states establish through institutions of global governance encourage cooperation and understanding.

Now test yourself

TESTED

4 Why are human rights so important to liberals?
5 Why do liberals support the expansion of democracy?
6 Why do liberals want to expand free trade?

Possibility of harmony and balance

REVISED

Liberals therefore believe that harmony and balance are possible in international relations when nation states make the rational decision to cooperate in institutions of global governance like the UN and of regional governance like the European Union (EU). These increase trust and understanding, since by having nation states work together towards collective outcomes, there is less likelihood of them acting as individual 'power maximisers'. The EU has, for example, helped to maintain peace between its members by deepening their connections.

Liberals welcome the involvement of non-state actors in global relations, since this further contributes to a cobweb model of global relations in which the centrality of individual nation states is reduced, therefore challenging warlike 'state egoism'. Such institutions of global and regional governance include: the UN (1945), the International Court of Justice (ICJ) (1945), the European Economic Community (EEC) (1957)/EU (1993), the WTO (1995) and the International Criminal Court (ICC) (2002).

In contrast to realism, which focuses on the sovereign interests of individual states, liberalism therefore takes a polycentric approach to international relations, by seeking to involve as many actors as possible in collective decision-making in shared institutions of governance.

Non-state actors Organisations which play a prominent role in global relations but are not nation states. These can include intergovernmental and regional organisations and non-governmental organisations such as charities, pressure groups and global foundations.

Now test yourself

TESTED

7 Define 'global governance'.
8 Give two examples of global governance.
9 Why do liberals support regional organisations like the EU?

Exam tip

Remember that realists, just as much as liberals, want to avoid conflict but they do it through strength not global governance.

17.3 Divisions between realism and liberalism

Human nature and power

REVISED

Realism and liberalism offer different interpretations of human nature and power. According to realism, nation states, like human beings, relentlessly seek supremacy and status. Thus, the potential for conflict is ever present in global relations. Therefore, to survive, nation states must be powerful enough to deter potential aggressors.

Since liberals believe human beings are rational and cooperative, they argue that peace is more likely than war. To encourage stability and harmony, they therefore advance institutions of regional and global governance in which nation states and non-state actors can combine to resolve shared dilemmas.

Order and security and the likelihood of conflict

REVISED

According to realism, all nation states are 'power maximisers' and possess ultimate sovereign power. Therefore, global relations are anarchic with no higher authority able to punish aggression and provide order. In these circumstances, as the political scientist John Mearsheimer states, it is better 'to be Godzilla than Bambi', since strength is the only way of guaranteeing security and autonomy.

Liberals respond that nation states are not hard-wired to engage in conflict out of the selfish desire to gain greater power. Instead, nation states are rational and cooperative, and can work together to achieve positive outcomes for all. Liberals further believe that conflict is best avoided by expanding free trade, democracy and human rights, since this creates shared values upon which global society can harmoniously unite.

Impact of international organisations and the significance of states

REVISED

Liberals argue that intergovernmental institutions of global and regional governance encourage peace and stability because they enable nation states to work together to enhance mutual understanding. Through collective endeavours to resolve world problems, state egoism is thus replaced by an internationalist world view. For example, the UN provides a framework for member states to collaborate in developing a global response to climate change.

In contrast, realists distrust intergovernmental institutions because they argue that they challenge state sovereignty. They believe that collective decision-making means that the interests of the individual nation state are insufficiently protected. For example, the US has not joined the ICC because it does not believe that an outside court can exercise jurisdiction over American citizens.

17.4 Main ideas of the anarchical society and society of states theory

Acceptance of anarchy in the global system

REVISED

In 1977, the political scientist Hedley Bull published *The Anarchical Society*, in which he acknowledged that although nation states are sovereign and act according to self-interest, this can still provide the foundations for global stability.

According to Bull, realists are right—nation states are sovereign and seek security in an **anarchic** world order without any higher authority able to impose order. However, nation states are also rational and can decide that they can achieve more for themselves through cooperation than through conflict. Consequently, a society of states can be created based on national self-interest.

'Society of states' theory differs from liberalism because the nation state remains the dominant player and chooses to cooperate for no higher purpose than its own ends.

> **Anarchical society and society of states** A theory developed by Hedley Bull which argues that nation states can maximise self-interest through cooperation. Consequently, global relations are not purely anarchic, as a society of states is possible.

163

However, it is also distinct from realism because it argues that nation states are not solely interested in power and prestige and can choose to work with other states to avoid conflict and maximise their security.

A practical example of this sort of approach to international relations is 'détente' in the 1970s. US President Richard Nixon (1969–74) and his key foreign policy adviser Henry Kissinger understood that, without sacrificing their principles, the US and the Soviet Union would enhance their security more through cooperation than through conflict.

17.5 An evaluation of the extent to which realism and liberalism explain developments (since 2000) in global politics

Table 17.1 highlights how liberal optimism about the direction of the twenty-first century has generally been replaced by more realist considerations.

Table 17.1 Replacement of liberal optimism about the twenty-first century by more realist considerations

	Liberalism	Realism
The state and globalisation	In the aftermath of the Cold War, liberals were confident that the centrality of the nation state in international relations would be reduced by the rise of economic and political institutions of global governance. In 1990, the management consultant Kenichi Ohmae predicted that we would become a 'borderless world'. A shared commitment to free trade, democracy and human rights would further make the differences between nations insignificant. The centrality of the nation state in international relations could thus be eroded.	The nation state has proved much more resilient than liberals expected. Globalisation has not encouraged greater dialogue and understanding. Instead, shifts in the economic and political balance of power have increased hostility and resentment. Rather than hollowing out nation states, globalisation can make them more powerful and nationalist. This is shown through China's global economic expansion through the Belt and Road Initiative.
Global governance: political and economic	In 2022, having lost a case at the ICJ and been condemned at the UN General Assembly by 116 votes to 6, the UK agreed to negotiate over the sovereignty of the Chagos Islands.	The WTO's Doha Round of trade negotiations failed because of disagreement between developed and developing countries. Recent Russian and Chinese challenges to US hegemony mean that the UN Security Council is paralysed by hostility between Russia and China, on one hand, and the US, France and the UK, on the other.
Global governance: human rights and environmental	UN Responsibility to Protect (2005) established the principle that the sovereignty of a nation state applies only if it does not commit or allow large-scale human rights abuses. In the Paris Treaty (2015), all Conference of the Parties (COP) members agreed to Nationally Determined Contributions (NDCs) to reduce their greenhouse gas emissions. At the Glasgow COP (2021), members recommitted themselves to the goal of ensuring temperature rise this century is below 1.5°C.	UN Responsibility to Protect (2005) is regularly ignored in conflicts like Yemen, Syria and Myanmar. The influence of the ICC remains limited as only 123 states accept its jurisdiction. Despite the warning from the Intergovernmental Panel on Climate Change (IPCC) that current NDCs were insufficient to keep temperature rise below 1.5°C, between the Glasgow and Sharm El-Sheikh COPs, only 34/194 agreed more ambitious targets.

	Liberalism	Realism
Power and developments	The EU is emerging as a significant global actor. Its €300 billion Global Gateway has been set up to advance sustainable development in the developing world.	Challenges to the balance of power from Russia and China have encouraged a more realist approach to international relations. In 2022 Russia invaded Ukraine. In 2022 Chinese President Xi Jinping increased pressure on Taiwan, telling the Communist Party National Congress that the 'complete reunification of our country must and will be realised'. In response to all of the above, western powers have increasingly focused on national defence. At the NATO summit in Madrid (2022), Finland and Sweden were fast tracked for membership. In 2021 a military alliance was established between Australia, the UK and the US (AUKUS) to maintain the existing balance of power in the Indo-Pacific.
Regionalism and the EU	Despite, the UK's withdrawal in 2020 (Brexit), the EU remains a powerful example of advanced regionalism. In 2022 its gross domestic product (GDP) was $16.6 trillion — equal to one-sixth of the global economy. The EU has some of the most ambitious greenhouse gas reduction targets in the world. By 2030, it is committed to cutting its carbon emissions to 55% of 1990 levels and being carbon neutral by 2050.	Regional organisations like the Association of Southeast Asian Nations (ASEAN), the Arab League, the US–Mexico Agreement (USMCA) and the African Union (AU) have made more limited progress towards greater integration.

Now test yourself

TESTED ⚪

10 What is anarchical society/society of states theory?

11 How do liberals and realists differ over human nature and why is this significant?

12 Give two examples of collective dilemmas (shared problems) which liberals believe nation states cannot resolve alone.

Case study

Perspectives on global relations

According to the noted realist Kenneth Waltz, 'With many sovereign states, with no system of law enforceable among them, with each state judging its grievances and ambitions according to the dictates of its reasons or desire — conflict, sometimes leading to war, is bound to occur.' Such a negative view of global relations defines realism.

In contrast, the former UN Secretary General Ban Ki-moon provides a powerful defence of liberalism: 'One of the main lessons I have learned during my five years as Secretary-General is that broad partnerships are the key to solving broad challenges.'

Critics warn that growing global tension between competing powers and claims of an inadequate response to climate change demonstrate the enduring power of realism. The extent to which liberalism can rise to the challenges of the twenty-first century thus defines global relations today.

My Revision Notes: Pearson Edexcel A-level Politics: UK Government and Politics, Political Ideas and Global Politics

Summary

+ The different approaches of realists and liberals towards international relations are founded on different views of human nature.
+ Realists are influenced by the negative attitude of Thomas Hobbes. Liberals are influenced by the more optimistic views of John Locke.
+ Realists argue that nation states play the dominant role in global relations and are self-seeking.
+ Liberals believe that nation states can be cooperative, so they favour regional and global governance.
+ According to the anarchic society/society of states theory, nation states can cooperate for reasons of self-interest.

Revision tasks

1 Produce four recent examples of nation states acting in a realist manner. Use examples not in this book.

2 Research the core thinkers Marx and Engels (socialism), John Stuart Mill (liberalism) and Robert Nozick (conservatism). Do you think they would be likely to support a realist or liberal approach to international relations? Be prepared to convince the rest of your class!

3 Debate the motion, 'Nothing is more important in global politics than the protection of human rights.' Be prepared to quote core thinkers on both sides of the argument and bring in political figures like Bernard Kouchner (liberalism) and Henry Kissinger (realism) to support your arguments.

Exam skills

Determining factors

+ The liberalism/realism 12-mark question is the only compulsory question on the specification.
+ Candidates must refer to core political ideologies (liberalism, conservatism, socialism) in Unit 1. The most effective way of doing this is by making explicit references to Thomas Hobbes' and John Locke's different views of human nature in your response.
+ Be prepared to connect liberalism and realism to recent developments in global relations.
+ It can be useful to refer to liberalism and realism when approaching 30-mark essays. This is not compulsory, but it can provide helpful context to your answer.

Exam practice

1 Analyse the differences that exist between realists and liberals over humanitarian intervention. In your answer you must discuss any relevant core political ideas.   (12 marks)

2 Analyse the differences that exist between realists and liberals over the most effective way of achieving peace and stability. In your answer you must discuss any relevant core political ideas.   (12 marks)

3 Analyse why realists and liberals view the role of the nation state in international relations so differently. In your answer you must discuss any relevant core political ideas.   (12 marks)

Answers at **www.hoddereducation.co.uk/myrevisionnotesdownloads**

18 The state and globalisation

18.1 The state: nation state and national sovereignty

Characteristics of a nation state and national sovereignty

REVISED ●

A nation state is a political community defined by shared citizenship and nationality. Nation states possess sovereignty, wielding ultimate authority within their territory. A nation state possesses recognised borders and a government capable of exercising authority. It should be acknowledged as a sovereign nation state by the rest of the international community.

Nation states are equal in terms of sovereignty. This means that, whatever the size of a state, it has the same sovereign jurisdiction over its citizens in terms of international law. The first chapter of the UN Charter (1945) recognises this, stating, 'The organisation is based on the principle of the sovereign equality of all its members.'

During the twentieth century, as empires declined, the number of nation states expanded dramatically. In 2023, 193 nation states were represented at the United Nations (UN).

Realists view nation states as the central actors in global politics and the relationship between them as defining the course of international relations.

According to the principles of the Peace of Westphalia (1648), which ended the Thirty Years War on the principle of non-interference, states are sovereign. Therefore there is no external authority capable of coercing them. Realists liken nation states to billiard balls constantly making contact with each other without damaging the hard shell of their sovereignty.

> **Sovereignty** The principle of unlimited authority which means that no outside power can exercise influence over a sovereign body.
>
> **Nation state** A sovereign political body whose people share a common citizenship.

18.2 Globalisation

The process of globalisation

REVISED ●

The centrality of the nation state in international relations has been challenged by globalisation. This is the process through which economic, financial, political and cultural exchanges increase the 'complex interconnectedness' between nation states.

Complex interdependence widens and deepens the connectivity between nation states and non-state actors. This means that the primacy of the nation state in international relations is replaced by a polycentric model of international relations in which power and influence are much more broadly shared.

> **Globalisation** The process by which nation states and their citizens become more closely interconnected, challenging the nation state as the principal actor in international relations.
>
> **Interconnectedness** The increased economic, political and cultural connectivity between nation states and their citizens, developing a cobweb of close and reliant global relationships.

Now test yourself

TESTED ⬤

1 List three characteristics of a nation state.
2 Define 'sovereignty'.
3 Define 'complex interdependence'.

Factors driving globalisation

REVISED ⬤

Globalisation is driven forward economically, politically and culturally. The internet enables the immediate exchange of ideas and capital flow, and the shared problems and common interests of nation states encourage greater connectivity between them.

Economic globalisation

+ Economic globalisation refers to the global spread of economic liberalism. This is known as the 'Washington Consensus' and is the process by which nation states eliminate the tariffs that protect their economies, engaging in free trade.
+ Since the collapse of the Soviet Union (1991), nation states globally have embraced free trade. This has led to rapid industrialisation in the developing world as it utilises its low-wage workforce to manufacture products for world markets.
+ Economic globalisation has been driven forward by the World Trade Organization (WTO) which negotiates free trade agreements among its 164 member states (2023).
+ Nation states and regional organisations can negotiate their own free trade agreements. In 2022, the Regional Comprehensive Economic Partnership (RCEP) agreement was agreed between the Association of Southeast Asian Nations (ASEAN), Japan, China, Australia, Japan and South Korea, making it the world's biggest free trade agreement.
+ The International Monetary Fund (IMF) and the World Bank further encourage economic liberalism through structural adjustment programmes which generally require recipient states to adopt free market reforms.
+ According to liberals, economic globalisation not only increases global wealth; it also serves a moral purpose by encouraging greater trust and understanding between nation states, thereby reducing conflict.

Political globalisation

+ Political globalisation is the process by which nation states negotiate with each other and with non-state actors in intergovernmental organisations (IGOs) to resolve collective dilemmas.
+ Examples of international intergovernmental organisations include the UN, the International Court of Justice (ICJ) and the International Criminal Court (ICC).
+ Global governance refers to the way in which nation states choose to work together and with non-state actors in collective organisations without abandoning their sovereignty. In contrast, world government would possess complete sovereign authority.
+ Regional organisations like the European Union (EU), the African Union (AU) and ASEAN provide another way for nation states to approach decision-making from a collective perspective.
+ By establishing institutional frameworks for cooperation, political globalisation encourages a less state-centric attitude towards international relations, as nation states and non-state actors work together to achieve mutually beneficial shared outcomes. This is referred to as a polycentric approach to global relations.

Economic globalisation
The process through which national economies become more closely connected and reliant on each other through free trade (economic liberalism) and capital investment.

World Bank The world's largest source of funding and knowledge for developing countries. It encourages long-term development through loans which are generally conditional on the recipient country implementing free market structural adjustment programmes.

Political globalisation
The establishment of intergovernmental organisations like the UN which enable nation states to work together and with non-state actors to resolve collective dilemmas.

World government This would be globally sovereign and would require nation states to abandon their sovereignty and accept the complete supranational authority of a single world power.

Cultural globalisation

+ Cultural globalisation involves the transmission of new cultural experiences across borders, challenging the traditional cultures of sovereign states.
+ This is facilitated by global trade, multinational corporations (MNCs), film, television and the internet, so that people globally access the same food, clothing and entertainment.
+ Cultural globalisation has generally been associated with Americanisation, so that global culture has become indistinguishable from US culture based on the world appeal of US entertainment, food and clothing.
+ Critics associate Americanisation with cultural homogenisation, so that what makes individual cultures unique is replaced by bland and superficial materialism.
+ The creation of a global 'monoculture' based on Americanisation is sometimes referred to as 'coca-colonisation'. According to the US sociologist Benjamin Barber, Hollywood has created a 'McWorld' based on consumerism and brand culture.
+ However, cultural globalisation can also provide greater choice. The internet provides access to a world of ideas, commodities and cultural experiences which do not have to be American.
+ Netflix, for example, provides a global audience for international films and television. Hollywood and Nollywood films generate a global following.

Cultural globalisation The spread of global values and material aspirations, so that the distinctiveness of national cultures becomes increasingly insignificant.

Homogenisation and **monoculture** These refer to the rise of a materialistic world culture in which the same products dominate globally. Often referred to as 'coca-colonisation', homogenisation suggests a dull uniformity challenging the uniqueness of diverse cultures.

Now test yourself TESTED

4 What is economic liberalism?
5 Define 'political globalisation'.
6 Define 'cultural homogenisation'.

18.3 Debates about the impact of globalisation

The implications of globalisation for the nation state and national sovereignty REVISED

Globalisation has had a profound impact on the state system, widening and deepening the connections between nation states. Some of this has been positive:
+ Economic globalisation has encouraged dramatic growth rates in the developing world. According to the World Bank, the economic expansion of China has lifted 800 million people out of extreme poverty (measured as living on less than $1.90 per day) between 1980 and 2022. The proportion of the world's population living in extreme poverty fell from 36% to 9% between 1990 and 2021, as shown in Figure 18.1 (on the next page).

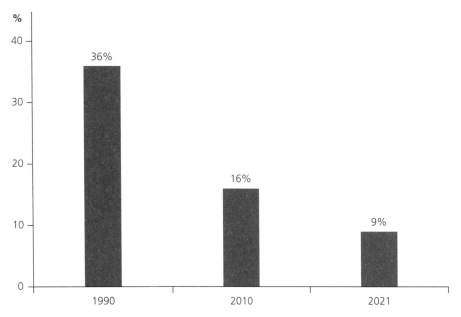

Figure 18.1 Percentage of the world's population living in extreme poverty

Source: World Bank

+ Political globalisation provides global forums for nation states to resolve collective dilemmas. Regular COP meetings coordinate a global response to climate change.
+ Cultural globalisation provides unprecedented global consumer choice, and the internet facilitates a global debate on pressing issues like climate change and racial intolerance.

More negatively:
+ Since the world is now so closely interlinked, economic crises have a global impact. The collapse of the US investment bank Lehman Brothers (2008) caused a worldwide recession.
+ Because of global travel the Covid-19 virus became a world pandemic.
+ Increased trade between nation states has massively increased carbon emissions, threatening dangerous global temperature rise above 2°C this century.
+ Instead of encouraging cooperation, free trade can lead to resentment as nation states in the developed world fear that they will lose manufacturing jobs to the developing world.
+ Rather than encouraging global dialogue and challenging borders, the internet encourages national and cultural echo chambers in which people only encounter information and prejudices that reinforce their existing prejudices. Consequently, foreign cultures and traditions are often attacked not embraced.

Now test yourself   TESTED ⬤

7 Distinguish between global governance and world government.
8 Give two ways in which globalisation has positively impacted on international relations.
9 Give two ways in which globalisation has negatively impacted on international relations.

The development of international law, humanitarian and forcible interventions

The collapse of the Soviet Union in 1991 conclusively ended the Cold War with the US, and human rights protection became more prominent in international relations. On several occasions western powers forcibly intervened in nation states for humanitarian rather than geo-strategic reasons (Figure 18.2).

Answers at **www.hoddereducation.co.uk/myrevisionnotesdownloads**

1992	President George H.W. Bush sent US troops to Somalia to 'end the starvation' which clan and ethnic rivalry was causing.
1993–2017	UN tribunal to try human rights abuses in the former Yugoslavia established.
1994–2016	UN tribunal to try human rights abuses in Rwanda established.
1995	NATO intervened in Bosnia following the Srebrenica Massacre.
1997–2022	International tribunal to try human rights abuses in Cambodia established.
1999	UN peacekeepers sent to East Timor to end the violence which was engulfing it following its separation from Indonesia.
1999	NATO intervened against Serbia to stop the government's policy of ethnic cleansing in Kosovo.
2000	UK military forces intervened in Sierra Leone to end its civil war.
2002–13	UN tribunal to try human rights abuses in Sierra Leone established.
2002	The ICC was established to try individuals accused of war crimes, genocide and crimes against humanity when national courts are not prepared to act.
2005	The principle of intervention on the basis of Responsibility to Protect (R2P) was adopted by the UN.
2011	NATO intervened in the Libyan civil war to protect civilians from retribution by the forces of the Gaddafi regime.

Figure 18.2 Forcible interventions by western powers in nation states for non-geo-strategic reasons

However, the extent to which human rights have become more central in international relations is hotly disputed:

+ Nation states retain ultimate jurisdiction over their citizens. Therefore, international courts are only effective if nation states are prepared to cooperate with them.
+ Three members of the Security Council (China, Russia and the US) do not recognise the authority of the ICC, significantly challenging its authority.
+ Humanitarian intervention did not take place to stop genocide in Rwanda in 1994.
+ The principle of Responsibility to Protect (R2P), adopted by the UN in 2005, states that the international community should be prepared to intervene, 'should peaceful means be inadequate and national authorities manifestly fail to protect their populations from genocide, war crimes, ethnic cleansing and crimes against humanity'. But the principle has been ignored despite massive human rights violations in Syria, Yemen and Myanmar.
+ Western support for humanitarian intervention is likely to further decline as the US and its western allies refocus on resisting Russian and Chinese attempts to expand their territorial influence.

> **Now test yourself** TESTED ◯
>
> 10 Define 'humanitarian intervention'.
> 11 List three humanitarian interventions.
> 12 What is the role of the ICC?

Does globalisation significantly challenge state sovereignty?

In the 1990s liberal theorists predicted that globalisation would lead to the rise of a post-sovereign state world as trade, migration and the internet increasingly made borders porous.

Were liberals right that globalisation would lead to the rise of a post-sovereign state world?

Yes	No
+ States cannot protect themselves from cross border challenges like the Covid-19 pandemic. + International free trade means that nation states need to integrate into the world market by adopting free market economic policies. + The internet and cultural globalisation are flattening out the unique heritage of nation states. + According to the UN's R2P, sovereignty is conditional on nation states protecting the human rights of their citizens.	+ During the pandemic, nation states closed their national borders to protect their citizens. + Nation states can restrict access to their markets. The Biden administration has maintained tariffs on China and has launched a 'Buy America' initiative to protect US manufacturing jobs. + R2P is ignored in cases like the Rohingya genocide in Myanmar, allowing nation states to abuse their citizens with impunity. + States can use the internet to destabilise rivals through cyber-terrorism and fake and damaging news. Powerful authoritarian states like China and Russia can restrict internet access, bolstering the government's power over its citizens.

The liberal and realist response to globalisation

Liberal and realist responses to globalisation are listed in Table 18.1.

Table 18.1 Liberal and realist responses to globalisation

Liberal	Realist
+ Liberals view globalisation positively. They believe that greater economic, political and cultural connections between nation states encourage trust and understanding, therefore contributing to global peace and stability. + Liberals believe that free trade reduces the risk of war because if nation states share the same global supply chain, it would be self-defeating for them to break this by going to war. + Liberals believe that, by encouraging global connectivity, the centrality of nation states is diluted, so reducing conflict.	+ Since realism is based on the inviolability of state sovereignty, realists distrust globalisation. + Realists argue that institutions of global governance lack legitimacy and do not have the authority to compel nation states to act in a certain way. + Liberalism's encouragement of democracy and human rights troubles realists, since they believe that respect for state sovereignty provides the basis for global stability.

The debate between hyper globalisers, globalisation sceptics and transformationalists

The views of hyper globalisers, globalisation sceptics and transformationalists about globalisation are summarised in Table 18.2.

Table 18.2 Views of hyper globalisers, globalisation sceptics and transformationalists on globalisation

Hyper globalisers	Hyper globalisers believe that globalisation creates so many economic, political and cultural connections that the borders between nation states are becoming porous, making national sovereignty increasingly irrelevant. Global problems like poverty, climate change and the future of artificial intelligence are so complex that nation states cannot solve them alone. This will further erode the nation state as the main actor in international relations.

Globalisation sceptics	According to globalisation sceptics, the impact of globalisation is exaggerated. Nation states remain the dominant force in international relations. Nation states still pursue their own interests and choose the extent to which they engage in free trade and cooperate in institutions of global and regional governance.
Transformationalists	Transformationalists agree that the impact of globalisation is unavoidable. However, they argue that it increases rather than lessens the power and influence of nation states. For example, China and India have become more powerful and assertive because of the wealth they have accumulated through economic globalisation.

> **Exam tip**
>
> The ideas represented by hyper globalisers, globalisation sceptics and transformationalists are complicated but important, so do learn them.

18.4 The ways and extent to which globalisation addresses and resolves contemporary issues

The ways and extent to which globalisation addresses poverty, conflict, human rights and environmental issues are debated in the following boxes.

Does globalisation resolve poverty?

Yes	No
+ By providing manufacturing jobs in the developing world, global poverty has been drastically reduced. + Wages in manufacturing are higher than in subsistence agriculture, with the possibility of greater responsibility and promotion. + Women gain factory employment. This provides them with more financial security and reduces pregnancy rates. (Large families in the developing world contribute to poverty.)	+ Globalisation leads to a 'race to the bottom' as MNCs maximise profits by providing low wages and limited health and safety provisions. + Industrialisation breaks up traditional communities, with a significant cost to human well-being. + Powerful nation states exploit the raw materials of the developing world, so they remain in a state of neo-colonial dependency (see Chapter 19 for world systems/dependency theory).

Does globalisation reduce conflict?

Yes	No
+ Economic liberalism creates closer bonds between countries, reducing the risk of conflict. This is known as the Dell Theory (Thomas Friedman) because states in the same Dell supply chain will not want to suffer economically by going to war with each other. + Political globalisation creates intergovernmental bodies like the UN to resolve conflict. + Globalisation encourages the spread of liberal democracy, so discouraging conflict. + Cultural globalisation spreads a world culture, challenging the differences between states.	+ Economic liberalism has shifted the balance of power towards emerging nations like China, encouraging the potential for conflict with the US. + The loss of manufacturing jobs to the developing world fuels resentment in the developed world. + There is little evidence that globalisation has encouraged liberal democracy. + The internet can encourage nationalism, hatred of outsiders, and conflict.

Are human rights better protected because of globalisation?

Yes	No
+ The ICC tries individuals accused of war crimes, crimes against humanity and genocide. + There have been successful humanitarian interventions (Bosnia, Kosovo, East Timor) based on the principle of our shared humanity. + R2P (2005) makes sovereignty conditional on nation states not committing human rights abuses. + Cultural globalisation spreads liberal and progressive values, encouraging LGBTQ+ and women's rights.	+ The ICC does not possess world jurisdiction as only 123 nation states (2023) accept its jurisdiction. + Further western-led humanitarian interventions are unlikely because the focus of western countries is now on resisting Russian and Chinese expansion. + R2P (2005) has not been invoked to stop human rights abuses in Syria, Myanmar, and Yemen. + 67/193 states still criminalise same-sex relations (2023). The UN has failed to protect women's rights in Afghanistan.

Does globalisation threaten the environment?

Yes	No
+ Carbon emissions have dramatically increased because of industrialisation. + Industrialisation causes environmental degradation in the developing world. + Cultural and economic globalisation encourages consumerism and materialism, which use up the planet's resources.	+ The UN provides a framework for COP members to come together regularly to work out solutions to climate change. + Globalisation encourages innovatory responses to climate change, as there is a global exchange of ideas. + At COP conferences, developed nations have agreed to provide $100 billion to developing countries to reduce the impact of climate change.

Now test yourself

 TESTED

13 Distinguish between hyper globalisers and globalisation sceptics.

14 Give two reasons why liberals support globalisation.

15 What has been the impact of economic globalisation on global poverty?

Case study

US brands in the Soviet Union

In 1990, the first McDonald's restaurant opened in Moscow to massive queues. The arrival of McDonald's in the Soviet Union proclaimed the global triumph of capitalism over communism and the Americanisation of world culture. A year later, in 1991, the Soviet Union collapsed and the 'McDonaldisation' of Russia seemed complete with the number of its restaurants expanding from 224 in 2009 to 850 in 2022.

However, in 2022, following the Russian invasion of Ukraine, McDonald's ceased its operations in Russia, as did all other US restaurant chains, including KFC, Pizza Hut and Starbucks. The global triumph of the American way of life suddenly seemed rather more doubtful.

Summary

+ The nation state has since the Peace of Westphalia (1648) become the dominant influence in global politics.
+ According to the billiard ball model of global relations, nation states are the dominant players in international relations.
+ However, the centrality of the nation state has been challenged by economic, political and cultural globalisation. This refers to the establishment of institutions of global governance (political globalisation), the spread of economic liberalism/ Washington Consensus (economic globalisation) and greater cultural exchanges (cultural globalisation).
+ Globalisation sceptics, transformationalists and hyper globalisers differ over the extent to which globalisation impacts on state sovereignty.
+ Realists suggest that recent events, such as the rise of China and the Russian invasion of Ukraine, indicate that the nation state remains the dominant force in global politics and that the impact of globalisation has been exaggerated.
+ Although globalisation has reduced global poverty, it has had little impact on reducing conflict and improving human rights.
+ By increasing growth rates in the developing world, globalisation has also increased carbon emissions.

Revision tasks

1 List the top ten most popular brands and restaurants in the world and the ten highest-grossing films this year. Does your evidence suggest that cultural globalisation has created a monoculture based on Americanisation?

2 Debate the motion, 'Globalisation has made the world a better place.'

3 Research three of the most recent decisions reached by the ICJ. Were they obeyed and what does this suggest about the influence and authority of the ICJ?

4 Produce three revision plans explaining what hyper globalisers, globalisation sceptics and transformationalists believe. Then add the evidence they use to support their explanations, and explain which theory you find most convincing.

Exam skills

Determining factors

+ When answering essay questions (30 marks) on globalisation, it can be helpful to contextualise your response within the globalisation sceptic/hyper globaliser/ transformationalist debate.
+ In essays, continually judge the extent to which the impact of economic, political and cultural globalisation has been positive or negative.
+ Remember to evaluate the effect of globalisation by considering its impact on poverty, conflict, human rights and the environment.

Exam practice

1 Examine the main ways in which economic globalisation and cultural globalisation impact on nation states. (12 marks)

2 Examine the impact of globalisation on the environment and human rights. (12 marks)

3 Evaluate the view that economic globalisation has had a more positive impact on the developing world than political globalisation. (30 marks)

4 Evaluate the view that the impact of globalisation on the sovereignty of nation states has been much exaggerated. (30 marks)

19 Global governance: political and economic

Since nation states possess sovereignty there is no supranational authority (power above the nation state) to compel their obedience. Therefore, global relations are anarchic because nation states cannot be compelled by a higher body to act in a particular way.

However, this does not mean that international relations are simply a Hobbesian 'war of all against all'. This is because nation states have established intergovernmental organisations (IGOs) to bring some order and stability to international relations.

19.1 Political

United Nations

REVISED

The United Nations (UN) is the world's biggest and most influential IGO with 193 member states (2023). It was founded at the end of the Second World War (1945) to encourage dialogue, goodwill and understanding between its members and to promote development and respect for human rights.

> **United Nations** The world's biggest IGO with 193 member states, focusing on peace, security and development.

The 1945 Charter

All members of the UN are bound by its Charter. This commits nation states:
+ 'To practice tolerance and live together in peace with one another as good neighbours'.
+ 'To unite our strength to maintain international peace and security'.
+ 'To employ international machinery for the promotion of the economic and social advancement of all peoples'.

However, such liberal attempts to build a global community are balanced in the Charter by the realist acknowledgement that nation states still possess sovereignty.

The UN is based on the principle of the sovereign equality of all its members (UN Charter, Article 1, Chapter 2). This, of course, significantly limits the authority of the UN, since its Charter recognises the sovereign independence of states.

Role and significance of the UN

Security Council

The Security Council is the UN's most important body, since it decides on the action necessary to protect international peace and security. Chapter 7 of the UN Charter allows the Security Council to 'determine the existence of any threat to the peace, breach of the peace, or act of aggression'. If economic and diplomatic pressure is insufficient, then the Security Council may 'take such action by air, sea, or land forces as may be necessary to maintain or restore international peace and security'.
+ The five permanent members of the Security Council are the US, the UK, Russia, China and France. They are joined by ten non-permanent members, which are elected by the General Assembly and serve for two years.
+ For a UN resolution to pass, a minimum of nine of the 15 states on the Security Council must support it. However, the five permanent members possess a veto which means that they can stop resolutions which they disagree with. Therefore, the Security Council often fails to agree resolutions to resolve international threats to peace because a resolution conflicts with the strategic interests of the 'Permanent Five', which thus

> **Security Council** The UN's most powerful body. Its five permanent and ten non-permanent members decide on matters connected with international peace and security.

choose to veto it. The Security Council can also be slow to react. For example, it failed to act quickly enough over Rwanda in 1994, allowing genocide to take place as 800,000 Tutsi were murdered by the Hutu.

+ Since the geo-strategic interests of the Permanent Five are so often in conflict, with Russia and China pitted against the US, France and the UK, it is increasingly difficult to obtain agreement to use Chapter 7. The UN also does not have its own standing army, which further limits the effectiveness of interventions since the deployment of necessary force is unlikely to be immediate.

+ The Security Council has authorised several important peace-keeping operations, including a UN mission to restore stability in East Timor as it transitioned to independence from Indonesia in 1999. In 2023, 12 UN peace-keeping missions were in operation. The biggest was in South Sudan where 17,000 UN personnel were attempting to stop ethnic violence and provide humanitarian relief to 7.8 million people facing famine or acute malnutrition.

Examples of UN action and the strengths and weaknesses of the UN Security Council are summarised in Tables 19.1 and 19.2.

Table 19.1 Examples of UN action and inaction

Following Iraq's invasion of Kuwait (1990), the Security Council passed UN Resolution 678, which authorised the UN to use 'all necessary means' to liberate Kuwait.
As a result of Sudan's policy of ethnic cleansing in Darfur, UN resolution 1590 (2005) authorised a UN mission to protect the population and provide emergency relief.
In 2022, a UN resolution called upon Myanmar's military junta to take 'concrete and immediate actions' to end violence and re-establish democracy. However, no reference was made to the use of military intervention, since Russia and China would have vetoed this.
In 2022, Russia vetoed a Security Council resolution condemning its annexation of four regions of Ukraine as a 'threat to international peace and security'.

Table 19.2 Security Council: strengths and weaknesses

Strengths	Weaknesses
+ The Permanent Five's veto power means that military action can only take place when there is full agreement. + This means that UN peace-keeping and peace-making missions possess strong legitimacy. + If majority voting were introduced on the Security Council, this could allow interventions which major powers disagreed with, massively increasing tension between them. + All member states of the UN can be elected to the Security Council as non-permanent members for two years, 'Due regard being specially paid, in the first instance to the contribution of Members of the United Nations to the maintenance of international peace and security and to the other purposes of the Organization' (UN Charter, Chapter 5).	+ The veto power of the Permanent Five gives them disproportionate influence and means intervention cannot occur against their will. + From 1945 to February 2023, the Soviet Union/Russia had vetoed 152 resolutions and the US 87. The Security Council has therefore often been unable to act. + France and the UK no longer have the global influence they had in 1945, so their permanent status is now controversial. + Despite the global balance of power shifting away from the West, three of the Permanent Five are western powers. + China is the only emerging/Asian power on the Security Council. + No African power has permanent status, even though most peace-keeping missions have occurred in Africa.

Now test yourself

TESTED

1 List the five permanent members of the Security Council.
2 What is the significance of Chapter 7 of the UN Charter?
3 Why is the veto power of the Permanent Five so significant?

General Assembly

The General Assembly:

+ consists of all 193 members of the UN, which have equal representation
+ votes on the Secretary General and the ten non-permanent members of the Security Council; it also determines the UN budget
+ is responsible for annually electing the Economic and Social Council (ECOSOC) of 54 member states for three-year terms
+ has endorsed milestone decisions like the UN Declaration of Human Rights (1948) and the Millennium (2000–15) and Sustainable (2015–30) Development Goals
+ provides a global forum to debate pressing international issues

Although they are non-binding, recommendations by the General Assembly provide an important way of establishing an international consensus on demanding global issues, such as combating climate change. The General Assembly has ensured that this has become an issue of global significance. Every September, world leaders address the General Assembly on the most urgent issues facing the world.

Table 19.3 summarises the strengths and weaknesses of the General Assembly.

Table 19.3 General Assembly: strengths and weaknesses

Strengths	Weaknesses
+ The UN General Assembly is the only body in which all nation states are equally represented. + Its debates can achieve a global consensus for action on issues such as climate change. + It can be addressed by globally influential people like Greta Thunberg (2019), contributing to a global debate on vital issues. + The UN Secretary General's annual address to the UN focuses attention on the world's most urgent priorities.	+ Since all nation states are represented in the General Assembly, consensus can only rarely be achieved. + Recommendations by the UN General Assembly lack coercive power, leading to claims that it is irrelevant. + Critics claim that the General Assembly can be used for partisan/one-sided political purposes. + For example, world leaders can use their addresses to the General Assembly to attack their enemies. + In 2018 President Trump used his address to condemn 'globalism'. + In 2022, António Guterres warned that the 'solidarity envisioned in the UN Charter is being devoured by the acids of nationalism and self-interest'.

> **Now test yourself**   TESTED ◯
>
> 4   How many nation states are represented in the UN General Assembly?
> 5   List two strengths and two weaknesses of the UN General Assembly.
> 6   Name the current UN Secretary General.

Economic and Social Council

The Economic and Social Council (ECOSOC) oversees the work of the UN's social and economic development agencies. ECOSOC:

+ coordinates the work of bodies promoting just and sustainable international development, such as the World Health Organization (WHO) and the International Labour Organization (ILO)
+ is reported to by the World Bank and the International Monetary Fund (IMF)
+ has five regional commissions that oversee development in Africa, Europe, Latin America and the Caribbean, Asia and the Pacific, and western Asia

Answers at **www.hoddereducation.co.uk/myrevisionnotesdownloads**

+ coordinates the Sustainable Development Goals (SDGs)
+ 'may make or initiate studies and reports…and may make recommendations' in areas connected with economic and social development, according to the UN Charter
+ has established conferences such as a Development Cooperation Forum and a Youth Forum to drive forward global debate on sustainable development

The strengths and weaknesses of ECOSOC are listed in Table 19.4.

Table 19.4 ESOSOC: strengths and weaknesses

Strengths	Weaknesses
+ ECOSOC provides a global forum to develop policies and programmes for sustainable development. + ECOSOC can initiate debate on challenges to development like the Covid-19 pandemic. + The WHO played a significant role in encouraging immunisation during the Covid-19 pandemic. + ECOSOC consults widely with **non-governmental organisations** (NGOs) to develop economic and social policy. + The 54 member states elected to ECOSOC provide a fair geographical balance of influence.	+ ECOSOC's powers are limited since, although organisations like the WHO report to it, they are not accountable to it. + The World Bank and the IMF report to ECOSOC, but ECOSOC has no operational influence over them. + ECOSOC reports are simply advisory. + ECOSOC's SDGs have no enforcement power to make nation states achieve them. + Confusingly, developmental agencies like the World Food Programme and the UN Development Programme report to the UN General Assembly not to ECOSOC.

Non-governmental organisations Non-profit-seeking bodies which seek to influence global politics, aiming to advance economic, social and political causes that empower individuals and communities.

International Court of Justice

+ The International Court of Justice (ICJ) was established in 1945 by the UN. Sometimes known as the World Court, the ICJ judges disputes involving nation states. Cases brought by nation states against each other are known as 'contentious cases'. ICJ judgements in contentious cases are binding on nation states. However, since nation states are sovereign and the ICJ lacks coercive power, it must rely upon the cooperation of member states for its judgements to be enforced.
+ The ICJ also provides advisory opinions. These can be requested by other UN bodies, most usually the General Assembly. Although non-binding, ICJ advisory opinions are significant because they represent the 'authority and prestige' of the UN.

The strengths and weaknesses of the ICJ are listed in Table 19.5.

Table 19.5 ICJ: strengths and weaknesses

Strengths	Weaknesses
+ As the legal arm of the UN, the ICJ enjoys strong legitimacy. + ICJ judgements can be followed by nation states which understand the value of upholding international law even at the expense of national self-interest. + ICJ judgements are important in expressing and developing global rules and setting international standards for future behaviour.	+ The ICJ cannot initiate cases and so lacks proactive influence. + Its judgements require consent to be upheld. It therefore lacks compulsory power. + Only 73 of the 193 member states of the UN (2023) recognise the compulsory jurisdiction of the court, agreeing beforehand to be bound by its judgements.

The effectiveness of the ICJ is covered further in Chapter 20.

179

TESTED ◯

7 What is the role of ECOSOC?

8 Distinguish between ICJ judgements in contentious cases and ICJ advisory opinions.

9 List a strength and a weakness of the ICJ.

North Atlantic Treaty Organisation

REVISED ◯

NATO and the Cold War

The North Atlantic Treaty Organisation (NATO) was created in 1949 during the Cold War to deter further Soviet expansion.

Article 5 of the NATO Treaty commits member states to the principle that 'An armed attack against one or more of them in Europe or North America shall be considered an attack against them all.' This is known as collective security and is designed to discourage a potential aggressor from risking war with any NATO member for fear of an overwhelming joint response.

From 1949 to 1991, NATO provided the basis for western defence against the Soviet Union.

In 1955, the Warsaw Pact was created, which pitted communist eastern European states led by the Soviet Union against NATO countries led by the US.

> **North Atlantic Treaty Organisation** A defensive military alliance which protects its members on the principle of collective security.

The changing role of NATO since the end of the Cold War

When the Warsaw Pact was dissolved and the Soviet Union collapsed in 1991, some critics suggested that NATO was no longer necessary. However, NATO did not disband. Instead, it developed beyond its defensive origins to engage in peace-making and nation-building operations in the Balkans. Its changing role is outlined in Figure 19.1

1995	Following the Srebrenica massacre, NATO launched the Operation Deliberate Force air campaign against the Bosnian Serbs. Subsequently, NATO peace-keeping forces helped stabilise Bosnia.
1999	NATO carried out a 78-day bombing campaign against Serbia to stop its policy of ethnic cleansing in Kosovo. When Serbia withdrew its forces, NATO forces (KFOR) replaced them. In 2023, KFOR was still engaged in supporting 'the development of a stable, democratic, multi-ethnic and peaceful Kosovo'. Czech Republic, Poland and Hungary joined NATO.
2001	When the September 11 terrorist attacks on the US occurred, Article 5 was invoked for the first time as US forces targeted al Qaeda bases in Afghanistan.
2003–21	From 2003 to 2014, NATO members participated in NATO's International Security Assistance Force in Afghanistan. From 2015 to 2021, NATO members engaged in the Resolute Support Mission supporting the Afghan government against terrorism and insurgency.
2004	Bulgaria, Estonia, Latvia, Lithuania, Slovakia and Slovenia joined NATO.
2009	Albania and Croatia joined NATO.
2011	NATO intervened in the Libyan civil war. Although mandated by UN resolution 1973 to protect civilians, it went beyond this by helping topple the Gaddafi regime.
2017	Montenegro joined NATO.
2020	North Macedonia joined NATO.
2023	Finland joined NATO. Sweden's membership is anticipated.

Figure 19.1 The changing role of NATO

TESTED ⬤

10 Define 'collective security'.

11 List three NATO peace-keeping operations.

12 How many members does NATO currently have?

The expansion of NATO, 1999–2023

Since the end of the Cold War, NATO has steadily expanded eastwards and into the Balkans. New states have joined to enhance their security through the principle of collective security.

✚ NATO expansion has been controversial. Despite new members exercising their sovereign right to determine their own defence policy, Russia has claimed that NATO expansion has been directed against Russia and that, far from being defensive, NATO has expanded western influence into the Balkans at Russia's expense.

✚ Russia has asserted that NATO's eastwards expansion threatens Russia's vital security interests. This is because countries which were once in the Soviet Union (Latvia, Lithuania, Estonia) or the Warsaw Pact (Poland, Czech Republic, Slovakia, Hungary, Bulgaria and Romania) are now allied with the US in NATO.

✚ A major reason why Russia annexed Crimea from Ukraine in 2014 and invaded Ukraine in 2022 was therefore to reassert its influence abroad and forestall any possible attempt by Ukraine to join NATO.

✚ In his speech in February 2022, justifying the invasion of Ukraine, President Putin warned, 'As NATO expands to the east, with every passing year, the situation for our country is getting worse and more dangerous.'

✚ However, supporters of NATO expansion respond that, far from being provocative, this has provided fledgling democracies with vital protection against Russian attempts to re-establish regional hegemony.

✚ In 2022, because of the Russian invasion of Ukraine, Finland and Sweden formally applied for NATO membership. Bosnia and Herzegovina, Georgia and Ukraine have also expressed a desire to join NATO.

Back to basics?

Although NATO acted significantly 'out of area' after the Cold War, by 2023 NATO had returned to its original purpose of protecting its members against threats from authoritarian states.

At the Madrid summit (2022), NATO Secretary General Jens Stoltenberg stated that 'Moscow and Beijing are openly contesting the rules-based international order' and so argued that NATO must 'strengthen our Alliance and keep it agile in this more dangerous world'.

The strengths and weaknesses of NATO are listed in Table 19.6.

Table 19.6 NATO: strengths and weaknesses

Strengths	Weaknesses
✚ NATO is the most powerful military alliance in the world. The number of members spending 2% or more of gross domestic product (GDP) on defence increased from three in 2014 to ten in 2023, further strengthening its power and cohesion. ✚ NATO had the military strength to carry out successful nation-building missions in Bosnia and Kosovo. ✚ By 2023 NATO had expanded to 31 members, extending collective security to potentially vulnerable states. ✚ If Hungary and Turkey were not in NATO, this would provide a major geo-strategic challenge to western interests.	✚ Most NATO members fail to fulfil their commitment to spend 2% of their GDP to defence. ✚ It can be difficult ensuring unity in such a large military alliance. NATO intervention in Afghanistan divided the alliance. Hungary (a NATO member) has blocked closer NATO cooperation with Ukraine. ✚ NATO expansion eastwards and in the Balkans has reignited Cold War tensions, destabilising Europe. ✚ NATO members should commit to democracy, but there are concerns that Hungary and Turkey are increasingly authoritarian and insufficiently committed to this requirement.

181

Now test yourself   TESTED ●

13 List the countries which have joined NATO since 1999.

14 What percentage of their GDP should NATO members spend on defence?

15 How many currently reach this target?

19.2 Economic

The aim of economic global governance is to encourage global economic stability and foster development. Central to economic global governance are the International Monetary Fund, the World Bank and the World Trade Organization. Collectively known as the Bretton Woods institutions, they originate from the Bretton Woods conference in 1944. This provided mechanisms to encourage global financial certainty and promoted free trade between states as the most effective way of encouraging economic development and cooperation.

International Monetary Fund

REVISED ●

The International Monetary Fund (IMF) was established in 1944 at the Bretton Woods Conference. In 2023, 190 nation states were members of the IMF, which seeks to promote international financial stability in three main ways:

+ **Surveillance:** The IMF monitors global economic conditions and warns of the potential for risk from the economic policies being carried out by its member states. In 2022, the IMF cautioned that the Truss government's proposed tax cuts and increased borrowing would increase inflation.

+ **Lending:** The IMF is a 'lender of last resort'. This means that if any member state is in such economic difficulty that it cannot pay for its imports or pay off its debts (a balance of payments crisis), the IMF will lend it the necessary funds in special drawing rights. In return for loans, recipient countries will generally be expected to introduce IMF-endorsed structural adjustment programmes (SAPs). The knowledge that the IMF can be relied on to save national economies from collapse provides vital reassurance to the global economy.

    + During the global economic crises caused by the collapse of Lehman Brothers (2008) and the Covid-19 pandemic (2020–), IMF loans ensured that nation states could carry on trading.

    + From 2020 to 2022, the IMF made available $650 billion to member states to cushion them from the worst effects of the pandemic.

+ **Capacity development:** The IMF provides knowledge assistance to countries. For example, it provides advice on how to introduce the free market and reform fiscal policy (public spending and taxation).

A number of criticisms are made of the IMF:

+ The IMF is controversial because critics claim that it is too ideologically committed to the free market (economic liberalism/the Washington Consensus).

+ Following the east Asian financial crisis (1997), South Korea and Thailand underwent free market structural adjustment programmes but recovered more slowly than Malaysia, which refused an IMF loan.

+ Its managing director is traditionally European (Kristalina Georgieva since 2019) and the US has 16.5% of the votes in its board of directors, leading to claims that it is not sufficiently responsive to the needs of the developing world.

+ IMF surveillance has often failed to warn against impending crises like the east Asian financial crisis (1997) and the financial crisis provoked by the collapse of Lehman Brothers investment bank (2008).

International Monetary Fund A major financial institution based in Washington DC. Its purpose is to encourage global financial stability among its 190 member states (2023) by providing technical advice, warning of potential financial crises and acting as lender of last resort.

Structural adjustment programmes Free market policies including privatisation, trade liberalisation and high interest rates, often required by the IMF and World Bank as a condition of their loans.

The IMF's strengths and weaknesses are summarised in Table 19.7.

Table 19.7 IMF: strengths and weaknesses

Strengths	Weaknesses
+ As a lender of last resort, the IMF provides the global economy with greater stability. + Although free market reforms are controversial, they are necessary. + Member states like India, which have carried out IMF free market structural reform programmes, have been better able to exploit the opportunities of economic globalisation. + The IMF is flexible in its response to global financial crises and challenges. Since 2005, it has supported debt relief in the world's poorest countries via initiatives such as the Heavily Indebted Poor Countries Initiative (HIPC). + The IMF is increasingly focused on social, political and environmental issues. + The IMF is committed to the UN's SDGs and promotes inclusive development policies. + For example, the IMF is advising India on how it can combine economic growth with reducing its carbon emissions. + The IMF provides regular financial/political updates. In 2023, the IMF noted that it was 'concerned about recent developments in Tunisia' as its government became more authoritarian and threatened civil liberties.	+ SAPs are a form of 'shock therapy' which can damage vulnerable economies. + Too often the IMF is not aware of the social and political consequences of its economic policies. + The cuts in public spending (austerity) required by SAPs can have a devastating impact on social welfare and human capital. + They are especially damaging in the developing world. According to the economist Jeffrey Sachs, cuts in public spending represents 'belt-tightening for people who cannot afford belts'. + IMF loans to Sudan have meant the removal of government fuel subsidies, despite almost half the population living in poverty. Critics suggest this has encouraged political instability. + The dramatic public spending cuts the IMF required in Greece following the Eurozone crisis increased poverty and encouraged the rise of political extremism.

World Bank

REVISED ●

The World Bank also dates from the Bretton Woods conference in 1944. Whereas the IMF concentrates on sudden shocks to the global financial system, the World Bank focuses on long-term development.

Like the IMF, the World Bank generally requires countries to undergo free market SAPs in return for loans. This is known as conditionality. It has been accused of a free market western bias because its President is by convention American, and the US has most voting power (9.86%).

However, its supporters respond that as well as encouraging free market reforms, the World Bank has become increasingly committed to sustainable development, debt relief and gender equality, while its community-based projects empower people by making them accountable for the support they receive. The strengths and weaknesses of the World Bank are summarised in Table 19.8.

Table 19.8 World Bank: strengths and weaknesses

Strengths	Weaknesses
+ Evidence suggests that free market reforms can enable developing countries to utilise the opportunities offered by globalisation. + By cutting excessive government spending and reducing debt, developing countries attract foreign investment. + Since 1999, the Comprehensive Development Programme has placed a greater emphasis on human development. This has led to a greater focus on community-based projects, lessening corruption which is a major barrier to growth. + The Accelerate Equality Initiative demonstrates the World Bank's commitment to advancing gender equality in the developing world. + World Bank infrastructure projects are required to be 'inclusive and sustainable'. + The World Bank encourages developing states to expand digital technology so they can better connect with the global economy. + Like the IMF, the World Bank supports the HIPC Initiative. + During the Covid-19 pandemic the World Bank provided emergency funds to developing countries to distribute vaccines and protect jobs.	+ SAPs impose inappropriate free market reforms on developing countries. + The structural dominance of the US in the World Bank means that it is ideologically committed to economic liberalism. + Cuts in public spending impact most on the poorest who rely on welfare, which is morally unacceptable. + Reductions in health and education spending undermine human capital, which is essential to economic growth. + According to world systems theory, by abandoning tariffs, developing countries become dependent on cheap imports from the developed world, so stopping their industrialisation.

16 What are the Bretton Woods institutions?

17 Define 'structural adjustment programmes'.

18 What is the significance of conditionality?

Exam tip

Remember that although they both impose SAPs, the IMF and World Bank possess different priorities.

World Trade Organization

REVISED ⬤

Although the World Trade Organization (WTO) was created in 1995, it is still referred to as a Bretton Woods institution. The successor to the General Agreement on Trade and Tariffs (GATT, 1947), the WTO is committed to multilateralism and encourages free trade between its 164 member states (2023).

World Trade Organization
An international body established in 1995 to encourage free trade between its members and resolve trade disputes.

+ WTO trade rounds are designed to liberalise trade in specific areas. For example, the Doha trade round (2001) attempted to open markets in the developed world to products from the developing world.

+ However, the Doha trade round collapsed because it was impossible to achieve consensus between developed and developing countries.

+ The Appellate Body is the WTO's final court of appeal and has final authority in arbitrating trade disputes between member states to stop them becoming trade wars.

+ For example, in 2015, China accepted a WTO ruling that its restrictions on the export of rare earth metals were illegal. Since China dominates this market and such metals are vital in the manufacture of mobile phones, the judgement was highly significant.

+ In 2021, Ngozi Okonjo-Iweala became the first WTO Director General from the developing world.

The strengths and weaknesses of the WTO are listed in Table 19.9.

Table 19.9 WTO: strengths and weaknesses

Strengths	Weaknesses
+ The WTO provides equal influence for all members, making it the most democratic institution of economic global governance. + Unlike the IMF and the World Bank, there is no expectation that the Director General should be from the developed world. + The WTO has resolved complex trade disputes between member states, encouraging a rules-based approach to global trade. + For example, the WTO has ruled that the US has illegally subsidised Boeing, while EU subsidies to Airbus have broken international trade rules. In 2021, both sides agreed to remove $11.5 billion worth of tariffs which they had imposed on each other in retaliation. + According to the WTO, if member states believe 'fellow-members are violating trade rules, they will use the multilateral system of settling disputes instead of taking action unilaterally'. + If states have not established their own individual free trade agreements, they will trade under WTO Most Favoured Nation terms. In 2021 these had been lowered to on average 9%, so facilitating global free trade.	+ WTO trade rounds require unanimity to be successful. The principle of 'nothing is agreed until everything is agreed' makes decision-making difficult. + 'Our consensus decision-making approach, while democratic and egalitarian…often leads to gridlock since just one member can hold up what might be a good agreement supported by many' (Ngozi Okonjo-Iweala). + Although the WTO is based on democratic consent, powerful member states can afford permanent representation at Geneva, giving them undue advantage in negotiations. + Regional organisations and nation states therefore often prefer making trade deals outside the WTO. + The WTO's focus on free trade means that it ignores the importance of labour rights, sustainable development and environmental protection. + Since 2019, the Appellate Court has not functioned because the US has blocked the appointment of new judges. + Member states can ignore WTO arbitration and still engage in trade wars.

19 List two strengths and two weaknesses of the World Bank.

20 List two strengths and two weaknesses of the IMF.

21 What is the purpose of the WTO?

Answers at **www.hoddereducation.co.uk/myrevisionnotesdownloads**

Group of Seven

Established in 1976, the Group of Seven (G7) is an informal forum for the most advanced democratic economies in the developed world to consult regularly. Its membership consists of the UK, the US, Canada, France, Germany, Italy, Japan and the EU. From 1997 to 2014 it was known as the G8 when Russia was a member, but it reverted to the G7 when Russia was expelled following the annexation of Crimea.

+ Although the EU is a full member, it does not host meetings.
+ Originally the G7 focused on economic issues, but it now consults on any issue of pressing concern. Therefore, recent meetings of the G7 have deliberated over a collective response to climate change, the Covid-19 pandemic and the Russian invasion of Ukraine.
+ The G7 does not make binding decisions. However, its meetings do enable the leaders of the Global North to discuss issues of mutual concern and work towards collective responses.
+ At the conclusion of a G7 summit, a joint communiqué will thus be released, establishing areas of agreement between its members and the policies which they collectively agree to follow.
+ For example, one of the agreements reached by the G7 at Hiroshima (2023) was that members would 'support a free and open Indo-Pacific and oppose any unilateral attempts to change the status quo by force or coercion'.

The strengths and weaknesses of the G7 are summarised in Table 19.10.

> **Group of Seven** An informal intergovernmental organisation which enables the leaders of the biggest democratic economies in the developed world to consult regularly on world issues.

Table 19.10 G7: strengths and weaknesses

Strengths	Weaknesses
+ The G7 provides the leaders of the Global North with an important opportunity to meet regularly to formulate collective responses to global problems. + Since the Global North represents the world's most economically developed liberal democracies, it is essential that its leaders are closely in touch. + G7 meetings have achieved significant agreement on how critical world challenges should be faced. + For example, in 2021 G7 finance ministers agreed to minimum 15% corporation tax levels to ensure that MNCs pay adequate tax.	+ By representing the biggest economies in the Global North and not the Global South, the G7 perpetuates structural imbalances in global politics. The G20 (see below) therefore provides a much less elitist forum for discussion between the world's biggest economies. + The existence of the G20 means that the G7 is no longer required, especially as the G7 encourages resentment from the developing world. + G7 communiqués generally provide statements of intent and are not enforceable. Therefore, their impact is limited as they have no legal status.

Group of Twenty

Established in 1999, the Group of Twenty (G20) brings together the leaders of the biggest economies in the Global North and the Global South for regular conferences to try to establish a shared response to global challenges. Since it includes major developing countries in the Global South like China, India, Brazil, Argentina and Indonesia, the G20 can claim enhanced legitimacy as a forum for international debate.

+ Members of the G20 are: Argentina, Australia, Brazil, Canada, China, the EU, France, Germany, India, Indonesia, Italy, Japan, Mexico, Russia, Saudi Arabia, South Africa, South Korea, Turkey, the UK and the US.
+ Like the G7, the G20 issues non-binding communiqués (areas of agreement) at the conclusion of its annual conferences. Since the interests of its members are often so different, critics claim that to achieve consensus the resulting communiqués are so generalised as to be valueless.
+ However, given the geo-strategic and economic differences between so many members of the G20, its supporters counter that it provides a regular and important forum at which issues of mutual concern can be discussed and areas of suspicion and hostility be addressed.

> **Group of Twenty** An informal intergovernmental organisation which brings together the leaders of the world's biggest economies for regular consultation.

The strengths and weaknesses of the G20 are outlined in Table 19.11.

Table 19.11 G20: strengths and weaknesses

Strengths	Weaknesses
+ The G20 is a much less elitist organisation than the G7. Its members represent 85% of global GDP, providing it with greater legitimacy than the G7. + During global crises it can provide vital leadership. + For example, at the London G20 meeting (2009), members agreed not to raise tariffs following the 2008 banking crisis. This stopped trade wars breaking out and facilitated the global recovery. + Its annual meetings provide a vital opportunity for emerging powers like Turkey, Mexico and Indonesia to make their views known. + Growing hostility between several members of the G20 makes these opportunities for face-to-face meetings increasingly important.	+ As in the G7, G20 communiqués are non-binding and so rarely have a meaningful impact. + Since all member states need to agree to the summits' communiqués, they are often bland. + Significant differences over responses to climate change, the Russian invasion of the Ukraine and US/Chinese geo-strategic rivalry have made consensus even more difficult to achieve. + For example, the G20 meeting at Bali (2022) could not agree a collective response to the Russian invasion of Ukraine, simply acknowledging 'that security issues can have significant consequences for the global economy'.

Now test yourself TESTED ⬤

22 What is the main difference between the memberships of the G7 and the G20?

23 List two successes and two weaknesses of the G7.

24 List two successes and two weaknesses of the G20.

Exam tip

Update your notes with the most recent G7 and G20 summits.

How effectively does global economic governance deal with the issue of poverty?

REVISED ⬤

Orthodox and alternative measurements of poverty

The orthodox measurement of poverty and its alleviation focuses on how many people have been lifted out of extreme poverty (wages of less than $1.90 a day). This measurement prioritises the growth of GDP as the best way of determining poverty reduction.

The alternative measurement of poverty approaches the issue from more than just an economic angle. Instead, it focuses on other important indicators such as access to health and education, human rights protection, gender equality and environmental protection.

The North–South divide

The principle of the North–South divide derives from the Brandt Report (1980). In this report the former West German chancellor, Willy Brandt, referred to the Global North as the developed world and the Global South as the developing world.

According to the Brandt Report, the Global North is defined by greater wealth and industrialisation whereas the Global South is much poorer, primarily focusing on the export of agricultural and raw materials. The financial sector, innovation and investment have also been more advanced in the Global North than in the Global South and overseas aid travels from the richer North to the poorer South.

'The Brandt Line' divides the world into the Global North and the Global South. The North–South divide is a political rather than a geographical line because some countries which are geographically in the Global South, such as Australia and New Zealand, are counted as Global North. According to some critics the term has also lost its meaning since several countries in the Global South, such as China and India, are now challenging the Global North in terms of wealth, industrialisation, enterprise, and innovation.

North–South divide The concept that there is a significant gap in wealth and development between the industrialised Global North and more agricultural Global South. It is a political rather than a geographical term.

Answers at **www.hoddereducation.co.uk/myrevisionnotesdownloads**

TESTED

25 What is the orthodox measurement of poverty?

26 What is the alternative measurement of poverty?

27 Define the North–South divide.

Classical economic development theory

Classical economic development theory is based on the principle that free markets and free trade maximise global trade and investment, therefore creating greater global wealth and opportunity. In contrast, tariffs and subsidies limit global trade, drive up domestic prices and, by discouraging competition, reward inefficiency.

Free trade thus enables nation states to export commodities in which they enjoy a 'comparative advantage' and to import cheap products from other nation states, maximising their own comparative advantage. As economist Milton Friedman put it, 'the most important central single fact about a free market is that no exchange takes place unless both parties benefit'.

Examples of the positive impact of classical economic development theory are:
+ From 1980 to 2022, China lifted 770 million people out of poverty, utilising its cheap labour force in manufacturing for world markets.
+ More advanced economies like Germany benefit from low-cost manufactured products from China, while maximising their own comparative advantage in motor vehicles, chemicals and machinery.

World systems/dependency theory

Critics of classical economic theory argue that, rather than providing worldwide opportunities for economic progress, it reinforces existing structural inequalities in economic power.

According to world systems/dependency theory, free trade enables the Global North to sell cheap products to the Global South. Developing countries then become dependent on these imported goods and so have no incentive to industrialise themselves. Additionally, MNCs in the developed world exploit the raw materials and cheap labour of the developing world, further reinforcing the Global North's dominant economic status.

In world systems/dependency theory, Global North countries are referred to as 'core' states and Global South countries as 'peripheral'. Some critics have even suggested that these structural inequalities are a form of neo-colonialism whereby powerful states continue to exercise control over less powerful states through economic rather than political means.

> **World systems/ dependency theory** This suggests that economic liberalism makes developing countries reliant on cheap imports from the developed world, so they never break free from a state of neo-colonial dependency.

TESTED

28 What is classical economic development theory?

29 According to world systems theory, how does free trade encourage dependency?

30 Define 'neo-colonialism'.

Role of global political and economic governance in resolving contemporary issues

REVISED

The following box (over the page) debates the extent to which global economic governance has been successful, while Table 19.12 considers the significance of global political and economic governance in resolving issues involving conflict, poverty, human rights and the environment.

Is global economic governance a success?

Yes	No
+ The IMF is an indispensable 'lender of last resort' during global economic crises. + In 2023, Sri Lanka received a $2.9 billion loan to stop it defaulting on its debts. + The IMF and World Bank provide specialist advice on how countries can develop their economic potential. + The World Bank is increasingly focused on community-based projects and sustainable development. + The WTO has resolved significant trade disputes. + The WTO, unlike the IMF and the World Bank, provides equal representation for developing and developed states. + World trade has increased dramatically because of the commitment of GATT (1947) and the WTO (1995) to free trade. + The increase in global trade has strikingly reduced global poverty, leading to growing convergence between the Global North and the Global South.	+ The US wields too much influence on the World Bank and the IMF. + World Bank and IMF SAPs impose inappropriate free market reforms on the developing world. + The IMF has often failed in surveillance, not alerting the world to impending financial crises. + The WTO does not protect workers' rights or the environment. + Divisions in the WTO between the developed and developing world make trade agreements difficult, as the failure of the Doha round illustrates. + Since 2019, the WTO's appellate court has not functioned, undermining the WTO's conflict resolution role. + Nation states can negotiate trade deals between themselves without going through the WTO.

Table 19.12 Role and significance of political and economic global governance in resolving issues involving conflict, poverty, human rights and the environment

Conflict	+ The UN has mandated peace-keeping missions in East Timor, the Democratic Republic of the Congo and Darfur. + However, the Permanent Five's veto on the Security Council means that conflict resolution often fails to happen. + Peace-keeping missions are often under-resourced (Rwanda, Libya). + In 2022, Russia ignored an ICJ judgement that it should immediately suspend military operations in Ukraine. + Russia has ignored condemnation at the General Assembly for its invasion of Ukraine and subsequent annexation of four regions of Ukraine.
Poverty	+ The Millennium Development Goals (2000–15) and Sustainable Development Goals (2015–) have provided a coordinated approach to poverty reduction. + UN aid agencies like the World Health Organization (WHO), the World Food Programme (WFP) and the UN Development Programme (UNDP) provide essential aid. + However, blurred accountability between ECOSOC and the General Assembly leads to unnecessary overlap and confusion. + IMF and World Bank SAPs have been criticised for negatively impacting on the poorest most. + In 2021, Kenya received a $2.3 billion loan from the IMF on the condition that it freeze public sector wages and increase food taxes. + From 1950 to 2021, encouraged by GATT and the WTO, the value of world trade increased by 347 times, significantly reducing poverty. + From 1995 (when the WTO was established) to 2021, the value of world trade increased by 6%. + In 2022, the G7 summit at Schloss Elmau agreed the Partnership for Global Infrastructure and Investment, which will provide $600 billion of funding for the developing world.
Human rights	+ The UN Declaration of Human Rights provides an international standard for human rights protection. + The Office of the UN High Commissioner for Human Rights highlights human rights abuses. + A General Assembly resolution condemning the UK's continued control of the Chagos Islands by 116 votes to 6 has encouraged the UK to negotiate over their sovereignty. + However, since member states are sovereign, the UN is unable to enforce human rights. + In 2022 Israel strongly condemned the General Assembly's request for a judgement on the legality of Israel's control of the Occupied Territories as politically motivated. + Although a UN resolution (80/29) criticising Iran's treatment of minorities was passed in 2022, it has had no impact on Iran's domestic politics.
The environment	+ UN Conference of the Parties (COP) meetings provide a unique forum for the world to address climate change. + However, the UN cannot impose mandatory cuts on member states' carbon emissions. + At the Carbis Bay summit (2021), the G7 committed to action to keep the global temperature rise to no more than 1.5°C. However, this is a statement of intent and is not mandatory. + In 2022, the World Bank was still spending £15 billion on fossil fuel projects despite COP26 (Glasgow) agreeing to 'phase down' coal use in 2021.

Answers at **www.hoddereducation.co.uk/myrevisionnotesdownloads**

Role of NGOs in resolving contemporary issues

Table 19.13 summarises the role of NGOs in resolving contemporary issues involving conflict, poverty, human rights and the environment.

Table 19.13 The role of NGOs in resolving issues in global civil society

Conflict	
	+ Several NGOs are involved in the peaceful resolution of conflicts.
	+ Accord is an NGO encouraging 'the constructive resolution of disputes, by the peoples of Africa'.
	+ The Berghof Foundation encourages dialogue between opposing groups to develop areas of mutual understanding.
Poverty	+ International foundations like the Gates, Carter and Clinton Foundations encourage overseas development.
	+ NGOs like Oxfam and the Red Cross support long-term development projects and provide emergency relief during crises.
	+ The actor Ben Affleck has established the Eastern Congo Initiative to support 'health, freedom and prosperity' in a notoriously troubled region.
Human rights	+ International pressure groups like Amnesty International, Human Rights Watch and Global Rights expose human rights abuses and press for action.
	+ Global celebrities can advocate for change. The Clooney Foundation for Justice was established by the actor George Clooney to make states more accountable for human rights abuses.
	+ Malala Yousafzai, who was almost killed by the Taliban, has established the Malala Fund to advance girls' education.
The environment	+ NGOs such as Greenpeace and Friends of the Earth create pressure for environmental action.
	+ The internet provides greater opportunities for global opinion-formers like the broadcaster and naturalist David Attenborough to press for faster action on climate change.
	+ The Earthshot Prize encourages global engagement with sustainable development.
	+ Actor Leonardo DiCaprio has established the Leonardo DiCaprio Foundation to preserve endangered wild places.

Case study

Globalisation and income inequality

As a result of the developing world being able to utilise its low-paid workforce in cheap global manufacturing, its growth rates have dramatically increased. In 2023, three of the ten biggest economies were in the developing world: China (2), India (5) and South Korea (10).

However, critics of economic globalisation respond that it has led to greater income inequality. This is measured by the Gini coefficient. The higher this number, the greater the inequality in wealth and so the greater the risk of resentment and social unrest. According to the UN, a score above 0.4 indicates concerning levels of societal income inequality. In 2000, China had a Gini coefficient of 0.41. By 2022 this had risen to 0.47. Significantly, the 20 countries with the highest Gini coefficient were all in the developing world (2023).

This suggests that economic globalisation is not 'raising all boats equally' in developing countries. Whether a growth in income inequality matters divides politicians. When Margaret Thatcher was told by an MP that her policies had made the UK richer but also increased income inequality, she retorted that 'he would rather the poor were poorer provided the rich were less rich'.

Summary

+ The UN was established in 1945 to encourage international peace, stability and development.
+ The UN Security Council consists of five permanent and ten non-permanent members and has the authority to decide on the action necessary to maintain peace and stability.
+ The UN General Assembly represents all UN members and ECOSOC coordinates some of the UN's development programmes.
+ The UN Security Council has been criticised because the Permanent Five possess the veto, which gives them disproportionate influence.
+ The UN General Assembly has been criticised for its lack of coercive power.
+ ECOSOC's effectiveness is undermined by unclear and conflicting jurisdiction.
+ Although known as the World Court, the ICJ's authority is challenged by state sovereignty.
+ NATO was established in 1949 to protect western democracies from the threat of Soviet expansion.
+ Collective security (Article 5) means that an attack on one member will generate a collective NATO response.
+ When the Cold War ended, NATO developed a peace-making and peace-keeping role in the Balkans and beyond.
+ NATO's expansion has contributed to increased tension with Russia. This has contributed to NATO once again focusing on defending its members from potential Russian aggression.
+ The IMF, World Bank and WTO are Bretton Woods institutions which contribute towards global economic governance.
+ The IMF provides loans to countries in emergencies and the World Bank provides loans for long-term development.
+ The WTO encourages free trade between its member states, but its most recent Doha trade round failed.
+ The G7 represents the most powerful democratic economies in the developed world and the G20 the biggest economies in the developed and the developing world.
+ Both meet regularly but have been criticised for not providing resolutions which are binding on their members.

Revision tasks

1 Debate the motion, 'The United Nations is now a failed organisation.'
2 Research the significance of the most recent NATO summit.
3 Produce a diagram highlighting the successes and failures of the IMF, the World Bank and the WTO. Having done this, answer the question 'Is global economic governance working?'
4 Produce brief case studies of economic development in India, China, Nigeria, Ghana, Brazil, Ethiopia, Vietnam and South Korea. Does your evidence suggest that classical development theory works or does it support world systems/dependency theory?

Exam skills

Determining factors

+ Even though you are a political scientist, you need to think like an economist! Therefore, you should thoroughly grasp the meaning of classical economic development theory and world systems/dependency theory.
+ Be clear what you mean by 'economic global governance'.
+ Be prepared to connect the information in this chapter to the previous chapter on globalisation and the following chapter on human rights.
+ You need to understand fully that there are several ways in which the North–South divide is used to explain the differences between the developed world and the developing world.

Exam practice

1 Examine the main differences between classical economic development theory and world systems/dependency theory. (12 marks)
2 Examine the main strengths and weaknesses of the UN Security Council and the General Assembly. (12 marks)
3 Evaluate the view that economic and political globalisation are both equally in retreat. (30 marks)
4 Evaluate the view that NATO now provides a more effective way of maintaining world peace than the UN. (30 marks)

Answers at **www.hoddereducation.co.uk/myrevisionnotesdownloads**

20 Global governance: human rights and the environment

20.1 Human rights

Origins and development of international law and institutions

REVISED

Human rights are the rights which all humans possess by virtue of their shared humanity. Nobody can be denied their human rights. All humans, whatever their race, gender, religion or sexual orientation, possess the same rights. They are therefore referred to as universal human rights.

Philosopher John Locke established the principle of natural rights in his *Second Treatise on Government* (1689), stating that men are 'all free, equal and independent'.

In 1948, these ideas were powerfully enshrined in the UN Declaration of Human Rights, which affirms 'the dignity and worth of the human person' and 'the equal rights of men and women'. The Declaration provides a global standard of human rights protection which all members of the United Nations (UN) should uphold.

Since the Declaration, the protection of human rights has advanced.
+ In 1950, the Council of Europe drew up the European Convention on Human Rights. All members of the Council are bound by its rulings.
+ The UN has adopted conventions clarifying the scope of international human rights law and committing member states to upholding it. These include the 1948 Genocide Convention, which made genocide a crime punishable in international law, the 1979 Convention on the Elimination of All Forms of Discrimination against Women and the 2006 Convention on the Rights of Persons with Disabilities. The position of UN High Commissioner for Human Rights was established in 1993 to monitor human rights violations. The current UN High Commissioner for Human Rights is Volker Türk (2022–), who works closely with the UN's Human Rights Council (2006) in promoting human rights.
+ In 1966, the Universal Declaration of Human Rights was amended to include economic and social rights such as adequate social welfare provision and political rights such as freedom of thought, religion and expression. The resulting International Bill of Human Rights has the force of international law and is binding on all member states of the UN.
+ In 2002, the Rome statute established the International Criminal Court (ICC) to try individuals accused of the most heinous human rights abuses when domestic courts cannot or will not provide justice.

Despite these significant advances, global human rights protection remains very difficult to enforce. There are several reasons for this:
+ Nation states are sovereign. Therefore, their commitment to upholding international human rights law is difficult to enforce. This is especially true of powerful states, which can generally act with impunity. For example, when President George W. Bush was criticised for the US occupation of Iraq, he joked, 'International law?…I better call my lawyer. He didn't bring that up to me.'
+ Nation states often act out of realist self-interest and can approach human rights hypocritically.
+ Critics claim that while the US has been keen to condemn human rights abuses in Iran, it has been much less prepared to hold its ally Saudi Arabia to the same standards.

> **Human rights/universal human rights** These refer to the rights which all human beings enjoy by virtue of their humanity. The same human rights cannot be denied to any member of the human race.
>
> **International law** Law which governs the relationship between nation states. Nation states are expected to obey international law even if it conflicts with their national interests.
>
> **International Criminal Court** Established in 2002, the ICC is a permanent court which tries individuals accused of genocide, crimes against humanity and war crimes.

+ The UN Security Council is the ultimate body which can enforce human rights, but it is too divided to do this. Two of its permanent members have also been accused of significant human rights abuses: Russia (in Ukraine and Syria) and China (in Tibet and claims of genocide against the Uighur Muslims).
+ Different cultures interpret human rights differently. For example, western democracies tend to emphasise the individual's right to self-determination. In contrast, Asian and African societies are more traditional and conservative, focusing on the rights of society over the individual.
+ Consequently, respect for women's rights and LGBTQ+ rights are dependent less on international law than on the cultural traditions of individual nation states.

> **Now test yourself**   TESTED ◯
>
> 1 Define 'human rights'.
> 2 What is the significance of the Universal Declaration of Human Rights?
> 3 List two reasons why it is difficult to enforce a universal standard of human rights protection.

> **Exam tip**
>
> Research new cases in international human rights law. This will ensure your writing is impressively relevant and up to date.

International Court of Justice

The International Court of Justice (ICJ) was established in 1945. It judges disputes between nation states and delivers legally binding judgements in contentious cases between nation states, and non-binding advisory opinions in cases brought by a UN institution.

Although the ICJ possesses strong legitimacy as part of the UN, state sovereignty significantly challenges its effectiveness. Its strengths and weaknesses are summarised in Table 20.1.

> **International Court of Justice** The ICJ is sometimes known as the World Court. Established in 1945, it is a UN court and judges cases involving nation states.

Table 20.1 ICJ: strengths and weaknesses

Strengths	Weaknesses
+ Despite its structural limitations, nation states respect the ICJ's independence and neutrality and therefore often comply with hostile judgements. + Since it is under the jurisdiction of the UN, the ICJ possesses international legitimacy. + The ICJ has settled several border disputes including those between Niger and Benin (2005) and Niger and Burkina Faso (2013). + In 2012, the ICJ ruled that Senegal must try the former president of Chad, Hissène Habré, who had fled there. Senegal complied and put Habré on trial for 'crimes against humanity and torture'. He was sentenced to life imprisonment. + In 2022, Uganda complied with an ICJ judgement that it should pay $325 million to the Democratic Republic of the Congo for infringing its territory during the civil war.	+ The ICJ cannot prosecute cases itself, so must wait for cases to be brought to it. + Only 73 of the 193 UN member states have agreed to be bound by ICJ rulings in all circumstances. + The Permanent Five's veto power on the Security Council means they are not meaningfully accountable to the ICJ. This challenges the principle of equality on which international law should be based. + If states do not accept an adverse ruling, the Security Council could theoretically compel compliance. However, this is highly unlikely, so the ICJ has practically no enforcement power. + In 2022, Russia ignored an ICJ judgement that it should 'immediately suspend' its 'military operations' against Ukraine. + In 2022, when the UN General Assembly requested the ICJ declare on the legality of its control of the Occupied Territories, Israel refused to cooperate.

UN tribunals

Following massive and sustained human rights violations, the UN established four international tribunals (see Table 20.2) which have helped in the work of post-conflict resolution. They have been significant in prosecuting egregious human rights abusers and, in some cases, advancing international human rights law.

> **International tribunals** Four tribunals established to try human rights abuses committed in Rwanda, the former Yugoslavia, Sierra Leone and Cambodia.

However, critics claim that UN tribunals represent victors' justice. The tribunals have also failed to discourage future state-led atrocities in, for example, Syria, Myanmar, Ukraine and Yemen. Ultimately, there have been relatively few prosecutions despite the massive scale of the atrocities committed.

The successes and failures of the tribunals are summarised in Table 20.2.

Table 20.2 The four international tribunals: successes and failures

Tribunal	Successes	Failures
Former Yugoslavia (1993–2017)	+ 90 war criminals have been convicted including Radovan Karadžić and Ratko Mladić (both imprisoned for life). + The tribunal exposed atrocities like the Srebrenica massacre (1995).	+ The court has not encouraged reconciliation as many Serbs believe it was biased against them. + The NATO bombing of Serbia (1999) killed between 489 and 528 civilians but NATO has not been held accountable.
Rwanda (1994–2016)	+ The tribunal established vital new precedents in international law (e.g. that the media can be complicit in encouraging genocide, and rape can be prosecuted as a way of perpetrating genocide). + The former Rwandan prime minister, Jean Kambanda, was convicted for his role in the genocide. + This established the precedent that heads of government cannot claim 'state immunity' from prosecution.	+ Although 800,000 Tutsis were killed in the genocide, only 61 individuals were convicted of participating in it. + Although there were allegations of post-genocide Tutsi-led atrocities, these were not tried by the court.
Sierra Leone (2002–13)	+ The former president of Liberia, Charles Taylor, was sentenced to 50 years' imprisonment for his intervention in the Sierra Leone civil war. As a former head of state, his conviction confirmed that 'state immunity' provides no defence in international law. + The court set the precedent that forced marriage can be prosecuted as a crime against humanity.	+ The tribunal's funding by the UK, US, Canada and the Netherlands led to claims that it represented a western agenda. + In 2009, the US ambassador to Liberia, Linda Thomas-Greenfield, stated, 'The best we can do for Liberia is to see to it that Taylor is put away for a long time.'
Cambodia (1997–2022)	+ Three Khmer Rouge leaders (Nuon Chea, Kaing Guek Eav and Khieu Samphan) were imprisoned for life for encouraging the Cambodian genocide. + Young people were encouraged to engage with the trial to educate them about the genocide.	+ Although 2 million died in the genocide, there were only three convictions. + Critics claim the government discouraged the prosecution of middle-ranking officials who served future governments for fear of embarrassing political consequences.

Now test yourself

TESTED ◯

4 What is the purpose of the ICJ?
5 List two strengths and two weaknesses of the ICJ.
6 List five successful prosecutions carried out by the UN tribunals.

Exam tip

Do not confuse the cases before the UN tribunals with the cases tried by the International Criminal Court.

International Criminal Court

The International Criminal Court (ICC) was established by the Rome statute (2002). As of 2023, 123 nation states accept its jurisdiction. It is a permanent court which tries individuals accused of crimes against humanity, war crimes and genocide when it is not possible to obtain justice through domestic courts.

+ Unlike the ICJ, the ICC has a special prosecutor (Karim Khan, 2021–) who can authorise investigations and initiate cases.
+ Critics note that its authority is severely limited, as the US, China, Russia and India do not recognise its jurisdiction. This demonstrates how state sovereignty undermines international human rights law.

193

Some successes and failures of the ICC are presented in Table 20.3.

Table 20.3 International Criminal Court: successes and failures

Successes	Failures
+ The ICC convicted Thomas Lubanga and Germain Katanga of atrocities carried out during the Congolese civil war. + The ICC is developing new precedents in international human rights law (e.g. Ahmad al-Mahdi has been convicted of 'cultural terrorism' in Mali for destroying religious buildings). + ICC investigations are now taking place globally, not just in Africa (e.g. Ukraine, Venezuela, Myanmar, Afghanistan and the Occupied Palestinian territories). + In 2022, the trial began of Ali Kushayb, who commanded the Janjaweed militia during the genocide in Darfur.	+ Three of the five permanent members of the Security Council (the US, Russia and China) do not accept the ICC's jurisdiction, significantly undermining its legitimacy. + Uighur demands that the ICC investigate the alleged genocide of Uighur Muslims by China have failed because China is not a member of the ICC. + In 2018, the Philippines withdrew from the ICC in retaliation for its investigation into its controversial war against drugs. This highlights how state sovereignty challenges the ICC's effectiveness. + From 2002 to 2023 the ICC has secured ten convictions and made four acquittals. All ten convictions were of Africans, encouraging claims that the ICC is partisan.

European Court of Human Rights

In 1959, the European Court of Human Rights (ECtHR) opened. It represents the judicial arm of the Council of Europe, which was established in 1949 to encourage human rights, the rule of law and democracy across Europe.

+ The ECtHR is the final court of appeal in cases involving the European Convention on Human Rights (ECHR, 1950).
+ It has 46 member states (2023), compared with 27 members of the European Union (2023).
+ Belarus is not a member and Russia was expelled in 2023 because of its invasion of Ukraine.
+ Although member states are obliged to comply with its judgements, the ECtHR lacks effective enforcement mechanisms. However, ECtHR judgements have put significant pressure on member states to reform legislation to make it compatible with the ECHR.

> **Exam tip**
>
> Avoid confusing the European Court of Human Rights (ECtHR) with the European Union's Court of Justice (ECJ).

Some successes and failures of the ECtHR are detailed in Table 20.4.

Table 20.4 European Court of Human Rights: successes and failures

Successes	Failures
+ In *Smith and Grady* v *the UK* (1999), the ECtHR stated that a ban on LGBTQ+ people serving in the military was contrary to their human rights. Consequently, the law was changed. + Despite the parliamentary vote not to comply with the ECHR, the government subsequently allowed limited prisoner voting rights enabling the UK to comply with the ECHR. + When a court in Malta convicted a journalist for defamation of a politician's character, the ECtHR stated in *Falzon v Malta* (2019) that his criticisms were in the public interest. Consequently, Malta's restrictive laws on press freedom were changed. + In 1990 when the French police tapped the phones of Jacques and Janine Huvig, the ECtHR judged that their right to privacy had been breached, leading to much stricter limits on police surveillance.	+ In 2022, Russia ignored a judgement from the ECtHR demanding that it withdraw its forces from Ukraine. + On several occasions, the UK has ignored the rulings of the ECtHR. In 2011, the House of Commons voted not to extend voting rights to prisoners in defiance of the ECHR. + Despite demands by the ECtHR that Turkey drop legal proceedings against the civil rights activist Osman Kavala, in 2022 he was sentenced to life imprisonment. + In 2023, Poland ignored an ECtHR ruling that it restore to office judges who had opposed the government's judicial reforms.

> **Now test yourself** TESTED ◯
>
> 7 How is the ICC different from the ICJ?
> 8 List three ICC convictions.
> 9 What is the purpose of the European Court of Human Rights?

Answers at **www.hoddereducation.co.uk/myrevisionnotesdownloads**

Rise of humanitarian interventions in the 1990s

Humanitarian intervention is the principle that if human rights are being abused in a nation state, then outside powers may intervene to protect those rights.

+ It derives from the liberal principle of our shared humanity, so that we have an obligation to 'save strangers'.
+ Humanitarian interventions should therefore not offer any geo-strategic advantage for an intervening power. The sole motivation should be to reduce suffering and protect the threatened and vulnerable.

In the 1990s, the Security Council was less divided than it had been during the Cold War and several humanitarian interventions were launched. This established the principle that there could be intervention within a nation state to uphold human rights, therefore challenging the principle of state sovereignty.

A timeline of humanitarian interventions since 1992 is shown in Figure 20.1.

> **Humanitarian intervention** The forcible intervention in a state to stop sustained and widespread human rights abuses.

1992	**Somalia:** When Somalia descended into civil war and the country faced famine, President George H.W. Bush dispatched 28,000 US military forces to bring relief.
1995	**Bosnia:** Following the collapse of Yugoslavia, civil war broke out in Bosnia. UN forces tried to maintain peace from 1992, but effective humanitarian intervention only occurred when NATO sent in peacekeepers with a robust nation-building mandate.
1999	**Kosovo:** When Serbia launched policies of ethnic cleansing in Kosovo, NATO launched a 78-day bombing campaign of Serbia which led to the withdrawal of Serbian forces and their replacement by a NATO/UN stabilisation force.
1999	**Tony Blair's Chicago speech:** During the Kosovo War, Tony Blair clarified the principle of humanitarian intervention, stating that 'acts of genocide can never be a purely internal matter'.
1999	**East Timor:** Following its referendum to declare independence from Indonesia, East Timor was engulfed by violence. UN resolution 1264 endorsed an Australian-led UN peace-keeping force which restored peace and stability.
2000	**Sierra Leone:** During its civil war, the population suffered mass atrocities. UK forces in the region were confident that they could end the violence, so Prime Minister Tony Blair authorised them to intervene.
2005	**UN Responsibility to Protect:** The UN world summit endorsed humanitarian intervention in 'Responsibility to Protect' (R2P), which stated that sovereignty is conditional on nation states being able to protect their citizens' human rights; otherwise the international community has an obligation to intervene.

Figure 20.1 Examples of humanitarian intervention

> **Now test yourself** TESTED ⬤
>
> 10 Why were there so many humanitarian interventions in the 1990s?
> 11 What is the significance of UN Responsibility to Protect (R2P)?
> 12 Why is humanitarian intervention a liberal principle?

> **Exam tip**
>
> Do not refer to the interventions in Iraq (1991, 2003) and Afghanistan (2001) as humanitarian. They were geo-strategic, although they had humanitarian elements.

Reasons for selective humanitarian interventions

Before a humanitarian intervention occurs, many questions need to be asked and much planning completed:

+ The occupying force must have a strong mandate and have sufficient strength to make an effective difference.
+ There needs to be a long-term commitment to nation building.
+ A successful intervention requires international legitimacy.
+ There should be significant support from within the country for an occupying force.
+ If an occupying force is seen as illegitimate and unwelcome, success is unlikely.

Therefore, even though a humanitarian intervention may be morally necessary, it should only be launched if it has a good chance of success.

20 Global governance: human rights and the environment

195

Examples of successful and unsuccessful interventions are given in Table 20.5.

Table 20.5 Humanitarian interventions: successes and failures

Successful	Unsuccessful
+ **Bosnia (1995):** In Operation Deliberate Force, NATO had a powerful military mandate to make peace. NATO forces then engaged in well-resourced nation building. + **Kosovo (1999):** Once Serbian forces withdrew from Kosovo, NATO undertook an extensive and long-term role restructuring civil society. In 2023, NATO forces were still in Kosovo. + **East Timor (1999):** Well-armed UN forces were able to disarm criminal gangs and support legitimate democratic structures. + **Ivory Coast (2011):** Following a disputed election, French military forces swiftly intervened in sufficient strength. The former president, Laurent Gbagbo, was arrested and the rightful government installed.	+ **Somalia (1992):** US forces in Somalia soon became embroiled in bitter criminal, clan and ethinc rivalry. Without a legitimate government to support, they were increasingly pulled into a quagmire. + **Rwanda (1994):** Although there was a UN force in Rwanda in 1994, it was under-strength and was only mandated to monitor the situation. When a larger contingent arrived with a more robust mandate, most of the killing was over. + **Democratic Republic of the Congo (DRC) (1999–):** UN forces in the DRC have been hampered by the immense size of the country, complex tribal differences and outside interference by neighbouring states. Limited numbers and a limited mandate to take sides has undermined their effectiveness. + **Libya (2011):** NATO intervention under a UN mandate contributed to the overthrow of the Gaddafi regime. However, there was no subsequent nation building, allowing Libya to descend into chaos.

Double standards and hypocrisy

Western powers are often accused of double standards and hypocrisy for intervening in some cases but ignoring others.

Do allegations of double standards undermine the case for humanitarian intervention?

Yes	No
+ Western powers have not intervened in the Syrian civil war despite the UN estimating the civilian death toll to be 306,000 (2022). + China is alleged to be carrying out genocidal policies against the Uighur Muslims. However, the response of the West has been limited. + Although the military junta in Myanmar is systematically persecuting the Rohingya Muslims, there has been no western intervention. + As the government of Tunisia becomes more authoritarian, human rights are increasingly being threatened. However, the western focus on the war in Ukraine means this has been little reported. + Despite the UN estimating in 2022 that 250,000 people may have died in Yemen, western powers have avoided intervening in the conflict or criticising Saudi Arabia's involvement. + Critics of western-led humanitarian interventions argue that too often they conceal geo-strategic self-interest (e.g. Bosnia and Kosovo).	+ Humanitarian intervention should only take place when it has a good chance of success. Given the complications of the Syrian civil war, this was unlikely to be the case. + Since it would be practically impossible for the West to intervene militarily in China, this is not double standards. + A humanitarian intervention against the military junta in Myanmar would be costly and could risk conflict with China. + According to the former UK foreign secretary, Douglas Hurd, 'We should do good where we can, but not pretend that we can do good everywhere.' + The West has intervened in some crises (e.g. Somalia, Sierra Leone and the Ivory Coast) when it might have been politically easier to have ignored them. + President Clinton was unwilling to intervene militarily in either Bosnia (1995) or Kosovo (1999) and only did so when the moral case for a humanitarian intervention became unavoidable.

Now test yourself — TESTED ○

13 List three examples of successful interventions.

14 List three examples of unsuccessful interventions.

15 How have claims of double standards and hypocrisy been used to discredit humanitarian intervention?

Answers at **www.hoddereducation.co.uk/myrevisionnotesdownloads**

Limits of humanitarian intervention

Realists claim that respect for state sovereignty provides the basis for global stability. Therefore, humanitarian interventions challenge the foundations of world order by infringing sovereignty.

Humanitarian interventions can be used as a justification for an expansionist foreign policy by predatory nations. For example, Russia claims that NATO's intervention in Kosovo (1999) was designed to expand western influence in the Balkans. Russia has itself used unverified claims of genocide in the Donbass to justify its war against Ukraine.

Failed attempts at nation building in Afghanistan and the growing geo-strategic challenge to western influence posed by Russia and China suggest that there is little appetite for further humanitarian interventions on the scale of the 1990s.

Is humanitarian intervention/UN Responsibility to Protect justified?	
Yes	**No**
✦ UN Responsibility to Protect (R2P) recognises the principle that whenever possible there is an obligation to save strangers as part of our shared humanity. ✦ Unpunished human rights violations embolden repressive regimes. Western failure to intervene in Syria has caused immense suffering and provoked enormous regional instability. ✦ Humanitarian interventions can restore stability and reduce suffering as Sierra Leone, East Timor, Bosnia, and Kosovo demonstrate. ✦ Although humanitarian interventions in South Sudan, the Democratic Republic of the Congo, Mali and the Central African Republic have been limited, the suffering would have been much worse without them.	✦ By infringing Westphalian principles of state sovereignty (see Chapter 18), humanitarian intervention threatens the basis of global order. ✦ Western humanitarian interventions provide a dangerous precedent for authoritarian regimes to claim the same mandate. ✦ The selective way in which humanitarian interventions occur undermines the principle. ✦ Humanitarian interventions risk unintended violent consequences, as occurred in Somalia and in Libya after the overthrow of the Gaddafi regime.

Now test yourself — TESTED ○

16 Why do realists criticise humanitarian intervention?

17 Why have there been fewer humanitarian interventions in recent years?

18 List three ongoing humanitarian interventions.

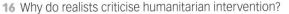

20.2 The environment

As a result of the dramatic increase in greenhouse gas emissions since the industrial revolution, the climate is threatened by dangerous temperature rise. Scientists warn that the higher the temperature rises, the more cataclysmic the results will be.

Despite this, recent research (2023) suggests that action to resolve the problem has been insufficient and there is a strong possibility that by 2027 temperature rise will already have gone beyond 1.5°C, above which irreversible climate change will take place.

The two ways of responding to climate change are mitigation and adaptation:
✦ Mitigation means that efforts are made to reduce the temperature increase in order to lessen the impact of climate change.
✦ Adaptation acknowledges that temperature rise and climate change are now a reality, so humanity must adapt by, for example, building flood defences and improving irrigation techniques.

United Nations Framework Convention on Climate Change

At the Rio Earth Summit in 1992, the United Nations Framework Convention on Climate Change (UNFCCC) was agreed. The UNFCCC requires its signatories to reduce greenhouse gas emissions to stop 'dangerous anthropogenic [human-caused] interference with Earth's climate system'.

+ The signatories to the convention are required to gather regularly at Conferences of the Parties (COP) meetings to assess progress and discuss further ways of limiting greenhouse gas emissions.
+ The UNFCCC separates the more developed countries from the least developed, recognising that since they have been polluting longer and are wealthier, they should contribute more to resolving the problem.
+ As a legally binding agreement, it commits all its members to working together to reduce harmful gas emissions. By 2023, 198 parties had ratified the UNFCCC, including the European Union (EU). The UNFCCC is crucial to combating climate change because it provides an annual opportunity for nation states and regional organisations like the EU to resolve the collective challenge of climate change.

> **United Nations Framework Convention on Climate Change** Established at the Rio Earth Summit in 1992, the UNFCCC is an international treaty which arranges regular COPs to combat 'human interference' in the environment.

Intergovernmental Panel on Climate Change

The Intergovernmental Panel on Climate Change (IPCC) was created in 1988. It brings together scientists from across the globe who analyse the significance of the most recent data on climate change. This enables the IPCC to 'provide policymakers with regular scientific assessments on climate change, its implications and potential future risks', and to 'put forward adaptation and mitigation options'.

Significantly, since the IPCC is a global body and politically neutral, its findings are very highly regarded since they objectively record and interpret the current scientific understanding of climate change. Its reports are therefore eagerly anticipated by policy makers and the public.

+ In 2022, the IPCC climate report warned that on current trajectories the temperature would rise by 3.2°C this century, significantly above the recommended IPCC limit of 1.5°C. The report thus concluded that much more urgent action must be taken by COP members this decade to halt catastrophic and irreversible climate change.
+ In 2023, an IPCC report concluded that there was a 66% chance that temperature rise would overshoot 1.5°C by 2027, requiring much more urgent action from governments now.

> **Intergovernmental Panel on Climate Change** An intergovernmental body which collates the most accurate and independently researched scientific data on the present state of climate change.

> **Exam tip**
> Show up-to-date knowledge by noting the significance of IPCC reports as they are published.

20.3 The ways and extent to which institutions address and resolve contemporary global issues

Competing views about how to tackle environmental issues

REVISED ●

Despite the UNFCCC establishing a framework for climate change conferences and the IPCC providing regular updates on how the climate is changing, progress on reducing greenhouse gas emissions has been slow.

Shallow-green ecology versus deep-green ecology

Shallow-green ecology provides a human-centred (anthropocentric) approach to the challenge of climate change. Its supporters argue that action needs to be taken to reduce the impact of climate change to safeguard humanity.

It therefore addresses the challenge of climate change from a practical perspective.

Shallow-green ecologists acknowledge that humans are accelerating the pace of climate change and that greenhouse gas emissions must be urgently reduced. However, they believe that sufficient action can be taken without dramatic changes being made to our consumer lifestyles and without abandoning free market economic development.

Deep-green ecology provides a radically different approach to the environment. Closely associated with the pioneering work of Arne Naess, deep-green ecology emphasises the interconnectivity of all life. It argues that the ecosystem needs to be treated with reverence and the planet protected because it is the source of all living things and the means of sustaining them. Deep ecologists therefore demand a radical restructuring of humanity's relationship with the planet, involving significant restrictions on capitalism, consumerism and materialism.

In his Gaia hypothesis (1972), scientist James Lovelock argued that the earth itself is a living entity, interacting with the organisms which it nurtures: 'Perhaps the single most important thing we can do to undo the harm we have done is to fix firmly in our minds the thought: the earth is alive.'

The spiritual/philosophic elements of deep-green ecology contrast with the transactional approach of shallow-green ecology, which focuses solely on protecting humanity's continued existence without dramatic alterations in how we live our lives.

Sustainable development

In 1987 the UN's 'Our Common Future' (the Brundtland Report) defined sustainable development as development which meets 'the needs of the present without compromising the ability of future generations to meet their own needs'. Sustainable development recognises that economic development can have negative consequences for the planet in terms of increased greenhouse gas emissions.

> **Sustainability/ sustainable development** Development which provides for the needs of the present without jeopardising the needs of the future.

Unlimited consumption and excessive consumerism place huge burdens on the ecosystem, so sustainable development seeks to achieve present-day development without ruining the earth's natural resources so that it cannot sustain future generations. This means that we must make ourselves accountable for our actions by recognising that what we do now will impact on how our descendants are able to live their lives. For example, if sustainable development does not take place, increased greenhouse gas emissions will lead to higher temperatures and more extreme weather events with incalculable consequences later in the century.

The UN recognised the vital importance of sustainable development with the launch of its Sustainable Development Goals in 2015.

If climate change is not halted, the human rights of people living in vulnerable areas will be severely impacted by increasing natural disasters such as droughts, famines and rising sea levels.

The tragedy of the commons

In 1968, the ecologist Garett Hardin published an article, 'The Tragedy of the Commons'. In it, Hardin argued that the resources of the planet are being inexorably depleted because states and non-state actors such as multinational corporations are placing their immediate material advantage above that of the well-being of the planet. Consequently, the global commons which sustain us (the atmosphere, the oceans and the Antarctic) are becoming so polluted by individual greed that the whole global community is being made to suffer. Even when global actors appreciate the damage that their actions

> **Global commons** Our shared environment, such as the oceans, the atmosphere, the Antarctic and outer space. These are under the jurisdiction of no state, so their protection requires collective endeavour.

are doing to the global commons, they often fail to act in the hope that others will act. They can therefore 'free ride' on the positive deeds of others.

The tragedy of the commons thesis helps to explain why sustainable development is difficult to achieve.

Now test yourself TESTED

19 Distinguish between shallow-green and deep-green ecology.
20 Define 'sustainable development'.
21 What is the 'tragedy of the commons' thesis?

Obstacles to international cooperation and agreement

The UNFCCC has been successful in arranging regular COP meetings since 1995. These have provided a unique forum for the global community to debate a collective response to climate change.

However, progress has been hampered by differences between developed and developing countries over how cuts in carbon emissions should be fairly shared. Member states have been unwilling to accept mandatory cuts in their carbon emissions.

The principle of the 'tragedy of the commons' has undermined progress, since states are often unwilling to make the necessary carbon cuts because of the negative economic consequences.

Successes and failures of the COP climate change agreements since 1992 are summarised in Table 20.6.

Table 20.6 COP climate change agreements: successes and failures

Conference	Successes	Failures
Rio de Janeiro (1992)	+ 178 nation states were represented, and 117 heads of government attended. This, for the first time, ensured that the problem of climate change was globally recognised. + Rio was important in establishing the UNFCCC under which annual climate change conferences take place. + The Rio Declaration stated the goal of sustainable development.	+ No binding targets were agreed on carbon reduction. + The conference highlighted substantial differences between developed (Annex 1) and developing countries over whose obligation it was to reduce carbon emissions.
Kyoto (1997)	+ The Kyoto Protocol was agreed. This set binding carbon-reduction targets for 37 (Annex 1) developed countries. + Kyoto introduced the principle of 'emissions trading' to incentivise carbon reduction.	+ Kyoto further emphasised global disunity over the responsibility for cutting carbon emissions. + The US argued that they were unfairly expected to reduce carbon emissions despite no action being required from developing countries like China and India which were becoming major carbon emitters. Consequently, the US did not ratify the Protocol.
Copenhagen (2009)	+ Member states agreed that the temperature rise must not go above 2°C this century. + Major emitters led by China and the US promised to reduce their greenhouse gas emissions. + By 2020, developed (Annex 1) countries would work towards allocating $100 billion annually to support developing countries respond to 'climate change'.	+ Although developed and developing countries agreed that greenhouse gas emissions should be reduced, no specific targets were agreed. + The balance of responsibility between developed and developing countries for reducing greenhouse gas emissions was left unclear. + No enforcement power was agreed, so nation states could not be held legally accountable for lack of action.

Conference	Successes	Failures
Paris (2015)	✦ The unworkable Kyoto Protocol was replaced by the Paris Treaty. ✦ 174 countries committed to keeping global temperature rise beneath 2°C with an aspirational goal of 1.5°C. ✦ Signatories committed to setting their own carbon reduction targets known as Nationally Determined Contributions (NDCs). ✦ As a major greenhouse gas emitter, US commitment to the treaty was a vital step forward.	✦ Although 174 nation states agreed to reduce greenhouse gas emissions, their NDCs are self-imposed. Consequently, most countries have committed to inadequate NDCs rather than the ambitious ones required. ✦ There is no mechanism for holding member states accountable for not reaching their NDC targets. ✦ Although progress was made, the conference did not generate the necessary urgency of action.
Glasgow (2021)	✦ Member states agreed to aim for no more than a 1.5°C temperature rise by 2100. ✦ 137 COP members agreed to 'halt and reverse forest loss and land degradation' by 2030. ✦ There was consensus among 190 COP members to 'phase down' coal use. This is important as coal represents 40% of greenhouse gas emissions. ✦ 100 countries agreed to a 30% reduction in methane by 2030.	✦ India and China blocked attempts to make a commitment to 'phase out' coal. ✦ China, Russia and India emit large quantities of methane but made no pledge to reduce them. ✦ As with the Paris Treaty, agreements reached at Glasgow depend upon the goodwill of states if they are to succeed.
Sharm el-Sheikh (2022)	✦ A 'loss and damage' fund was set up by developed states to help developing countries adapt to climate change. ✦ States promised to develop 'a clean energy mix, including low-emission and renewable energy'. ✦ A world market for trading carbon was created.	✦ No measurable targets were agreed. ✦ Carbon trading is controversial, and critics argue that the conference should aim to eliminate not trade it. ✦ Glasgow failed to generate more urgent action with just 34 COP members making their NDC more ambitious.

Now test yourself   TESTED ⬤

22 Distinguish between the IPCC and the UNFCCC.

23 List two agreements made in the Paris Treaty (2015).

24 List two successes and two criticisms of the Glasgow Conference (2021).

Role and significance of global civil society and non-state actors and the challenge of climate change

Although the decisions reached by nation states at COP meetings are crucial, this must not minimise the significant role of non-state actors.

Climate activists like David Attenborough and Vanessa Nakate raise global awareness of the need to meet the challenge of climate change. Global celebrities also advance action on climate change. The indigenous American model Quannah Chasinghorse campaigns against oil extraction and in favour of sustainable brands. The billionaires Bill Gates (co-founder of Microsoft), Jeff Bezos (founder of Amazon) and Jack Ma (co-founder of Alibaba) set up the Breakthrough Energy Alliance in 2015 to 'inspire the world to develop and scale the critical solutions we need to reach net-zero emissions'.

Prince William's Earthshot Prize globally publicises the necessity of radical new ideas in sustainable development.

The C40 Cities Climate Leadership Group brings 96 world cities together to develop strategies to ensure temperature rise does not exceed 1.5°C. Since these cities represent 20% of the world economy, this is very significant.

201

EU gross domestic product represents approximately one-sixth of the world economy. By 2030 it is committed to reducing carbon emissions to 55% of 1990 levels and by 2050 it aims to be carbon neutral.

Now test yourself

TESTED

25 Name three climate change activists.

26 List three non-state actors trying to resolve the challenge of climate change.

27 Which was the only climate change conference to make cuts in carbon mandatory?

Is significant progress being made to resolve the challenge of climate change?

Yes	No
✦ Regular COP meetings ensure that new initiatives and solutions to address climate change are being developed. ✦ There is a global consensus that humans are contributing to climate change and that temperature rise must not go beyond 1.5°C this century. ✦ Non-state actors are increasingly prominent in pressing for more urgent action. ✦ Developed countries now acknowledge the need to support developing countries with climate adaptation strategies.	✦ The IPCC warns that if current policies continue, temperature increase may exceed 1.5°C by 2027. ✦ NDCs are self-imposed and unenforceable. Consequently, most nation states have opted for inadequate targets. ✦ There is already striking evidence of climate change occurring (extensive flooding in Bangladesh), without provoking an urgent world response. ✦ COP members have not agreed to phase out coal burning, and net-zero emissions targets are too far in the future (China 2060, India 2070) to stop irreversible damage now.

Case study

The ICC and the invasion of Ukraine

In 2023, the ICC issued an arrest warrant for President Putin, accusing him of the forced deportation of Ukrainian children to Russia. According to its chief prosecutor, Karim Khan, 'We will not hesitate to submit further applications for warrants of arrest when the evidence requires us to do so'.

Russia reacted furiously, opening its own case against the ICC. As Russia has already been expelled from the Council of Europe for its invasion of Ukraine and been condemned by the ICJ, critics claim that the ICC's indictment is meaningless. Others respond that it shows that not even world leaders are beyond the reach of international law.

Summary

✦ The UN Universal Declaration of Human Rights (1948) established the human rights which all human beings possess.

✦ Four tribunals (Former Yugoslavia, Rwanda, Sierra Leone and Cambodia) were established to enforce human rights.

✦ However, state sovereignty makes it difficult to enforce international human rights.

✦ Consequently, international courts like the ICJ, the ICC and the ECtHR cannot enforce their judgements on unwilling states.

✦ Humanitarian intervention means intervention within a state to protect human rights. It should have no other purpose than this.

✦ In 2005, UN Responsibility to Protect recognised the principle of humanitarian intervention.

✦ Western-led humanitarian interventions have been criticised for double standards.

✦ Since the Rio de Janeiro Earth Summit in 1992 there have been regular climate change conferences.

✦ The UNFCCC provides the framework for these conferences and the IPCC provides governments with up-to-date information on the state of climate change.

✦ Progress on climate change has been hampered by nation states often being unwilling to cut greenhouse gas emissions sufficiently.

✦ The 'tragedy of the commons' thesis explains how self-interest hampers action on climate change.

✦ Sustainable development is development which does not negatively impact on future generations.

✦ Non-state actors are playing an increasingly important role in tackling climate change.

Answers at www.hoddereducation.co.uk/myrevisionnotesdownloads

Revision tasks

1 Research allegations of human rights abuses in Saudi Arabia, Iran, Turkey and Myanmar. Explain whether you agree that more should/could be done to stop them.

2 Debate the motion, 'Humanitarian interventions cause more harm than good.'

3 Create a diagram of the four most recent climate change conferences. For each, list four successes and four failures of the conference.

4 Research the most recent IPCC report. What are its most important findings? To what extent does it suggest that COP member states are taking sufficient action on climate change?

Exam skills

Determining factors

+ If you can memorise several cases connected with each of the courts and tribunals in this chapter, your writing will have real conviction.

+ Make a note of the ways in which the courts and tribunals have established new principles in international law.

+ It may seem tedious to learn detail about all the climate change conferences. However, if you can do this, it will enable you to write much more confidently about climate change.

Exam practice

1 Examine the successes and failures of two climate change conferences. (12 marks)

2 Examine the strengths and weaknesses of the ICC and the ICJ. (12 marks)

3 Evaluate the view that state sovereignty is the most important factor making international human rights enforcement difficult to achieve. (30 marks)

4 Evaluate the view that non-state actors are as important as nation states in resolving the challenge of climate change. (30 marks)

21 Power and developments

21.1 The different sorts of power in international relations

The American political scientist Joseph Nye defines two sorts of power in global relations.

According to Nye, 'When one country gets other countries to want what it wants, it might be called co-optive or soft power, in contrast with the hard or command power of ordering others to do what it wants.'

A combination of soft and hard power is known as smart power.

Hard power

REVISED

Hard power is coercive power. This means that it is power which creates compulsion to act in a desired way. In global relations, this is often exercised through military and economic force. The use, or the threat of the use, of military force can compel desired outcomes.

> **Hard power** The coercive utilisation of military and economic force to achieve desired outcomes.

✦ In 1991, Saddam Hussein was forced by superior military forces led by the US to withdraw from Kuwait.
✦ Russian military intervention in Syria in 2015 enabled the Assad regime to survive attempts to topple it.

Economic compulsion can be exercised through sanctions and by imposing tariffs on another power's imports. The World Bank and the International Monetary Fund (IMF) exercise economic hard power because their loans are often conditional on the introduction of free market reforms.

Realists emphasise the utility of hard power as the only way in which nation states can achieve security in an anarchic world.

Structural power

Powerful states are likely to possess significant structural power in intergovernmental organisations. For example, the five permanent members of the UN Security Council possess veto power, providing them with powerful structural influence.

The US enjoys substantial influence in the World Bank and the IMF because of its considerable voting power.

Soft power

REVISED

Soft power is the power of attraction, so that one nation state can encourage another to act in a certain way. Soft power can be exercised through cultural appeal and through a winning narrative. For example, the US has exercised significant global soft power through the appeal of its commitment to liberal democracy.

> **Soft power** The deployment of political and cultural attraction to persuade other states to willingly support chosen objectives.

✦ President Biden acknowledged this in his inaugural speech (2021) when he stated, 'We will lead not merely by the example of our power but by the power of our example.'
✦ Nation states can take advantage of major events which they host to expand their soft power influence. The UK used this highly effectively to showcase the dynamic appeal of multicultural Britain in the London Olympics (2012).
✦ The internet has increased the potential of soft power, since a popular narrative can be provided with global outreach.

- A persuasive story can be very powerful in gaining support, while a damaging story makes it much more difficult to lead by example. For example, President Zelensky's appearances in military fatigues have effectively encouraged western economic and military support for Ukraine. In contrast, Russia's lack of soft power limits its ability to exert influence in most nearby European countries.
- 'Right or wrong, it's a brand, a brand that sticks' (from the US western *Shane*, 1953).

Smart power

REVISED

Smart power represents a combination of soft and hard power. This can provide a highly effective way of achieving success. According to the American satirist P.J. O'Rourke, the US won the Cold War, 'Not just with ICBMs [intercontinental ballistic missiles] and Green Berets and aid to the Contras. These things were important, but in the end we beat them with Levi 501 jeans.'

Is hard power more important than soft power in global relations?

Yes	No
+ Superior military hard power enables nation states to protect themselves and achieve their objectives irrespective of soft power appeal. + Emerging powers like India, Turkey and Brazil possess outreach because of the strength of their economic and military power. + China asserts its growing global influence through agencies of economic hard power like the Asian Infrastructure Bank and the Belt and Road Initiative. + The EU exerts global influence because of the enormous economic hard power it deploys in trade negotiations. + Russia has deployed cheap energy exports to emerging countries like India to ensure they do not join the West in condemning their invasion of Ukraine (2022).	+ Soft power enables nation states to construct alliances based on shared values. + NATO has expanded because prospective members admire the liberal democratic values on which the alliance is founded. + By 2022, China had exported 476.8 million doses of Covid-19 vaccine, which helped to raise its influence among developing states. + Although the US had dominant military hard power in Iraq and Afghanistan, it failed in its objectives because it failed to win 'hearts and minds'. + Since its invasion of Ukraine, Russia has contrasted its conservative moral values with the more progressive West to win support in Africa and Asia.

Now test yourself

TESTED

1 Distinguish between soft and hard power.
2 Define 'smart power' and give an example.
3 Define 'structural power' and give an example.

21.2 State power classifications

Great powers

REVISED

Great powers wield significant global influence. They do this through their economic, political and military power, while they are also likely to exert significant influence through institutions of regional and global governance. Great powers:

- are likely to possess significant cultural outreach as, for example, the UK does through the Commonwealth
- possess a strong diplomatic global presence and are self-confident in international dialogue
- include India, Brazil, France and the UK, while the EU has many of the characteristics of a great power

> **Great power** A great power possesses considerable structural, diplomatic and economic influence without being able to exert global dominance over other states.

205

Superpowers

A superpower is able to assert its economic, political and military influence globally. According to the political scientist, W.T.R. Fox (1944), a superpower is 'a great power plus great mobility of power'.

✚ The US meets the criteria necessary to be a superpower because, despite challenges, it can still project its influence globally.

✚ There is a strong case that China is an emerging superpower because its economic influence through the Asian Infrastructure Bank and the Belt and Road Initiative provides it with global outreach. However, its lack of worldwide military and cultural outreach indicates to some political scientists that it is not yet a superpower.

> **Superpower** A superpower is a dominant power that can exert its military, economic and diplomatic influence across the world.

Emerging powers

Emerging powers wield rising influence in global affairs and their leadership will be increasingly assertive. Emerging powers:

✚ possess all the characteristics of a great power, such as global economic, military, diplomatic and cultural outreach

✚ are new to global influence, which is why India, China, Brazil and the EU are often classified as emerging powers and France, the UK and Japan are not

> **Emerging power** A power which can increasingly assert economic, diplomatic and military influence in international relations, so challenging the existing balance of power.

The economist Jim O'Neill has coined two acronyms to represent prominent emerging powers: he has referred to **B**razil, **R**ussia, **I**ndia, **C**hina and **S**outh Africa as the BRICS and **M**exico, **I**ndonesia, **N**igeria and **T**urkey as MINT countries.

However, critics note that Russia has more of the characteristics of a declining superpower and South Africa has too many unresolved domestic problems to claim great power status.

> **Now test yourself** TESTED
>
> 4 Define a superpower and give an example.
> 5 Define a great power and give an example.
> 6 Why are China, India and Brazil termed 'emerging' powers?

21.3 Polarity

The implications of polar structures for global stability

Unipolarity/hegemony

In global politics, polarity refers to the location of power. In a **unipolar** balance of power, one dominant power exercises global domination (hegemony). The hegemonic power can thus project its power anywhere in the world.

✚ The values of a hegemon will have global appeal and lesser states will bandwagon behind it.

✚ A hegemon will be so powerful that no other power can contest its dominant position.

✚ There have been few periods in history when the balance of power has been unipolar. For example, the Roman Empire possessed hegemonic power within the western world.

✚ When the Cold War ended in 1991, the US achieved hegemonic status. When and whether this hegemonic status has ended invites much debate.

According to some political scientists, like John Mearsheimer, unipolarity/ hegemony encourages international stability because the hegemon can act as a global police force, maintaining order and encouraging a shared commitment to the same values. This is known as the 'benign hegemonic theory'. This was the case during the *Pax Romana* (Roman Peace) in the ancient world. Similarly, in 1990, when Iraq attacked Kuwait, President George H.W. Bush utilised US hegemonic influence to establish a global coalition to repel the invasion.

Critics of unipolarity respond that there is a danger of the hegemon acting above the law, as there are no constraints on it. This is sometimes known as 'malign hegemonic theory'. Some political scientists claim this occurred after the terrorist attacks on New York and Washington DC in 2001, when President George W. Bush was accused of acting beyond international law during the 'war on terror'.

If a hegemon is perceived to be in decline, this may encourage potential rivals to try to supplant it. This is known as 'power transition theory' and critics suggest that this may be the case today with China probing the limits of US power.

> **Exam tip**
>
> Be prepared to debate whether superpower status requires both hard and soft power influence.

Bipolarity

In a bipolar distribution of power, two competing powers confront each other for dominance.

+ The Cold War provides a good example of bipolarity. From c.1947–c.1989 the US and the Soviet Union challenged each other for geo-strategic supremacy.
+ Realists favour a bipolar distribution of power because they argue that it encourages a stable balance of influence. Both sides are so evenly balanced that they have no incentive to risk conflict.
+ Bipolarity may even encourage cooperation, since neither competing power can destroy the other. For example, détente (loosening of tension) took place in the 1970s between the US and the Soviet Union.
+ Critics respond that, rather than bipolarity creating an equilibrium (equal balance of influence), each side will attempt to expand its influence at the expense of the other. This occurred during the Cold War with indirect (proxy) conflict between the superpowers in Vietnam, South America, the Middle East and Africa.
+ Since bipolarity is based on mutual suspicion, there is the ever-present chance of a crisis escalating into conflict, as almost happened in 1962 when the Soviet Union placed nuclear missile bases in Cuba, threatening the US.

> **Polarity** The different ways in which power can be distributed in international relations.
>
> **Unipolarity** In a unipolar distribution of power, a globally dominant power, known as a hegemon, can exert complete world influence without being challenged by a rival.
>
> **Bipolarity** In a bipolar distribution of power, two superpowers compete for global influence.
>
> **Multipolarity** In a multipolar distribution of power, several great powers compete for regional and global influence.

Multipolarity

In a multipolar distribution of power, global influence is shared between several states of relatively equal influence.

+ Multipolarity is the most difficult configuration of power to predict the consequences of.
+ If states are prepared to cooperate and respect institutions of global governance, a relatively stable balance of power can be created.
+ Realists contend that multipolarity is the most dangerous configuration of power. This is because nation states are power maximisers and a fluid balance of power can encourage ambitious states to challenge other states for influence.

Consideration of the changing nature of world order since 2000

REVISED

In 2000, the US was the dominant world power (global hegemon). Since then, emerging powers like China have challenged its world influence. Russia has also attempted to regain influence at the expense of the US.

Have emerging powers significantly altered the global balance of power?

Yes	No
+ Russia's annexation of Crimea (2014) and invasion of Ukraine (2022) represent a significant challenge to the balance of power. + China's approach is increasingly assertive, threatening Taiwan and extending Chinese military influence by constructing naval bases in the Indian Ocean ('String of Pearls' strategy). + China and Russia are together challenging US influence. In 2023, at a Moscow summit, they agreed to extend their 'strategic partnership'. + Significant regional powers like India, Egypt, Iran and South Africa maintain good relations with Russia, suggesting a potential shift of power away from the US.	+ The Russian invasion of Ukraine has demonstrated significant weaknesses in Russia's military capability and encouraged NATO enlargement. This suggests that western influence is undiminished. + Although China's economic influence has dramatically increased, its military outreach is not yet global. In contrast, the US military maintains global outreach. + China has just one overseas naval base at Djibouti compared to approximately 800 for the US. + NATO is still the world's most advanced military alliance. The establishment of AUKUS (2021) between Australia, the UK and the US demonstrates that western powers still project a powerful military presence in the Indo-Pacific region.

Now test yourself

TESTED

7 Distinguish between a bipolar and a unipolar distribution of power.

8 What is a multipolar distribution of power?

9 List three ways in which US claims to global hegemony are being challenged.

21.4 Different systems of government

Characteristics, examples and consequences for global order of different systems of government

REVISED

Democratic states

+ **Democratic states** are accountable to their citizens in regular elections.
+ In democratic states, the rule of law and civil liberties are upheld and there is a free media.
+ Liberals claim that democratic states contribute to stability because they are accountable to their citizens and the public do not want conflict.
+ Democracies also favour free trade and, according to liberals, free trade encourages so much interconnectivity and mutual interest that it reduces the risk of conflict.
+ Democracies are more likely to pool sovereignty (share the decision-making powers) in regional organisations and respect human rights and institutions of international law. Consequently, the theory of democratic peace suggests that the global expansion of democracy encourages peace and stability, since democracies are more likely to respect international law and avoid conflict.
+ Realists claim that the type of state is irrelevant, since all states are power maximisers.

> **Democratic state** A state in which the government is accountable to the public in regular elections and where the rule of law is paramount.

+ They argue that democracies can risk provoking conflict to advance their interests. For example, in 1956, France, the UK and Israel (democracies) went to war with Egypt (autocracy/dictatorship) to safeguard their interests in the Middle East. The US intervened in Vietnam (1960s/1970s) and invaded Iraq (2003) to advance its global security interests.

+ It is misleading to suggest that democracies always advance free trade and respect international law. An example of this is the US not recognising the jurisdiction of the International Criminal Court (ICC). Both the Trump and Biden administrations have pursued more protectionist policies.

+ Realists believe that the western emphasis on human rights protection may even provoke destabilising wars of humanitarian intervention, such as occurred in Libya (2011).

Semi-democratic, non-democratic and autocratic states

Semi-democratic states possess democratic institutions, but their importance is undermined by a shift towards authoritarianism (dictatorial power) by the government and challenges to media freedom and the rule of law. There is a strong case that Belarus and Russia are semi-democratic states because, although they have regular elections, opposition politicians are persecuted and media are a mouthpiece for the government.

Non-democratic states possess no popular legitimacy. China and Saudi Arabia are non-democratic states because their citizens cannot elect their governments and so have no political rights.

Autocratic states can arbitrarily imprison their citizens. The rule of law, an independent judiciary and media freedom are non-existent. Saudi Arabia, Syria and Russia are examples of autocratic states.

+ According to some critics, autocratic states challenge world stability most. This is because their leaders can try to achieve legitimacy through military success. For example, in 1980 the Iraq dictator Saddam Hussein invaded Iran and in 1990 he invaded Kuwait to enhance his reputation through military achievement. In 1982, Argentina's military junta invaded the Falklands in a bid to restore the regime's flagging popularity.

+ Since they control the media and opposition is banned or severely limited, authoritarian states can risk warfare without being held accountable for potential failures.

+ Lack of civil rights may mean that leaders of these states are less concerned about the human cost of launching conflicts.

> **Semi-democratic state** A state in which the effectiveness of democratic institutions has been undermined by authoritarianism.
>
> **Non-democratic state** A state which possesses no democratic institutions and where authority rests in the governments which is not accountable to the people. Citizens have no political rights and their civil rights are unprotected.
>
> **Autocratic state** A state where a single ruler has absolute power and is not democratically accountable to the public. Its government does not respect the rule of law and there is no human rights protection.

Now test yourself

TESTED ○

10 Define an autocratic state.

11 Define a democratic state.

12 List three ways in which it has been suggested autocratic states encourage conflict.

Failed states

+ In failed states governing structures have completely broken down. Consequently, they become a haven for criminal gangs, people-traffickers and terrorist organisations. One example of a failed state is Somalia which, due to its ungovernability, provides a refuge for the Islamist terrorist group Al-Shabaab, transnational crime networks and human smugglers. Another example is Libya where, in the confusion following the overthrow of the Gaddafi regime in 2011, military equipment was seized by extremists, destabilising North Africa and provoking an Islamist insurgency in Mali.

> **Failed state** A state in which the government is no longer able to exert its authority and where law and order has consequently broken down.

209

+ Neighbouring states can intervene in a failed state to advance their geo-strategic interests, encouraging regional instability. Since the 1990s, Uganda, Rwanda, Burundi and Kenya have all intervened in the Democratic Republic of the Congo.
+ The Syrian civil war has created a destabilising refugee crisis and encouraged the intervention of rival states like Iran, Turkey and Russia, further exacerbating regional tension.

Rogue states

+ Rogue states threaten their neighbours and so challenge regional and global stability.
+ They carry out systematic human rights violations and defy international human rights law.
+ Rogue states are linked to international terrorist/criminal groups and illegally seek to acquire weapons of mass destruction. North Korea is the most recognised example of a rogue state because the regime carries out massive human rights abuses, is illegally acquiring a nuclear capability, threatens its neighbours and supports the terrorist group Hezbollah.
+ The term 'rogue state' is controversial because critics claim that it can be used in a subjective way by the US to 'delegitimise' enemies such as Iran, Syria, North Korea and Venezuela. It is therefore difficult to agree a definitive list of rogue states.
+ There is a strong case that Russia is a rogue state given its invasion of Ukraine, President Putin's indictment for human rights abuses by the ICC and allegations of state terrorism, including the attempted assassination of former Russian intelligence agent Sergei Skripal and his daughter Yulia in Salisbury in 2018. The 'Wagner Group', the Russian paramilitary organisation, has been classified as a transnational criminal organisation by the US Department of the Treasury.
+ Some critics have suggested that China's threats towards Taiwan and its policies towards the Uighur Muslims make it a rogue state.
+ The term 'rogue state' is also controversial because once a state is classified as 'rogue' it can be more difficult for other states to make diplomatic progress with it.

> **Rogue state** A state that engages in extensive human rights violations, threatens its neighbours and acts in defiance of international law.

Now test yourself TESTED ◯

13 Define a failed state and give two examples.

14 Define a rogue state and give two examples.

15 List two ways each in which rogue states and failed states can threaten peace and security.

> **Exam tip**
>
> Be prepared to explain why the term 'rogue state' is more contested than 'failed state'.

21.5 Development and spread of democracy

When the Cold War ended, the American political scientist Francis Fukuyama predicted the global triumph of liberal democracy in his book, *The End of History and the Last Man* (1992). However, in recent years the spread of democracy has been reversed with governments including Russia, Poland, Hungary and Tunisia becoming increasingly controlling. Consequently, the Biden administration launched a series of 'Summits for Democracy' aimed at restoring global faith in democracy. In 2023, Vice President Kamala Harris also led a 'goodwill tour' of Africa designed to encourage enthusiasm for US liberal democracy and limit Chinese and Russian influence.

Post-Cold War optimism that liberal democracy possesses irresistible global appeal has thus been replaced by the belief that the case for democracy still has to be made and its values fought for and protected.

21.6 The ways and extent to which the changing relationships and actions of states in relation to power and developments address and resolve contemporary global issues

As we have seen, at the end of the Cold War, liberal political scientists like Frances Fukuyama expected that globalisation would advance liberal economics, the rule of law and democracy. This would mean, it was hoped, that globally nation states would embrace free market economics, adopt democracy, and uphold the civil and political rights of their citizens.

The reality has, though, been much more complex.

Conflict

REVISED

+ Realists argue that the changing balance of world power has encouraged the risk of conflict. This is because it is creating a period of power transition in which the US is trying to maintain its hegemonic dominance against the challenge of aspiring powers like Russia and China.
+ The political scientist Graham Allison has referred to this as the 'Thucydides Trap', since the ancient Greek historian Thucydides argued that the Peloponnesian War (431–405 BCE) was made inevitable by 'the rise of Athens and the fear that this inspired in Sparta'.

Poverty

REVISED

+ The emergence of rising powers like China and India has helped to lift unprecedented numbers of people out of poverty. The World Bank estimates that from between 1980 and 2022 China's engagement in the global free market raised 800 million people out of poverty.
+ In 1990, 36% of the global population lived in extreme poverty. By 2019, this had fallen to 9.2% (World Vision).
+ Covid-19 had a negative impact on global poverty reduction. However, in 2023, the World Bank estimated that extreme global poverty remained at 9.2%, which is considerably less than it was in 1990.
+ The Brookings Institution (a non-profit research organisation based in Washington DC) suggests that, although the only Asian countries unlikely to have eliminated extreme poverty by 2030 are Afghanistan, Papua New Guinea and North Korea, sub-Saharan Africa is unlikely to see any reduction.

Human rights

REVISED

+ Progress on international human rights protection has been set back by the changing balance of power.
+ China's poor record on human rights means that its emergence as a global leader has challenged the western focus on human rights protection.
+ Since the western countries' geo-strategic focus is now on resisting Chinese and Russian expansion, they are no longer able to provide leadership over humanitarian intervention.

The environment

REVISED

+ By encouraging industrialisation in the developing world, economic globalisation has led to a massive increase in carbon emissions. The biggest global carbon emitters are shown in Figure 21.1.

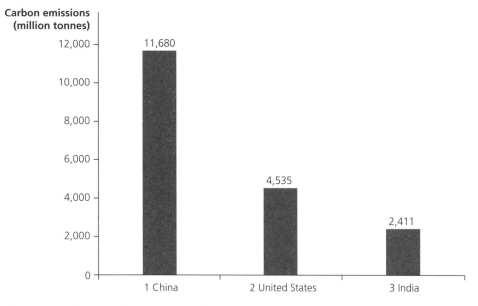

Figure 21.1 The top three carbon emitters, 2020

+ Organs of political globalisation, such as COP meetings, attempt to resolve this problem, although critics claim their actions have been inadequate.

See Chapter 20 for a debate on how much progress has been made to resolve the challenge of climate change.

Case study

On the right side of history?

At a meeting with President Putin in Moscow in March 2023, President Xi Jinping praised the two countries' 'neighbourliness, friendship and mutually beneficial cooperation', stating that China was 'on the right side of history'.

In response, the US secretary of state, Anthony Blinken, condemned China's 'illiberal' vision of the future and condemned Russia for encouraging 'world disorder'. Over 30 years after Francis Fukuyama predicted that the spread of liberal democracy would lead to 'the end of history', some critics began to claim that western democracy was under greater threat than at any time since the 1930s.

Summary

+ Soft, hard and smart power all provide ways in which global powers exert influence.
+ Hard power (economic, political and military) is coercive. In contrast, soft power utilises the power of cultural attraction.
+ When the global distribution of power is unipolar, one power (hegemon) dominates. When it is bipolar, two rival powers bid for influence. A multipolar distribution of power means that several evenly matched states compete for influence.
+ Each of these power distributions has consequences for global stability.
+ Emerging powers are challenging the existing balance of power, leading to claims that global politics has now entered an unstable period of power transition.

+ Liberals claim that democracies encourage peace and stability, and semi-democratic states and autocracies are more likely to provoke war.
+ Realists believe that all states are power maximisers and so can equally engage in conflict.
+ Rogue states seek weapons of mass destruction and do not act according to accepted standards of international behaviour. Failed states lack properly functioning governments, and so provide a haven for terrorists and criminals.
+ The term 'rogue state' is controversial because critics claim the US uses it to discredit its opponents.
+ In recent years democracy and the rule of law has not advanced in the way that liberals expected.

Revision tasks

1 Create a list of rogue and failed states. Rank them in order of their threat to global peace and stability, and explain your reasoning.

2 Debate the motion, 'The US can no longer claim to be a global hegemon.'

3 Produce a set of revision cards on the possible consequences of bipolar, unipolar and multipolar distributions of global power. On one side have the potential advantages of each, and on the other, potential disadvantages.

4 Debate the motion, 'Soft power does not matter in global relations.'

Exam skills

Determining factors

+ The issues of power raised here mean that you should contextualise your writing within the realist/liberal debate.

+ Be prepared to debate how useful the term 'rogue state' is, since it is such a subjective term.

+ Do not confuse the terms 'superpower' and 'global hegemon'. A state can be a superpower without being able to claim hegemonic status.

+ Make sure you know why power transition is dangerous and have an informed view of whether the world is currently in power transition.

Exam practice

1 Examine the ways in which the US exerts soft and hard power. (12 marks)

2 Examine the ways in which rogue and failed states challenge regional and global stability. (12 marks)

3 Evaluate the view that the changing balance of world power means that the US can no longer claim hegemonic status. (30 marks)

4 Evaluate the view that democratic states encourage global peace and stability more than autocratic states. (30 marks)

22 Regionalism and the European Union

22.1 Regionalism

The different forms

Since the end of the Second World War (1945), states in a similar geographical location have combined in regional organisations.

Regionalism refers to the way in which states in specific geographical regions develop closer relations through shared institutions of governance.

Regionalism can have a political, economic or security motivation, or be based on a combination of all three.

> **Regionalism** A process of integration in which nation states in a specific region decide to develop their institutional connections to advance their joint interests.

Economic regionalism

+ Economic regionalism involves states in the same geographical area adopting free trade policies to encourage trade and prosperity.
+ States can also agree a common external tariff to protect themselves from outside competition.
+ The Association of Southeast Asian Nations (ASEAN) and the US–Mexico–Canada Agreement (USMCA) are primarily examples of economic regionalism.

Political regionalism

+ With political regionalism, cooperation between nation states enables them to resolve regional disputes.
+ Political regionalism allows states with a shared ethnic, religious and cultural perspective to present a united front in global politics.
+ The Arab League is an example of political regionalism.

Security regionalism

+ Security regionalism encourages states to combine their military, police and intelligence services.
+ This reduces the risk of conflict between them and enables them to pool their resources against external threats.
+ ASEAN and the European Union (EU) both possess significant elements of security regionalism.

The EU, ASEAN and the African Union (AU) possess elements of the three types of regionalism, although the EU is the most advanced.

The relationship between regionalism and globalisation

+ Globalisation encourages more trade, but also presents challenges like greater security threats from transnational criminal networks.
+ Regionalism therefore allows nation states to exploit the advantages and minimise the risks of globalisation. For example, the EU and ASEAN are successful in using their economic might to negotiate favourable trade deals.
+ ASEAN's Political and Security Community (APSC) and the EU's Agency for Law Enforcement Cooperation (Europol) coordinate security policy against terrorist and criminal threats.
+ The AU enables its members to express a united response to shared challenges such as climate change.

Answers at **www.hoddereducation.co.uk/myrevisionnotesdownloads**

Prospects for political regionalism and regional governance

REVISED ◯

Regionalism provides nation states with the opportunity to advance their interests. Therefore, regionalism is a significant force in international relations.

There is a strong case to suggest that regionalism has also been advanced by globalisation, as nation states decide that they can take better advantage of the opportunities offered by globalisation and limit its disadvantages by establishing regional organisations.

The impact on state sovereignty

REVISED ◯

Although the EU significantly impacts on the sovereignty of its member states, most other regional organisations pose less of a challenge to national sovereignty.

This has led some critics to suggest that the EU is a unique example of regionalism. Others, however, argue that the AU and ASEAN possess similar motivation and characteristics, and so will develop in a similar way to the EU.

22.2 Development of regional organisations (excluding the EU)

North American Free Trade Agreement/ US Mexico Canada Agreement

REVISED ◯

✦ The North American Free Trade Agreement (NAFTA) created a free trade area between the US, Mexico and Canada in 1994. However, it was controversial among blue-collar workers in the US, who feared job losses because Mexican factory production was cheaper.
✦ Due to pressure from the Trump administration, NAFTA was replaced with the US–Mexico–Canada Agreement (USMCA) in 2020.
✦ The focus of USMCA is the automobile, textiles and agricultural markets. It is therefore a limited free trade agreement. However, it does include some environmental protection and workers' rights.
✦ USMCA is not an advanced form of regionalism because it lacks shared governing bodies and in 2036 will lapse unless the US, Mexico and Canada agree to renegotiate it.

African Union

REVISED ◯

✦ The African Union (AU) dates from 2002. It is the successor to the Organisation of African Union (1963). All 55 African countries are members of the AU.
✦ In many ways the AU resembles the EU, since it possesses quite advanced governing institutions. These include the Pan-African Parliament, the Assembly of the African Union, which annually brings together the AU's heads of government, and the Peace and Security Council, which mandates peace-keeping operations in Africa.

215

+ The governing institutions of the AU lack supranational authority. For example, the parliament only makes suggestions for the AU's heads of government to discuss. Consequently, most decision-making within the AU remains intergovernmental, protecting the sovereignty of member states.
+ In contrast to the EU's commitment to 'ever closer union', the AU's constitution defends 'the sovereignty, territorial integrity and independence of its Member States'.
+ Although the AU's court and judicial commission on Human and Peoples' Rights interpret the AU's African Charter on Human and Peoples' Rights (1981), it has no precedence over domestic law.
+ The significant ethnic, tribal, linguistic and political differences between AU member states also make further integration difficult.
+ The AU commitment to a single currency and an African Central Bank remains a distant ideal.

However, the AU has achieved significant successes, including the following:
+ The AU possesses the right to intervene within member states to end conflict. AU peace-keeping operations have thus taken place in Somalia, South Sudan, Darfur, Mali, Burundi and the Central African Republic.
+ In 2022, the AU negotiated a peace deal between the Tigray People's Liberation Front and Ethiopia.
+ During the Covid-19 pandemic, the AU and World Bank successfully cooperated over the African Vaccine Acquisition Task Team.
+ In 2018, the AU established the African Continental Free Trade Area (AfCFTA) which, when complete, will represent the biggest free trade area in the world. In 2022, eight AfCTFA members negotiated the Guided Trade Initiative, allowing tariff-free trade in a limited number of goods.

Arab League

REVISED

+ The Arab League was created in 1945 to 'draw closer the relations between member states and coordinate collaboration between them'.
+ As an example of political and security regionalism, it should encourage stability and cooperation in the Arab world and represent Arab interests globally.
+ However, its influence is minimal because it possesses no supranational authority — its Charter states that decisions 'shall bind only states that accept them'.
+ Divisions within the Arab world also undermine its relevance. During both Gulf Wars (1991, 2003) it was divided over how to respond to US-led military operations against Iraq.
+ Although the Arab League suspended Libya and Syria during their brutal suppression of demonstrations, it has not provided leadership to resolve the Yemen civil war or Turkish incursions into Syria. It is divided over recognising Israel as a state.
+ In 2023, when President Zelensky attended an Arab League summit in Saudi Arabia he accused some members of 'turning a blind eye' to Russia's attack on Ukraine.
+ Unlike the AU, the Arab League has not developed an effective peace-keeping arm, meaning that it is generally a bystander in Middle East crises and conflicts.

Association of Southeast Asian Nations

REVISED

+ The Association of Southeast Asian Nations (ASEAN) dates from 1967. It was created to encourage economic and political ties between its members and to provide a geo-strategic counterweight to China and Japan.
+ Economically, ASEAN has achieved significant success. According to ASEAN, almost all goods traded within its free trade area are now free of tariffs, whereas they averaged 7% in 1996.

+ ASEAN has negotiated ambitious free trade agreements including the Regional Comprehensive Economic Partnership (RCEP) with China, Japan, South Korea, New Zealand and Australia in 2020.
+ In 2023, ASEAN was the world's fastest-growing trade bloc with exports worth $1.3 trillion.
+ In political and security issues, ASEAN is hampered by its commitment to the sovereign independence of its members, its lack of governing structures and its members' different political structures and aims. This means that ASEAN is unable to respond effectively to crises like the persecution of the Rohingya Muslims, the Myanmar military coup (2021) and Chinese military expansion in the South China Sea, which impacts the security of several ASEAN members.

> **Now test yourself** TESTED
>
> 4 In what ways is USMCA an example of economic regionalism?
> 5 Distinguish between the aims of the Arab League and ASEAN.
> 6 List two successes of the AU.

22.3 Factors that have fostered European integration and the major developments through which this has occurred

Formation, role, objectives and development of the EU

REVISED

+ **European integration** is rooted in the experience of the two world wars. The harrowing experience of total war persuaded liberal politicians across Europe that lasting peace could only be secured through pooling **sovereignty** in shared governmental bodies. By reducing the importance of borders, the nationalist hatreds which provoke war would be eliminated.
+ This aim was that European economic and political integration should be seen within a moral context, bringing peace and prosperity across the European continent.
+ States wanted to join the European Economic Community (EEC), a regional organisation created by the Treaty of Rome (1957), to share the prosperity of the free market. This later became known as the European Community (EC) and then the European Union (EU). Figure 22.1 shows the growth of the organisation over the years.
+ Former communist states which joined in 2004 (Estonia, Latvia, Lithuania, Czech Republic, Slovakia, Poland, Hungary and Slovenia) and in 2007 (Romania and Bulgaria) were eager to gain the benefits of shared security.

> **European integration**
> The process of 'ever closer union' through which decision-making in the EU is increasingly made by supranational institutions.
>
> **Sovereignty** Complete and absolute jurisdiction so that no higher power can legally compel a political entity to act in a certain way.
>
> **European Union** The world's most advanced regional organisation, in which decision-making between its 27 member states is made through supranational and intergovernmental institutions.

1957	France, West Germany, Italy, Belgium, the Netherlands, Luxemburg
1973	Ireland, Denmark, UK (withdrew 2020)
1981	Greece
1986	Spain, Portugal
1995	Austria, Finland, Sweden
2004	Estonia, Latvia, Lithuania, Czech Republic, Slovakia, Poland, Hungary, Cyprus, Malta, Slovenia
2007	Bulgaria, Romania
2013	Croatia

Figure 22.1 The process of EU enlargement from 6 to 27 members

217

Key treaties in the development of the EEC/EU

European expansion creates the challenge that the EU could become so large and diverse that it becomes impossible for it to make decisions. Therefore, the EU is based on the principle that, as its membership widens, successive treaties will deepen the connections between the member states. This is known as widening and deepening.

Each treaty has thus developed the power of the organisation's governing institutions, leading to greater federalism (unity) and so eroding the sovereignty of the member states (see Table 22.1).

> **Widening and deepening** A process whereby the EU expands its membership at the same time as it intensifies integration between members.
>
> **Federalism** The concentration of sovereign power in supranational institutions of governance, so reducing the sovereign independence of the EU's member states.

Table 22.1 Key treaties and agreements

Treaty/agreement	Provisions
Treaty of Rome (1958)	+ Established the principle of 'ever closer union' on which EEC/EU integration is based. + Introduced a common external tariff to protect the original six members. + Recognised the 'Four Freedoms' as the basis of economic integration: the free movement of goods, people, services and capital.
Single European Act (1987)	+ A European Single Market (tariff-free internal market) to be operational by 1992. + Direct elections to the European Parliament. + The opportunities for qualified majority voting (QMV) were increased on the Council of Ministers. This meant that decisions could be made when a sufficient majority vote was reached, reducing opportunities to use the national veto.
Maastricht Treaty (1993)	+ Established the EU based on shared citizenship, making it easier for EU citizens to cross national borders. + Maastricht's three pillars further advanced European integration by (1) committing the EU to monetary union by 2002; (2) forming an EU common foreign and defence policy; (3) advancing police and judicial cooperation.
Treaty of Nice (2003)	+ QMV was further increased on the Council of Ministers. + This was important to ensure that decision-making after enlargement in 2004 was not slowed down by more national vetoes.
Treaty of Lisbon (2009)	+ Established an EU President and EU High Representative for Foreign Affairs. + Provided the EU with a legal identity, so it could negotiate with other powers. + The EU's Charter of Fundamental Rights, which lists the rights of all EU citizens, was provided with legal force. + Further QMV was introduced on the Council of Ministers. + Decisions should be made as close to the people as possible (subsidiarity) and the right of states to leave the EU was recognised (Article 50).

> **Now test yourself**
>
> TESTED ●
>
> 7 What are the Four Freedoms?
>
> 8 How does QMV on the Council of Ministers impact on state sovereignty?
>
> 9 List three advantages of EU membership.

Answers at **www.hoddereducation.co.uk/myrevisionnotesdownloads**

Economic and monetary union

+ One of the key reasons why the EU is the world's most advanced regional organisation is that it is based on economic and monetary union (EMU).
+ EMU was established at the Maastricht Treaty (1993).
+ Twenty EU members have reached the most advanced stage of EMU through membership of the Eurozone. This means that they share the euro currency, so their monetary and fiscal policies are coordinated.
+ Denmark secured an opt-out from the Eurozone. However, Bulgaria, Czech Republic, Hungary, Poland, Romania and Sweden are required to join the euro when they have fulfilled the necessary economic criteria.
+ Future members of the EU are also expected to join the Eurozone.

> **Now test yourself**   TESTED
>
> **10** How did the Maastricht Treaty (1993) advance EU integration?
> **11** How did the Lisbon Treaty (2009) advance EU integration?
> **12** Define 'Eurozone'.

Supranational versus intergovernmental approaches

Since its foundation, the EEC/EU has balanced 'supranational' governing bodies, which encourage a more federal/unified Europe, with 'intergovernmental' bodies, which protect the sovereignty of the member states. The key EU institutions and their approaches to supranationalism and intergovernmentalism are listed in Table 22.2, with the year when they were established.

> **Supranationalism** Decision-making when member states of a regional or global institution agree to accept the decisions taken by a higher sovereign institution than themselves.
>
> **Intergovernmentalism** Decision-making in institutions of regional and global governance which relies on the consent of each member state. This protects their sovereignty.

Table 22.2 Key EU institutions and their differing approaches

EU institution	Role
The Commission (supranational), 1958	+ The 27 commissioners (one for each member state) recommend legislation. + The Commission is therefore the EU's governmental/executive body. + It is supranational since the commissioners represent the interests of the EU not their state. + Since 2019 the president of the Commission has been the former German minister of defence, Ursula von der Leyen.
Council of Ministers (supranational/ intergovernmental), 1967	+ The EU's decision-making body. Ministers from the EU's 27 member states reach decisions on Commission proposals. + Ministers attend when their interests are involved. For example, transport ministers attend meetings connected with transport. + Although increasing numbers of decisions are made by QMV, members still exercise the veto on key issues of sovereignty like foreign policy, defence, taxation and immigration.
European Council (intergovernmental), 1974	+ The EU's 27 leaders and foreign ministers meet four times a year to plan EU priorities with the president of the Council (Charles Michel, 2019–). + The European Council is intergovernmental as the veto can be exercised.

219

EU institution	Role
European Parliament (supranational), 1958	+ The EU's directly elected parliament, which shares legislative influence with the Council of Ministers in certain areas. + The 705 Members of the European Parliament (MEPs) are directly elected to serve five-year terms and sit according to shared political allegiance rather than representing national interests. + The parliament must agree the EU budget and confirm the choice of commissioners. + In 2019, the parliament rejected two commissioners over an alleged conflict of interests.
European Court of Justice (ECJ) (supranational), 1952	+ 27 judges representing each member state who interpret the meaning of EU law. + In cases where EU law exists, the ECJ takes precedence over domestic law. + The court determines whether member states are acting in accordance with the legally binding EU Charter of Fundamental Rights.
European Central Bank (supranational), 1988	+ The European Central Bank sets a single interest rate for all members of the Eurozone.

Now test yourself TESTED

13 What is the purpose of the EU Commission?

14 List the EU institutions which are fully supranational.

15 List the EU institutions which combine supranationalism with intergovernmentalism.

The impact of regional organisations like the EU on state sovereignty is summarised in Table 22.3.

Table 22.3 Impact of regional organisations on state sovereignty

Organisation	Impact
EU	+ Significant impact through supranational institutions like the Commission, the European Parliament and the ECJ. + Expectation that all EU members (except Denmark) will achieve full EMU in the Eurozone. + Member states protect their sovereignty in specific areas on the Council of Ministers and the Council. + The Lisbon Treaty (Article 50) provides a mechanism for states to leave the EU.
ASEAN	+ ASEAN's Charter is based on the 'principles of sovereignty, equality, territorial integrity, non-interference, consensus and unity in diversity'. + Consequently, ASEAN safeguards rather than challenging state sovereignty. + Its governing institutions are therefore intergovernmental, and decisions must be reached through consensus.
AU	+ The governing institutions of the AU are intergovernmental. + The AU's Charter recognises the 'inalienable right to independent existence' of its member states. + Very limited progress on economic and monetary union has been made. + Significantly, the AU's Charter does empower states 'to intervene in a Member State…in respect of grave circumstances, namely: war crimes, genocide and crimes against humanity'.
Arab League	+ The Arab League's Charter states that members must 'respect the systems of government established' in each state. + Decisions are only binding if unanimously agreed. Even then, a member state may implement them 'according to its respective laws'.
USMCA	+ USMCA has established rules regarding trade, workers' rights and environmental protection. However, its impact on sovereignty is limited since its members can decide not to extend it beyond 2036.

22.4 Significance of the EU as a global actor

+ The second pillar of the Maastricht Treaty (1993) established the principle of a common foreign and security policy.
+ The Lisbon Treaty (2009) provided more effective mechanisms through which the EU can exercise external influence. These included the establishment of a permanent office of EU President (Ursula von der Leyen, 2019–) and a High Representative of the European Union for Foreign Affairs and Security Policy (Josep Borrell, 2019–).
+ The Lisbon Treaty also provided the EU with its own legal identity, so that it can negotiate with other powers through its own diplomatic service. Therefore, the EU can exercise political, economic, structural and military influence in global politics.
+ The extent to which the EU has become a major global actor is contested by realists, who believe that it lacks the extensive military hard power necessary to exert world influence.

> **Global actor** A political entity which can extend its influence (economic, political or military) beyond its region and on a world scale.

> **Exam tip**
>
> Continually refresh your notes on the impact of the EU in global politics.

Is the EU now a significant force in global politics?

Yes	No
+ The size of the EU's economy provides it with strong negotiating power in international trade deals. + The EU is the world's biggest donor of international aid. Its $300 billion Global Gateway to encourage sustainable development in the developing world provides it with extensive influence. + The EU exerts extensive structural influence as a member of the World Trade Organization, G7 and G20. It is also a COP participant at climate change meetings. + The Russian invasion of Ukraine has encouraged greater unity in EU foreign and security policy. In the year following the invasion, the EU supplied Ukraine with €3.6 billion of military and non-military aid. + The EU provides an example of global leadership over climate change, pledging to be carbon neutral by 2050.	+ EU members often have different foreign policy objectives. Since foreign and defence policy requires unanimity, this is problematic. + The EU has thus failed to provide global leadership during crises like the civil war in Syria and Libya and did not achieve a collective response to human rights abuses in Myanmar and China. Five EU states (Cyprus, Greece, Romania, Spain and Slovakia) do not recognise Kosovo as a sovereign state (2023). + The EU is not a permanent member of the Security Council and only possesses observer status at the United Nations. + The EU does not have its own military capability and 22 members prioritise their security through NATO (see Chapter 21). This greatly reduces its hard power influence. + Slow action on climate change, the rise of authoritarian governments and global challenges to human rights demonstrate limits to EU soft power.

> **Exam tip**
>
> You may be asked to decide how much influence regional organisations have compared with powerful nation states. Be prepared to contrast the power of regional organisations with countries like the US, China, Russia and India.

> **Now test yourself** TESTED
>
> 16 How has the EU responded to the challenge of climate change?
> 17 Define 'widening and deepening' in the context of the EU.
> 18 List three ways in which the EU exerts global influence.

22.5 The ways and extent to which regionalism addresses and resolves contemporary global issues involving conflict, poverty, human rights and the environment

Regional organisations have had mixed success in resolving some of the world's most pressing global challenges, as shown in Table 22.4.

Table 22.4 Regional organisations addressing global challenges

Conflict	+ Small-scale EU peace-keeping operations have taken place in Bosnia, Macedonia, Chad, the Democratic Republic of the Congo and the Central African Republic. + The AU has launched peace-keeping missions in Burundi, Somalia, Darfur, Sudan and Mali. + AU forces have been used against the Lord's Resistance Army, Boko Haram and jihadists in the Sahel region. + The Arab League and ASEAN have failed to resolve conflicts among their members.
Poverty	+ The EU combats poverty through overseas aid and the Global Gateway, which encourages development. + EU regional development grants have encouraged growth among the poorest EU members. + Critics claim that the EU's external tariff and the Common Agricultural Policy, which keeps EU agricultural prices low, limit trading opportunities for the developing world. + ASEAN's commitment to free trade has encouraged rapid economic growth among its members. In 2022, its gross domestic product was US$3.2 trillion, making it the fifth largest economy in the world (US–ASEAN Business Council). + By increasing trade between its members, USMCA combats poverty, especially in Mexico. From 2019 to 2021 trade between its members increased by 6%. + The New Partnership for Africa's Development (NEPAD) is designed to eradicate poverty and provide sustainable development within the AU. However, little progress has been made on the African Continental Free Trade Area (AfCFTA).
Human rights	+ The EU Charter of Fundamental Rights is legally enforceable on member states through the ECJ. + USMCA provides some protection for workers' rights. + Since ASEAN, the Arab League and the AU all recognise their members' sovereignty, human rights are not enforceable in those countries.
The environment	+ The EU attends COP meetings and provides global leadership over climate change. + ASEAN and AU countries are particularly threatened by climate change. + ASEAN has established an Action Plan on Joint Response to Climate Change and is committed to net-zero carbon emissions by 2050. + In 2022, the AU launched its 'comprehensive strategy' to combat climate change, although it is not binding on member states. + The Arab League and USMCA do not have a coordinated response to climate change.

Now test yourself

 TESTED ○

19 In what different ways do regional organisations approach human rights?

20 Which regional organisations carry out peace-keeping operations?

21 Contrast the EU's attitude to sovereignty with other regional organisations.

Case study

The EU's Strategic Compass

In *Of Paradise and Power: America and Europe in the New World Order* (2004), the US political scientist Robert Kagan remarked that Europeans 'generally favour peaceful responses to problems, preferring negotiation, diplomacy and persuasion to coercion'. However, in 2023, the US Congressional Research Service noted that 'In March 2022, the EU released a new EU security and defence strategy — known as Strategic Compass — to improve EU military and defence capabilities by 2030.'

This has led some critics to suggest that Vladimir Putin has done more to make the EU militarily self-confident than any European leader since 1957.

Summary

+ Regionalism involves nation states in the same geographical location joining together in collective organisations to achieve the best outcomes for their members.
+ There are three types of regional organisation: political, economic and security. Some regional organisations combine these characteristics.
+ European integration has been strongly influenced by the experience of the two world wars.
+ The EU is the world's most advanced form of regionalism, combining intergovernmental and supranational institutions. It is the only regional organisation to have achieved monetary union.

+ The EU is based on the principle of 'ever closer union' (Treaty of Rome, 1957).
+ The EU has increased in membership (widening), while developing the ties between its member states (deepening).
+ ASEAN and USMCA have achieved significant economic success but do not challenge the sovereignty of member states in the same way as the EU.
+ The Arab League has been criticised for inaction.
+ The AU has achieved significant success in peace-keeping but its plans for economic and monetary union remain far in the future.

Revision tasks

1 Research the biggest challenges facing the EU. How well do you think that it has overcome them?

2 Debate the motion, 'The European Union has become a world power.'

3 Produce a summary of the most recent successes and failures of the AU, ASEAN and USMCA.

4 Debate the motion, 'Regional organisations have now replaced nation states as the main players in global politics.'

Exam skills

Determining factors

+ Be prepared to make detailed comparisons between the EU and the other four regional organisations.
+ To judge the effectiveness of each regional organisation, first determine with what purpose it was established.
+ Be aware of the historical background to European integration. This contrasts significantly with the origins of the other regional organisations.

Exam practice

1 Examine the different powers that supranational and intergovernmental institutions have in the EU. (12 marks)

2 Examine the purpose of ASEAN and the Arab League. (12 marks)

3 Evaluate the view that regional organisations have responded effectively to the challenge of globalisation. (30 marks)

4 Evaluate the view that the AU now resembles the EU in terms of power and influence. (30 marks)

223

Glossary

Theme 1 UK government and politics

Term	Definition	Page(s)
Additional member system (AMS)	An electoral system that uses two, separate, votes — one for a constituency representative and one for regional representatives on a top-up basis. It aims to create a more proportional result.	30
Authoritative works	Works written by political experts that have become recognised as useful guides to the UK political system.	54
Backbencher	An MP who does not hold a position within the government.	68
Cabinet	A group appointed by the prime minister that includes senior government ministers.	77
Class dealignment	The process of voters not associating themselves as belonging to a particular class.	41
Coalition government	A government formed after an election consisting of two or more parties that have formally compromised on common policy goals.	34
Collective responsibility	The expectation that ministers must support decisions publicly made by the cabinet, or resign.	82
Common law	Rules made by judges interpreting the legislative landscape.	54
Confidence and supply	The right of Parliament to remove government or withhold funding (supply) from it. Also the name of an agreement between two parties in which support is promised in votes of confidence and supply in return for policies.	80
Constitution	A set of principles that outline the political system and division of political power within a country.	52
Conventions	Unwritten traditions of the UK political system that influence how politics works.	54
Democratic deficit	A lack of democratic ideals seen in a political system, or where political decisions are taken by those without sufficient legitimacy.	10
Devolution	The sharing of political power, but not sovereignty.	55
Direct democracy	A political system in which the people make decisions themselves, rather than through an elected official acting on their behalf.	6
Elective dictatorship	The domination of Parliament by the government resulting in ineffective checks on government.	91
European Union	A political and economic union of European member states.	93
Executive	The branch of government responsible for implementing and enforcing law from the legislative branch.	77
First-past-the-post	A plurality electoral system used for UK general elections to Parliament.	29
Four freedoms	The EU principle of the free movement of goods, services, capital and people.	93
Franchise	The right to vote. It is also called 'suffrage'. The extent of the franchise refers to those with the right to vote, for example over-18s in the UK.	9
Governing competency	The perceived ability of a party to carry out the roles of government effectively.	43
Government department	A part of the executive, headed by a government minister, that oversees a particular policy area.	84
Head of state	The chief representative of a nation; different to the head of government.	92
House of Commons	One of two chambers of UK Parliament, forming the legislative branch. Considered the primary legislative chamber due to its elected status.	65
House of Lords	One of two chambers of the UK Parliament. Considered the secondary legislative chamber due to being unelected.	66
Judicial independence	The principle that judges should be free of influence from other branches of government when making their decisions.	88
Judicial neutrality	The principle that judges should not apply political opinion in their decision-making process, and judges should remain outside of party politics.	88

Answers at **www.hoddereducation.co.uk/myrevisionnotesdownloads**

Judicial review	The power of the judiciary to review the actions of other branches of government to determine whether they have breached the law or are incompatible with the Human Rights Act.	88
Left wing	Describes a set of political ideals that support increased social and economic equality, favouring increasing government intervention and challenging existing structures such as capitalism.	17
Legislative bills	These are bills created by Parliament. If they pass through the entire legislative process and gain royal assent, they become 'Acts of Parliament'.	69
Legal sovereignty	The legal right of an entity to exercise power in a political system.	95
Legitimacy	The rightful exercise of political power, usually by a government that gains legitimacy for its decisions from winning a free and fair election.	7
Lobbyist	A person or company that is paid to try to influence those in power, particularly when legislation is being considered.	11
Mandate	The authority to carry out the policies that are in a party's manifesto, and to govern the country.	32
Manifesto	A document containing the principles and policies that are a party's pledges to carry out if it wins an election.	44
Marginal seat	A constituency in which the winner in an election is not easily predictable and could be won by a number of parties. Also known as a 'swing seat'.	36
Minister	An MP or member of the House of Lords appointed to oversee the work of a government department or part of a government department.	82
Minority government	A government in which one party has a minority, but usually a plurality, of seats in Parliament, and chooses to form government alone.	35
New Labour	A Labour Party faction that accepts a greater role for the private sector and prioritises equality of opportunity.	20
New right	A Conservative Party faction that favours a smaller government, less state intervention and more responsibility for the individual.	19
Old Labour	A Labour Party faction that prioritises government intervention and control in order to achieve social equality.	20
One-nation conservatives	A Conservative Party faction that has a greater appreciation of the need for a welfare state due to the responsibilities of the noblesse oblige.	19
Opposition	MPs and Lords who are not from the governing party.	73
Parliamentary privilege	The right of MPs to speak freely on the floor of the House of Commons.	67
Parliamentary sovereignty	The principle that Parliament is the source of all political power in the UK.	56
Participation crisis	A situation in which few people take part in the political process and decision-making, undermining democratic legitimacy.	10
Partisan dealignment	The process of voters not having a long-term loyalty to a particular party.	41
Party system	Describes the number of parties in an election that have a realistic chance of forming government. This is usually the result of a chosen electoral system.	23
Political sovereignty	The political ability of an entity to exercise power in a political system.	95
Presidential government	A government in which the executive is dominated by one person with an individual mandate, and where power is separated between the branches of government.	80
Public bill committee	A committee created to consider a piece of legislation. These committees are created for a specific bill.	69
Rational choice	This refers to the theory that a voter will vote for a party that best serves the interests of that voter.	43
Representative democracy	A political system in which citizens elect a representative to make decisions on their behalf.	6
Right wing	Describes a set of political ideals that support individual rights and capitalism, which may result in inequality, often challenging increased government intervention in society.	17
Royal prerogative	A set of powers exercised by the prime minister on behalf of the monarch.	79
Rule of law	The law passed by Parliament applies equally to everyone.	52

225

Salisbury Convention	A convention that the Lords will not reject a bill put forward in a government's election manifesto.	71
Safe seat	A constituency that is highly likely to be won by a specific party due to a concentration of its voters in this area.	29
Secondary legislation	Powers of the government to make changes to the law within specific limits.	78
Select committee	A committee of backbench MPs that scrutinises the work of a specific government department.	73
Single transferable vote (STV)	A voting system in which voting places the candidates in order of preference, and that uses the Droop quota to proportionately allocate seats to parties.	30
Statute law	An act that is passed by UK Parliament, for example the Human Rights Act 1998.	54
Supplementary vote (SV)	A majoritarian electoral system in which voters can express two preferences, and a candidate needs to gain at least 50%+1 of the vote to win their seat.	31
Supreme Court	The highest court of the UK legal system.	87
Think tank	A group of experts on a particular policy area that produces research to try to influence the government. These groups may have a specific political leaning.	11
Uncodified	A constitution that is not written in one single document, but drawn from a range of sources.	52
Ultra vires	This means that a public body or government has acted beyond the power that it has.	90
Unitary	The idea that legal sovereignty resides in one place. In the UK, this is parliament.	59

Theme 2 Political ideas

Term	Definition	Page(s)
Altruism	Concern for the welfare of others based on social solidarity.	123
Anthropocentric	A view with humans at the centre of it and nature as a tool for humans to use for their own ends.	130
Anti-permissiveness	Rejecting permissiveness where people make their own moral choices and these choices are not objectively 'right' or 'wrong'.	109
Assimilation	The expectation of minority groups adopting the values and traditions of the majority group.	149
Atomism	Belief that society is made up of individuals who act in self-interested ways.	112
Authority	The idea that there is a hierarchy and those in higher positions are best placed to make decisions for the good of society.	107
Autonomy	Freedom to act without restriction from the state or other people.	124
Biocentric equality	All living livings are equal to one another.	133
Biodiversity	A wide diversity of species within nature helps to ensure balance and stability of nature.	128
Black nationalism	The idea that black people worldwide are part of 'one people'. It is a reaction to white oppression in the twentieth century.	158
Buddhist economics	A view of economics where human needs should be met to achieve maximum quality of life from minimal consumption.	133
Capitalism	An economic model in which wealth and the means of production are privately owned and goods are produced for the profit of the owners.	115
Change to conserve	Society should adapt incrementally to current circumstances in order to prevent revolutionary change.	109
Chauvinistic nationalism	Nationalism that believes one nation is superior to another.	155
Civic nationalism	Nationalism, which is based on the active participation of citizens in supporting the values of society.	154
Class consciousness	Social class is central to the ideas of socialism and the exploited class must adopt a revolutionary class consciousness to overthrow the exploiters.	115
Collectivisation	Abolish private property and replace it with common ownership.	126

Answers at **www.hoddereducation.co.uk/myrevisionnotesdownloads**

Common ownership	The ownership of the means of production by all those involved in the process, to benefit the whole of society.	114
Communism	An economic (and political) system in which the means of production are held in common ownership, society is classless and wealth is equally distributed.	118
Consumerism	The consumption of goods is a means to happiness.	130
Cooperation	Humans working collectively together for the benefit of all.	117
Cosmopolitan integration	The widest freedoms for all cultures to mix and learn from other cultures.	147
Cultural feminism	A form of difference feminism that looks to promote 'women's values' over male ones.	137
Culture	The shared values, customs and beliefs of a group.	144
Decentralisation	The process by which society is broken up into smaller societies that are more self-sufficient and therefore more sustainable and dependent on the natural world.	132
Developmental individualism	Individual freedom is linked to a society in which individuals can achieve their aspirations.	98
Dialectic	Where two opposing sets of values — often the exploiters and the exploited — clash to create a new society, over and over again creating new stages of history.	116
Difference feminism	Difference feminists argue that men and women are fundamentally different.	137
Direct action	Action taken by an individual, both non-violent and violent, beyond the traditional political framework of that individual.	125
Direct democracy	Citizens making law and policy directly, rather than through an elected government.	123
Diversity	Different races and cultures that exist within a state creating differences that should be celebrated.	148
Ecocentric	A nature-centred rather than human-centred view of the world.	130
Egoistical individualism	Individual freedom is linked to self-reliance and self-interest of individuals.	98
Empiricism	Knowledge comes from lived experience and not from abstract theories.	111
Enabling state	A state that helps individuals to achieve their potential and which is therefore often a larger state.	101
Environmental consciousness	A human consciousness in which people identify innately with the environment, as part of it not master of it.	129
Equality feminism	Equality feminists argue that men and women are fundamentally the same.	137
Equality of opportunity	All individuals have the same opportunity to succeed in life.	99, 138
Essentialism	Biology creates differences in the characters of men and women.	137
Ethnicity	The sense of belonging to a social group that shares commons characteristics such as culture, religion or language.	152
Evolutionary socialism	A gradual, reformist approach to achieve socialism via legal and political means.	116
Exclusive nationalism	A belief that to be a part of a nation, an individual should share the history, language etc. of that nation.	158
Formal equality	All individuals have the same political and legal rights in society.	99, 144
Foundational equality	All humans are born with the same rights and these cannot be removed. These are also known as 'natural rights'.	100
Fraternity	The bonds that naturally exist between humans sharing the same basic nature and outlook.	114
Gender equality	Treating everyone in society the same, regardless of their gender.	138
Government [anarchism]	The system and institutions of rule, which anarchists consider are based on deceit and violence.	122
Green capitalism	A capitalist free-market delivering more environmentally sustainable methods of production.	131
Group differentiated rights	Rights being given uniquely to groups including self-government, polyethnic rights and representation rights.	150

My Revision Notes: Pearson Edexcel A-level Politics: UK Government and Politics, Political Ideas and Global Politics

Harm principle	The theory that individuals should be free to do anything provided it does not cause harm to other individuals.	103
Hierarchy	A natural order to society arranged in fixed tiers that is not necessarily based on the ability of the individual.	107
Historical materialism	Where the method of material production influences the nature and organisation of society.	118
Human imperfection	Humans are naturally flawed and therefore not able to make good decisions for themselves.	107
Identity politics	The acceptance of a sense of identity by a minority group is an act of political liberation against oppression.	144
Imperialism/ colonialism	The control of one country by another.	155
Inclusive nationalism	Nationalism that believes that anyone can join a nation by choosing to.	158
Individualist integration	Everyone being treated on an individual basis when being integrated into a state, being given equal individual rights rather than rights based on difference.	146
Industrialisation	Largescale production and wealth accumulation with continuous, unlimited growth to satisfy consumerism.	130
Insurrection	Individuals elevating themselves beyond state institutions, so that the institutions decay and die away.	125
Integral nationalism	Intense form of patriotism that subsumes the individual in favour of the interests of the nation.	157
Intersectionality	A challenge to the idea that being a woman alone is the biggest cause of oppression; women have overlapping characteristics as well as gender, e.g. race, class and age, that cause differences in experience and oppression.	137
Keynesianism	An economic system in which the government has a greater role in order to achieve stability and full employment.	102
Laissez-faire	Describes a government that has minimal intervention in the economy and running of the state.	108
Laissez-faire capitalism	An economic system that has minimal government intervention, instead allowing the market to regulate itself.	102
Legal equality	The law applying equally to everyone, including women.	138
Liberal internationalism	Nations should cooperate and create mutual dependence to avoid international conflict.	154
Limited government	A government whose power is restricted by checks and balances and often through the separation of powers.	100
Limits to growth	Nature comprises of finite resources which require a need for limits to economic growth.	132
Marxism	An ideological strand of socialism based on the work of Marx and Engels in which capitalism will ultimately be replaced by communism.	118
Mechanistic view	A perception that the state is created to serve the interests of individuals.	102
Meritocracy	A society in which success and organisation are based on the ability and effort of individuals.	102
Minimal state	Where role of the state is limited in order to protect individual freedom.	99
Multicultural integration	Integration being different for different groups allowing for a sense of belonging to the whole group as well as minority groups/cultures.	145
Mutual aid	Humans are successful when they work cooperatively rather than compete as individuals.	126
Mutualism	Exchange of goods equitably between producers organised individually or in small-scale private property.	125
Negative freedom	Where individuals are free from constraints or limitations.	98
Noblesse oblige	The responsibility of those with power and wealth to help the less fortunate.	107
Otherness	The idea that women are defined in opposition to men, where men are the 'norm' and women are 'other'.	141
Political equality	The equal rights of women to vote and protest.	142

Answers at **www.hoddereducation.co.uk/myrevisionnotesdownloads**

Positive discrimination	Giving one group preferential treatment on the basis of historical oppression.	145
Positive freedom	The principle that freedom is linked to the opportunity to fulfil an individual's potential.	101
Power	The means by which the state enforces its authority, such as police, military and law.	122
Private sphere	The area of society in which relationships are private, i.e. those inside the family home.	136
Progressive	Nationalism that looks towards improving society by moving it forwards.	156
Public sphere	The area of society in which relationships are public, i.e. those outside the family home.	136
Radical	Drastic and extensive change in society, politics or the economy.	109
Rational	The result of logical reasoning and decision-making.	154
Regressive	Nationalism that looks to the past as the ideal of society and looks to move society back to this.	156
Revisionism	The attempt to redefine socialism to a less radical, more evolutionary movement.	119
Segregation	The separation of cultural groups based on their beliefs.	146
Social contract theory	Government is based on consent of the governed in exchange for a protection of freedoms, but consent can be removed if the government fails to protect these freedoms.	102
Socialist internationalism	Class divisions cut across geographical boundaries and are a more significant source of identity.	154
Social justice	The distribution of wealth in society to limit inequality.	119
Solidarity	Sympathy, cooperation and harmony between individuals therefore not requiring state regulation.	123
State	The sovereign body that exerts power over humans under its controlled area.	122
Sustainability	The ability of the environment to maintain health over time.	132
Syndicalism	A revolutionary movement with trade unions at its heart, using direct action to lead to revolution.	124
Tolerance	Respecting the beliefs of others, even if individuals disagree with them.	103, 148
Universalism	Some values are universally applicable regardless of culture, history or other differences.	147
Value pluralism	No one right or set of values is more or less important than any other.	149
Volksgeist	The unique identity of a national based on the culture of that nation.	153
Waves of feminism	The time periods during which feminism was targeting different goals or outcomes.	138

Theme 3 Global politics

Term	Definition	Page(s)
Anarchical society and society of states	A theory developed by Hedley Bull which argues that nation states can maximise self-interest through cooperation. Consequently, global relations are not purely anarchic, as a society of states is possible.	163
Autocratic state	A state where a single ruler has absolute power and is not democratically accountable to the public. Its government does not respect the rule of law and there is no human rights protection.	209
Bipolarity	In a bipolar distribution of power, two superpowers compete for global influence.	207
Complex interdependence	A liberal term sometimes known as the 'cobweb model of international relations', in which the close relationships that nation states establish through institutions of global governance encourage cooperation and understanding.	162
Cultural globalisation	The spread of global values and material aspirations, so that the distinctiveness of national cultures becomes increasingly insignificant.	169
Democratic state	A state in which the government is accountable to the public in regular elections and where the rule of law is paramount.	208

Dependency theory	This suggests that economic liberalism makes developing countries reliant on cheap imports from the developed world, so they never break free from a state of neo-colonial dependency.	187
Economic globalisation	The process through which national economies become more closely connected and reliant on each other through free trade (economic liberalism) and capital investment.	168
Emerging power	A power which can increasingly assert economic, diplomatic, and military influence in international relations, so challenging the existing balance of power.	206
European integration	The process of 'ever closer union' through which decision-making in the EU is increasingly made by supranational institutions.	217
European Union (EU)	The world's most advanced regional organisation, in which decision-making between its 27 member states is made through supranational and intergovernmental institutions.	217
Failed state	A state in which the government is no longer able to exert its authority and where law and order has consequently broken down.	209
Federalism	The concentration of sovereign power in supranational institutions of governance, so reducing the sovereign independence of the EU's member states.	218
Global actor	A political entity which can extend its influence (economic, political or military) beyond its region and on a world scale.	221
Global commons	Our shared environment, such as the oceans, the atmosphere, the Antarctic and outer space. These are under the jurisdiction of no state, so their protection requires collective endeavour.	199
Global governance	When sovereign nation states work together and with non-state actors in international/intergovernmental organisations (IGOs) (such as the UN) to address collective problems.	161
Globalisation	The process by which nation states and their citizens become more closely interconnected, challenging the nation state as the principal actor in international relations.	167
Great power	A great power possesses considerable structural, diplomatic and economic influence without being able to exert global dominance over other states.	205
Group of Seven (G7)	An informal intergovernmental organisation which enables the leaders of the biggest democratic economies in the developed world to consult regularly on world issues.	185
Group of Twenty (G20)	An informal intergovernmental organisation which brings together the leaders of the world's biggest economies for regular consultation.	185
Hard power	The coercive utilisation of military and economic force to achieve desired outcomes.	204
Homogenisation and monoculture	These refer to the rise of a materialistic world culture in which the same products dominate globally. Often referred to as 'cocacolonisation', homogenisation suggests a dull uniformity challenging the uniqueness of diverse cultures.	169
Humanitarian intervention	The forcible intervention in a state to stop sustained and widespread human rights abuses.	195
Human rights/ universal human rights	These refer to the rights which all human beings enjoy by virtue of their humanity. The same human rights cannot be denied to any member of the human race.	191
Interconnectedness	The increased economic, political and cultural connectivity between nation states and their citizens, developing a cobweb of close and reliant global relationships.	167
Intergovernmentalism	Decision-making in institutions of regional and global governance which relies on the consent of each member state. This protects their sovereignty.	219
Intergovernmental Panel on Climate Change (IPCC)	An intergovernmental body which collates the most accurate and independently researched scientific data on the present state of climate change.	198
International anarchy	Realists argue that there is no authority greater than the nation capable of imposing order, so nation states will pursue their individual interests, leading to a state of global anarchy.	160

Answers at **www.hoddereducation.co.uk/myrevisionnotesdownloads**

International Court of Justice (ICJ)	The ICJ is sometimes known as the World Court. Established in 1945, it is a UN court and judges cases involving nation states.	192
International Criminal Court (ICC)	Established in 2002, the ICC is a permanent court which tries individuals accused of genocide, crimes against humanity and war crimes.	191
International law	Law which governs the relationship between nation states. Nation states are expected to obey international law even if it conflicts with their national interests.	191
International Monetary Fund (IMF)	A major financial institution based in Washington DC. Its purpose is to encourage global financial stability among its 190 member states (2023) by providing technical advice, warning of potential financial crises and acting as lender of last resort.	182
International tribunals	Four tribunals established to try human rights abuses committed in Rwanda, the former Yugoslavia, Sierra Leone and Cambodia.	192
Liberalism	A theory of international relations founded on the principles that nation states are cooperative and so can work together in institutions of global governance, and that free trade, democracy, the rule of law and human rights are essential in international relations.	161
Monoculture (and homogenisation)	These refer to the rise of a materialistic world culture in which the same products dominate globally. Often referred to as 'cocacolonisation', homogenisation suggests a dull uniformity challenging the uniqueness of diverse cultures.	169
Multipolarity	In a multipolar distribution of power, several great powers compete for regional and global influence.	207
Nation state	A sovereign political body whose people share a common citizenship.	167
Non-democratic state	A state which possesses no democratic institutions and where authority rests in the governments which is not accountable to the people. Citizens have no political rights and their civil rights are unprotected.	209
Non-governmental organisations	Non-profit-seeking bodies which seek to influence global politics, aiming to advance economic, social and political causes that empower individuals and communities.	179
Non-state actors	Participants in international relations with significant power and influence, which are not states.	162
North Atlantic Treaty Organisation (NATO)	A defensive military alliance which protects its members on the principle of collective security.	180
North–South divide	The concept that there is a significant gap in wealth and development between the industrialised Global North and more agricultural Global South. It is a political rather than a geographical term.	186
Polarity	The different ways in which power can be distributed in international relations.	207
Political globalisation	The establishment of intergovernmental organisations like the UN which enable nation states to work together and with non-state actors to resolve collective dilemmas.	168
Realism	A theory of international relations based on the principle that nation states are self-seeking and power-hungry. Since according to realism there is no authority greater than the nation state, nation states must prioritise their own survival in a hostile world order.	160
Regionalism	A process of integration in which nation states in a specific region decide to develop their institutional connections to advance their joint interests.	214
Rogue state	A state that engages in extensive human rights violations, threatens its neighbours and acts in defiance of international law.	210
Security Council	The UN's most powerful body. Its five permanent and ten non-permanent members decide on matters connected with international peace and security.	176
Security dilemma	The problem that, when nation states maximise their power to deter aggression, this threatens other nation states, which then increase their own military spending, leading to distrust and arms races. Therefore, actions designed to make a state safer make it less safe.	161
Semi-democratic state	A state in which the effectiveness of democratic institutions has been undermined by authoritarianism.	209

My Revision Notes: Pearson Edexcel A-level Politics: UK Government and Politics, Political Ideas and Global Politics

Society of states	A theory developed by Hedley Bull which argues that nation states can maximise self-interest through cooperation. Consequently, global relations are not purely anarchic, as a society of states is possible.	163
Soft power	The deployment of political and cultural attraction to persuade other states to willingly support chosen objectives.	204
Sovereignty	The principle of unlimited authority which means that no outside power can exercise influence over a sovereign body.	167, 217
Structural adjustment programmes (SAPs)	Free market policies including privatisation, trade liberalisation and high interest rates, often required by the IMF and World Bank as a condition of their loans.	182
Superpower	A superpower is a dominant power that can exert its military, economic and diplomatic influence across the world.	206
Supranationalism	Decision-making when member states of a regional or global institution agree to accept the decisions taken by a higher sovereign institution than themselves.	219
Sustainability/ sustainable development	Development which provides for the needs of the present without jeopardising the needs of the future.	199
Tragedy of the commons	The theory that by putting their own material interests above that of the collective well-being of the planet, states and non-state actors deplete the earth's natural resources.	200
Unipolarity	In a unipolar distribution of power, a globally dominant power, known as a hegemon, can exert complete world influence without being challenged by a rival.	207
United Nations	The world's biggest IGO with 193 member states, focusing on peace, security and development.	176
United Nations Framework Convention on Climate Change (UNFCCC)	Established at the Rio Earth Summit in 1992, the UNFCCC is an international treaty which arranges regular COPs to combat 'human interference' in the environment.	198
Universal human rights/human rights	These refer to the rights which all human beings enjoy by virtue of their humanity. The same human rights cannot be denied to any member of the human race.	191
Widening and deepening	A process whereby the EU expands its membership at the same time as it intensifies integration between members.	218
World Bank	The world's largest source of funding and knowledge for developing countries. It encourages long-term development through loans which are generally conditional on the recipient country implementing free market structural adjustment programmes.	168
World government	This would be globally sovereign and would require nation states to abandon their sovereignty and accept the complete supranational authority of a single world power.	168
World systems/ dependency theory	This suggests that economic liberalism makes developing countries reliant on cheap imports from the developed world, so they never break free from a state of neo-colonial dependency.	187
World Trade Organization (WTO)	An international body established in 1995 to encourage free trade between its members and resolve trade disputes.	184

Answers at **www.hoddereducation.co.uk/myrevisionnotesdownloads**